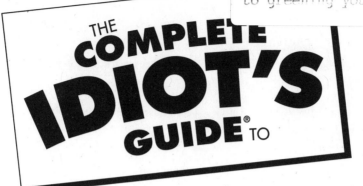

THE COMPLETE IDIOT'S GUIDE® TO

Greening Your Business

by Trish Riley and Heather Gadonniex

ALPHA

A member of Penguin Group (USA) Inc.

 Printed on recycled paper

ALPHA BOOKS

Published by the Penguin Group

Penguin Group (USA) Inc., 375 Hudson Street, New York, New York 10014, USA

Penguin Group (Canada), 90 Eglinton Avenue East, Suite 700, Toronto, Ontario M4P 2Y3, Canada (a division of Pearson Penguin Canada Inc.)

Penguin Books Ltd., 80 Strand, London WC2R 0RL, England

Penguin Ireland, 25 St. Stephen's Green, Dublin 2, Ireland (a division of Penguin Books Ltd.)

Penguin Group (Australia), 250 Camberwell Road, Camberwell, Victoria 3124, Australia (a division of Pearson Australia Group Pty. Ltd.)

Penguin Books India Pvt. Ltd., 11 Community Centre, Panchsheel Park, New Delhi—110 017, India

Penguin Group (NZ), 67 Apollo Drive, Rosedale, North Shore, Auckland 1311, New Zealand (a division of Pearson New Zealand Ltd.)

Penguin Books (South Africa) (Pty.) Ltd., 24 Sturdee Avenue, Rosebank, Johannesburg 2196, South Africa

Penguin Books Ltd., Registered Offices: 80 Strand, London WC2R 0RL, England

Copyright © 2009 by Trish Riley and Heather Gadonniex

International Standard Book Number: 978-1-59257-885-6
Library of Congress Catalog Card Number: 2008941484

11 10 09   8 7 6 5 4 3 2 1

Interpretation of the printing code: The rightmost number of the first series of numbers is the year of the book's printing; the rightmost number of the second series of numbers is the number of the book's printing. For example, a printing code of 09-1 shows that the first printing occurred in 2009.

Printed in the United States of America

Note: This publication contains the opinions and ideas of its authors. It is intended to provide helpful and informative material on the subject matter covered. It is sold with the understanding that the authors and publisher are not engaged in rendering professional services in the book. If the reader requires personal assistance or advice, a competent professional should be consulted.

The authors and publisher specifically disclaim any responsibility for any liability, loss, or risk, personal or otherwise, which is incurred as a consequence, directly or indirectly, of the use and application of any of the contents of this book.

Most Alpha books are available at special quantity discounts for bulk purchases for sales promotions, premiums, fund-raising, or educational use. Special books, or book excerpts, can also be created to fit specific needs.

For details, write: Special Markets, Alpha Books, 375 Hudson Street, New York, NY 10014.

Publisher: *Marie Butler-Knight*
Editorial Director: *Mike Sanders*
Senior Managing Editor: *Billy Fields*
Senior Acquisitions Editor: *Paul Dinas*
Development Editor: *Ginny Bess Munroe*
Production Editor: *Kayla Dugger*
Copy Editor: *Nancy Wagner*

Cartoonist: *Steve Barr*
Cover Designer: *Bill Thomas*
Book Designer: *Trina Wurst*
Indexer: *Heather McNeill*
Layout: *Brian Massey*
Proofreader: *Mary Hunt*

I'd like to dedicate this work to my children, Rachel and Bud, and to their children and your children and all the generations of the future, the ones who will most benefit from our work together in creating a healthier world and a healthier economy. I also dedicate this book to you, the reader, who is helping make these new ideas in business responsibility a reality. —Trish Riley

This book is dedicated to my grandfather, Wendell Shepherd. When I was a child, my grandfather taught me to always think critically about what others spoke and wrote and to research in order to make my own decisions. He also taught me to respect nature and be a steward for our environment. This served as the backbone for my developing worldview and allowed me to accept a new paradigm where social and environmental issues are intertwined with profits. I would also like to echo Trish's dedication to the reader, for without you to implement the suggestions found in these pages, sustainable business will remain a discussion topic for few instead of an answer for many. —Heather Gadonniex

Contents at a Glance

Part 1:   Greening Your Business: Why It's the Way to Go   1

    1   Welcome to the Green Revolution   3
       The world has awakened to environmental responsibility,
       and as a sustainable business owner, you'll be guiding us all
       into a brighter, healthier future.

    2   Green Is Gold   15
       Businesses lead the way to new sustainable industries and
       new green jobs. You, your business, and the world will
       benefit.

Part 2:   Getting Started on the Green Path   25

    3   Steps to Make It Happen   27
       Create your plan to make your business sustainable.

    4   How Does Your Business Impact the Environment?   43
       Take a hard look at the many ways your business is
       affecting the environment and the world.

    5   Implementing Your Plan   59
       Begin the process of making yours a green business.

    6   Calculating and Reducing Your Carbon Footprint   69
       Measure your resource use and emissions.

Part 3:   Your Business Environment and Operations   85

    7   Greening Your Space   87
       Make your building eco-friendly.

    8   Green Interiors and Indoor Air Quality   101
       Create a healthy indoor atmosphere to benefit staff,
       customers, and your business.

    9   Greening Your Landscape   117
       Eco-friendly grounds protect the environment and enhance
       your image.

   10   Greening Your Products   129
       Reduce energy use and toxic emissions with sustainable
       manufacturing practices.

11 Greening Retail Operations   143
    *Showcase your environmental commitment with your retail
    store.*

12 Greening Your Restaurant or Food Supplier   153
    *Food represents a major opportunity to go green and cut
    costs.*

13 Packaging Cost Benefits   163
    *Wrap and pack your products sustainably to save resources
    and save money.*

14 Cost Analysis of Getting to Market   171
    *Reduce the environmental impact of delivering your
    products.*

Part 4:   Your Business Practices and Cost Benefits   181

15 In-House Office Systems   183
    Save energy and save money in your business office.

16 Greening the Commute and the Workweek   195
    Make daily employee activities more sustainable.

17 Employee Issues   207
    Employees enjoy green benefits at work.

18 Green Your Company Events   217
    *Business meetings and events provide a great chance to go
    green and demonstrate your commitment to sustainability.*

19 Sustainability Reporting   231
    Assess your success at creating a sustainable business.

Part 5:   Marketing Your Green Message   247

20 Spreading the Word   249
    *Let shareholders and stakeholders appreciate your
    environmental responsibilities.*

21 Promote, Support, Expand   261
    *Let your customers know they're making the best choice
    when they do business with you.*

22 Stamp of Approval   271
    *Seek recognition and valuable endorsements for your green
    efforts.*

23 Green Partners   283
*Collaborate with other green organizations to increase your
sustainability and reduce expenses.*

24 Networking With Other Green Businesses   291
*Get to know your like-minded colleagues through
cooperation and celebration.*

Appendixes

A Glossary   303

B Resources for Going Green   313

   Index   333

Contents

Part 1: Greening Your Business: Why It's the Way to Go   1

1 Welcome to the Green Revolution   3

The Bottom Lines...4

Business Is Key to Success..5

  Business Drives Our Economy 6

  Sustainable Economy Thrives...7

  New Green Industries...7

  Green-Collar Jobs..8

  Benefiting Your Business's Bottom Line................................9

Good for the Planet 10

  Reduce Our Dependence on Oil..10

  Reduce Greenhouse Gas Emissions......................................11

Good for People..12

  Employees Are Attracted to Environmentally
    Responsible Employers...12

  Green Policies Benefit Families and Lifestyles........................13

  Impact of Healthy Industries on Life 13

2 Green Is Gold   15

Cost-Benefit Analysis of Going Green 15

  Save Energy, Save Money 16

  Reduce Waste, Transportation Expenses, and Supply Costs.........16

Sustainable Business Practices...17

  What Is Sustainability?..17

  Why Sustainability Is Important 18

  Enhance Stakeholder Relations..20

  Improve Brand Value..21

  Improve Employee Relations and Productivity 22

Part 2: Getting Started on the Green Path   25

3 Steps to Make It Happen   27

Visioning Your Green Business Reality......................................27

  Gather a Team from Your Business..29

  Define What Sustainability Means to Your Business...................30

  Determine Your Green Mission Statement and Priorities............32

Assessing Your Current Operations 33

Creating Your Green Goals..34
  What Would You Like to Achieve in Six Months? 35
  What Would You Like to Achieve in One to Three Years? 36
  Cost-Benefit Analysis of Green Goals 37
Establishing Environmentally Friendly Policies.......................37
Creating a Strategic Plan 38
  Prioritize Green Goals 38
  Develop Strategies to Achieve Green Goals 40
  Develop a Timeline for Achievement of Green Goals 40
  Establish Roles and Responsibility 41

4   How Does Your Business Impact the Environment?   43
Sustainability Audit and Assessment 44
  Environmental and Social Indicators 44
Water 47
  Measuring Your Inputs 49
  Assess Water Quality 49
Energy...50
  How Much Electricity Does Your Company Use? 51
  Survey Technology Usage 51
Waste 53
Fuel 55
Green Business Programs..56

5   Implementing Your Plan   59
Establish Environmentally Friendly Policies 59
  Office Practices 61
  Sustainable Supply Chain 62
Create Checklists 63
  Steps to Reduce Emissions..63
  Steps to Reduce Water Usage...64
  Steps to Reduce Waste 65
Strive for Continuous Improvement 65
  Small Changes Reap Big Gains..66
  Each Step Moves You Forward...66

6   Calculating and Reducing Your Carbon Footprint   69
What's Your Carbon Footprint?...70
  A Basic Calculation 70
The GHG Protocol...72
  The Example of Little Red Wagon, Inc. 73

Creating Your Greenhouse Gas Emissions Inventory 75
Greenhouse Gas Reporting Standards 77
Product Carbon Footprinting 78
Carbon Offsets 80
About Carbon Offsets 80
Are Carbon Offsets Sustainable? 81
Other Greenhouse Gases to Consider 82

Part 3:   Your Business Environment and Operations   85

7   Greening Your Space   87
The Benefits of Green Construction and Renovation 87
Environmental 88
Economic 88
Starting From Scratch 89
LEED for Existing Buildings: Operations and Maintenance 90
Enlightening Your Landlord 91
Commissioning and Retrofitting for Greater Efficiency 92
Renovating for Savings 92
Applying Green Principles 93
Local Materials 94
Natural and Rapidly Renewable Materials 95
Maximize Natural Light and Ventilation 96
Solar Power and Renewable Energy Credits 97
Reduce Toxic Materials and Emissions 98
Eco-Friendly Waste Disposal 98
Conserving and Reusing Water 99

8   Green Interiors and Indoor Air Quality   101
Indoor Air Quality 102
Dangerous Indoor Air Contaminants 102
Biological Contaminants 103
Paints and Fabrics 104
Formaldehyde 104
Interior Fabrics 106
Nontoxic and Natural Choices 106
Floorings 107
Flooring Options 107
Reduce Flooring Waste 108
Reduce Toxic Exposure 109
Increase Durability 110

Furnishings 110
   Sustainable Materials 110
   Healthy Choices 111
Lighting 111
   Daylight Harvesting 111
   Motion Detection 112
Equipment 112
   Energy Conservation 112
   Sustainable Materials 113
Bathrooms 113
   Efficient Toilets and Sinks 113
   Napkins Versus Blowers 114
   Nontoxic Soaps 114
Biodegradable and Nontoxic Cleaning Supplies 114
   Air Fresheners 115

9   Greening Your Landscape   117
The Benefits of a Green Landscape 118
Self-Maintenance Versus Professional Services 118
   Finding Eco-Friendly Lawn Care 118
   Time and Cost Assessment 118
Replace Your Lawn with Native Plants 119
   Plant Placement and Diversity 120
Avoid Synthetic "-Cides" 121
Water Conservation 121
   Drip Irrigation 121
   Sprinkler Timers Help Conserve 122
   Collecting Rainwater 122
   Reusing Water for Irrigation 125
   Terracing 125
Soil and Fertilizers 125
   Compost 125
   Collect Yard and Snack Room Scraps 126
   Use Natural Fertilizers 127
   Mulch to Nourish and Retain Moisture 127

10   Greening Your Products   129
Using Life-Cycle Assessment 129
   Addressing Life-Cycle Assessment 130
   Assessing Environmental Impacts of Materials 131
   Green Manufacturing 133

Biomimicry 134
   Learning from Nature 134
Cradle to Cradle 135
Choose Green Materials 136
   Minimize Adverse Health Effects 137
Sustainable Supply-Chain Policies 138
   Local Sourcing 138
   Cost Savings and Marketing Benefits 138
   Maintain Safety, Price, and Performance 138
Alternatives 139
   Seek Recycled Materials 139
Pollution Prevention 140
   Replace Traditional Solvents with Bio-Based Options 140
   Offset Emissions with Renewable Energy Credits 141

11 Greening Retail Operations   **143**
Creating a Healthy Store 143
Reducing Supply Costs 145
   Reducing Waste 145
   Recycling Used Products 146
   Reusable Packaging Materials 147
   Reducing Energy and Water Usage 148
Streamlining Fuel Expenses 150
   Reviewing Delivery Practices 150
   Encouraging Walk/Bike Traffic 150
Educating Customers 150
Selling Green Products 151

12 Greening Your Restaurant or Food Supplier   **153**
The Cost Benefit of Organic Foods 154
Food's Impact on the Environment 156
   Meat's High Carbon Footprint 156
   Chemicals in Foods 157
   Transportation Costs of Food 158
Organic Versus Conventional Food Purveyors 159
Green Restaurant Association Resources 159
   Electricity 160
   Water 160
   Waste 161
   Marketing Your Environmentally Responsible Food Offerings 162

13 Packaging Cost Benefits   163

Sustainable Packaging Resources and Information 163
Packing Materials *164*
Impacts of Packing Materials *165*
Examples of Biodegradable and Eco-Friendly
Packaging Options *165*
Shipping Cartons 166
Design for Disassembly and Reuse *166*
Help Customers Maximize Benefit *167*
Reduce Plastic 167
Weigh Your Options: Shrink-Wrap Plastic *168*
Replace Plastic Cases with Biodegradable Cardboard *168*
Biodegradable Packing Materials 168
Green Peanuts *168*
Post-Consumer Recycled Paper *169*
Reducing Package Weight 169
Using Less Packing Materials *169*
Reducing Package Size *170*
Cost Benefits of Reducing Package Weight 170

14 Cost Analysis of Getting to Market   171

Choosing a Green Vehicle 172
Hybrid SUVs *172*
Is Ethanol a Green Fuel Choice? *173*
Adapt Delivery Vehicles to Biodiesel Fuel *174*
Low-Carbon and Fuel Standard *174*
Freight Options 175
Hybrid Truck Fleets *176*
Rail Transit *176*
Choosing Existing Green Shippers *177*
Port Support *178*
Local Sales Focus 178
Increase Local Market to Increase Profits *178*
Reduce Shelf Time *179*
Reduce Transportation Costs *179*
Support Local Businesses *179*

Part 4: Your Business Practices and Cost Benefits 181

15 In-House Office Systems 183

Electronic Efficiency..184

Obsolete File Storage: Save to Disk................................. *184*

Electronic "Paperwork"... *184*

Power Down: Unplug Unused Equipment.......................... *185*

Greener Electronics 186

Purchasing and Manufacturing Processes *186*

Update Equipment... *187*

Managing E-Waste *187*

Reduce Paper 188

Use Recycled Paper.. *189*

Print on Both Sides... *190*

Recycle Waste Paper *191*

Reduce Toxics...192

Chlorine-Free Paper *192*

Soy-Based, Vegetable-Based, and Water-Based Inks.................. *193*

16 Greening the Commute and the Workweek 195

Support Mass Transit...195

Provide Public Transport Stipends.................................. *196*

Help Employees Green Their Commute.................................196

Carpooling.. *197*

Cash Incentives for Employee Bicycles and Hybrid Cars *199*

Parking Incentives for Hybrid Cars................................. *199*

Remote Employees...199

Telecommuting Full Time or Part Time *199*

Reduced Costs = Increased Profits *200*

Sales and Meeting Travel Offsets..200

Promote Efficient Business Travel................................... *200*

Reduce Business Travel.. *200*

Teleconferencing Instead of Fly-In Meetings.................... *201*

Purchasing Travel Offsets *202*

Sustainable Travel Choices.. *202*

Tinkering with Time Clocks...203

Flextime... *203*

Four-Day Workweek *204*

Increase Family Time *204*

17 Employee Issues   207

Employee Relations...208
   Build Green Values into Corporate Culture............................*209*
   Support Employee Creativity *210*
   Rewarding Employees *211*
Encouraging Healthy Food Choices 211
   Provide Incentives to Choose Healthy Lunches and
     Build Community..*212*
   Organize Meals Featuring Local Organic Produce *212*
   Think Green for Business Meeting Meals...........................*213*
Green Up the Snack Room..213
   Eliminate Disposables *213*
   Provide Recycling Receptacles..*214*
Employee Health Options 214
   Group Activities: Exercise, Yoga, Tai Chi, and Biking..............*215*
   Credit for Alternative Health Choices................................*215*

18 Green Your Company Events   217

Green Meeting Possibilities...218
Choose a Green Venue 218
   Seek Building Efficiency *220*
   Green Interiors..*221*
   Clean Cleaning Agents...*221*
   Convenient Location Reduces Transportation *221*
Help in Finding Green Space 223
   Firms Specialize in Connecting Venue to Client......................*223*
   Consultants Go Green *223*
   Reducing Waste Is Key...*224*
   Select Eco-Friendly Gifts *224*
Request Green Dining...225
   Locally Grown Menu Items *226*
   Reusable Dining Ware..*226*
   Request Bulk Condiments *226*
   Three Stream Waste Stations *227*
   Pitchers of Tap: Skip Bottled Water..................................*227*
Reduce Paper 228
   Communicate Electronically..*228*
   Electronic Registration...*228*
   Handouts on Jump Drive..*228*

Name Tags *228*
Provide Recycling Receptacles *229*
Cost-Benefit Analysis 229
Weighing Cost Savings Against Additional Expense to
Go Green *229*
Creating the Best Combination for You *229*

19 Sustainability Reporting   **231**

What Is a Sustainability Report? 231
The History of Sustainability Reporting *233*
The Business Value of a Sustainability Report 234
Enhancing Reputation *234*
Improving Internal Operations *235*
Building Relationships *235*
Who Will Use the Sustainability Report? *235*
Does This Apply to My Business? 236
How to Begin Your Sustainability Report 237
Build the Business Case *238*
Preplanning Decisions 238
Focus of Report *239*
Level of Integration *239*
Boundary of the Report *239*
Medium of Reporting—Printed or Electronic? *239*
Communications Messaging and Design of the Report *239*
Level of Verification or Assurance to Use *240*
Information Gathering 240
Map Out Sustainability Process *241*
Identify Key Issues and Map Data Points *241*
Stakeholder Engagement *241*
Develop Performance Indicators *242*
Collect Information and Data *243*
Prepare and Design the Report 244
Verification and Assurance *244*
Publish, Distribute, and Evaluate *245*

Part 5: Marketing Your Green Message   **247**

20 Spreading the Word   **249**

Develop Your Green Story 250
Why Is Your Company Green? *250*
How You Made the Transition *250*

How Are Your Products Green? 251
Guide to Greenwashing 252
   Make Sure Your Story Is Valid 252
   Greenwashing Sins 254
Environmental Marketing Guidelines 255
   Truth in Advertising 255
   Environmental Marketing Claims 256
Publicity 258
   Electronic Resources 259

21 Promote, Support, Expand   **261**
Who's Buying? 261
   Defining Conscious Consumers 262
   Defining Your Green Consumer 264
Value-Driven Purchasing 265
   Health and Safety 265
   Honesty 266
   Convenience 266
   Relationships 266
   Doing Good Feels Good 266
Conveying Your Green Status to Customers 267
   Educate Customers About Recycling Products 267
   Don't Overstate Benefits 268
Customizing Your Marketing Message 268
   Staff 269
   Customers 269
   Media 269
Measuring Your Success 270

22 Stamp of Approval   **271**
Navigating the Sea of Endorsements 272
   Understanding the Endorsement 272
   Accuracy in Verification 273
   Signs of Genuine Value 274
   Pseudo Sanctions 275
Third-Party Certifications 276
   Green Seal 276
   Scientific Certification Systems 277
   *LEED Certification: Leadership in Energy and
      Environmental Design* 277

Fair Trade..278
Government Eco-Labels...279
International Eco-Labels 280
Is It Worth It?...282

23 Green Partners **283**

Government and Organizations as Your Green Partners........283
Regulatory Bane or Benefit?...284
Tax Rebates in Strategic Areas.....................................285
EPA Green Power Partnership...286
Recognition for Reducing..287
Strength in Numbers 288
Energy Star Partners..288
Energy-Saving Resources...289
Choose Energy-Efficient Equipment..............................289

24 Networking With Other Green Businesses **291**

Cooperation Trumps Competition 292
Collaborating for Common Good...................................292
Benefits Beyond the Bottom Line..................................293
Networking Resources...293
Green America and the National Green Pages...............294
Other Sustainability Professional Organizations.............295
Green Festivals, Conferences, and Networking Groups.........295
Earth Day Network 296
Green Music Festivals...296
Business for Social Responsibility.................................296
Green Drinks..296
Net Impact..297
Social Venture Network..297
Working With Community Initiatives....................................298
Cause Marketing..298
Supporting Sustainable Community Programs................299
Assisting Nonprofits...299

Appendixes

A Glossary **303**

B Resources for Going Green **313**

Index **333**

Foreword

It can be rightly said that we live in a transformational era.

There is now a broad consensus that the new economy that will emerge from the current cycle of "creative destruction" will have to be green. Green business, green tech, green jobs … the list goes on. As our nation begins to truly support the growth of renewable energy and environmentally friendly policies and practices, sustainable businesses will be the order of the day.

The recognition of the challenge of global climate change, an ominous impending energy crisis, and a fundamental reformation of the prevailing economic worldview guarantee that things will definitely be different in the twenty-first century.

In the context of all this, the meteoric rise of green business will continue unabated. Every week, I talk to business executives, students, trade unionists, entrepreneurs, people I meet in the grocery store, investors, government office holders, even shoe shiners and bus boys in restaurants—all speak of the need to transform our habits of consumption, business practices, and our culture as a whole. The world is beginning to understand that the status quo can no longer be the status quo.

Fortunately, there is a rather elegant solution to our problems: green business. Many have been preaching the benefits of green business for years, and now corporations and businesses of all kinds have begun to recognize the inextricable links between preserving our shared assets like the air, water, weather, and wildlife, a healthy economy and society, and profitability. Business can be a serious engine of change for the earth, for profitability, and for sustainable growth.

Green business is not a marketing slogan. It is a proactive embrace of a holistic worldview that integrates sound business practices with values that promote the regeneration and sustainability of the health and vitality of all life on the planet.

The Complete Idiot's Guide to Greening Your Business is a timely and valuable resource to impel the transformations demanded by our age. It provides a comprehensive guide to best practices you can put into place today to propel your business into tomorrow's paradigm. Get your business ahead of the curve. If you want to build a sustainable business and make profits while protecting the planet and caring for its people, this is the book for you.

One day the concepts illustrated in this book will be conventional wisdom, but in the meantime, the path to this new wisdom will be long and complicated, and we'll all need guidance and help in forging the best road into the future. You will experiment, succeed, fail, and learn. But if you want to get started, if you want to absorb tomorrow's wisdom today, and you want to begin building your business on a sound foundation that will withstand the tests of time, read this book.

Dan Geiger
Executive Director
U.S. Green Building Council—Northern California Chapter

Introduction

The world is in trouble, but it has often been said that crisis brings about opportunities. That sage observation is truer now than at any time in history. We all have the opportunity to participate in the wave of sustainability to better our economy, environment, and society while improving our profit margins.

Our civilization has evolved in a way that is damaging our Earth and society. Since the Industrial Revolution, we've been driven by our desire for more money and constant growth—development and so-called improvements—and we've allowed those values to cloud our ability to understand resource capacity, the balance of natural ecosystems, and the value of quality of life. We've overlooked the fact that we need our natural resources to survive, and we've used and destroyed them relentlessly in our rampant rage through the twentieth century. Now we are facing the damage, and a new age is dawning in the twenty-first century. Collectively, we can act now to change the overconsumptive habits we have developed and leave a lasting, positive impact on our planet and society.

The International Panel on Climate Change, a consortium of scientists from around the world, reported in 2007 that global concentrations of carbon dioxide, methane, and nitrous oxide have increased markedly as a result of human activity since 1750 and now far exceed pre-industrial values. These greenhouse gases contribute to global warming, which leads to increased average air and ocean temperatures and widespread melting of snow and ice. This may not seem like a huge disaster, but the disruption of these fragile systems can lead to increased hurricanes, drought, flood, and famine. We're already seeing severe increases in these and other related problems, and scientists are fast-tracking their predictions, warning that the dangers associated with higher temperatures worldwide are happening much more rapidly than anticipated.

In addition to the release of greenhouse gases, we have been pouring toxins into the ecosystem and our bodies. Oftentimes these toxins bioaccumulate or remain in our tissue and ecosystem, building up over time. Over the past decade, we have felt the environmental and health effects of toxic substances, including now-banned chemicals for agriculture such as DDT the highly toxic pesticide made famous by acclaimed environmental author Rachael Carson, and polychlorinated biphenyl (PCBs), a known carcinogen banned in the 1970s that was the cause for the massive Hudson River cleanup. Our water, air, and soil are saturated with synthetic petrochemicals, and they are threatening the health of our planet and all life on Earth.

As citizens of the earth, we are contributing to these problems. But we have the knowledge and ability to change the course of this environmental and social crisis brought about in large part by our use of fossil fuels. The question looming over our heads is: can we mobilize the population to make the necessary changes in timely enough fashion to restore balance? We won't be able to stop global warming completely—too much damage has already been done. But we can certainly change the disastrous path we're on and avert the worst-case scenarios projected.

Resource scarcity coupled with the consumer demand for green products and company transparency is defining today's marketplace. This new opportunity represents one of restoration, not destruction. We have the ability to change the habits and industrial systems we've developed over the past century. New technology makes it easier to leave less of an impact on the earth, and innovation allows us to develop creative ways to engage our employees and give back to our communities.

Businesses can make a substantial impact on our environment and on society by leading the way into a more sustainable future. Because business represents a large share of activity around the world, making changes to more environmentally friendly operations can achieve the scale of conversion that is necessary to truly affect our climate, our environment, and our society.

We, Heather Gadonniex and Trish Riley, met at the National Association of Home Builders Green Trends trade show in Orlando in 2007, and struck up a conversation about finding a way to work together to help spread the message about the importance of going green. We arranged to meet again at the United States Green Building Council's Green Build conference in Chicago in 2008, where we joined an amazing crowd of more than 20,000 green businesspeople to hear green business visionary Paul Hawken speak about the importance of the movement. "It's not about the money," said Hawken, "It's about meaning."

As we watched green business owners and innovators network together and learn from one another, we were truly awestruck by the realization that the green movement is not so much a part of the future; it is in full force right now. Since attending her first GreenBuild in 2003, Heather was particularly inspired by the drastic increase in attendance each year at GreenBuild. There is no longer a question of whether we can make the changes we need to ensure a sustainable and healthy future. The only question is how fast can we turn the tide away from the course we've been on—which we now know is significantly damaging the earth and our health—and toward a healthy new environment and lifestyles for our children. The masses of young, smart attendees at the USGBC conferences make it clear that the young professionals of today are taking their businesses in the right direction. They recognize that profit is not the only benefit from business. Building satisfying lives and protecting the planet and our health are just as important.

Business is the engine that drives our economy. It operates on a world stage and at the large scale necessary to really make the good ideas science offers us work for sustainable and renewable industries. It's an exciting time to be on the verge of a new green industry and green economy, and a great opportunity for businesses to not only reap the benefits of the wealth of new information coming to market each day, but also to become sustainable leaders in their communities and fields.

We are pleased to provide this step-by-step guide to help small businesses make the responsible move into healthy practices that will protect our air, water, and soil as well as your customers and employees. While you're doing the right thing for people and the planet, you'll be doing the best thing for your bottom line at the same time. Let us show you how.

How to Use This Book

This book is divided into five parts to make the process of greening your business as easy and successful as possible.

In **Part 1, "Greening Your Business: Why It's the Way to Go,"** you will learn why sustainable business is the way of the future and how to develop your plan to green your business.

In **Part 2, "Getting Started on the Green Path,"** we'll help you assess your green potential and develop plans to achieve it.

In **Part 3, "Your Business Environment and Operations,"** we help you make your place of business and products more environmentally friendly.

In **Part 4, "Your Business Practices and Cost Benefits,"** we discuss ways to green your office systems, employee practices, and business events.

Part 5, "Marketing Your Green Message," helps you let customers and others know the important step you've taken, and helps you develop working relationships with like-minded businesses to capitalize on your success.

The back of the book contains a glossary of definitions with terms you may not be familiar with. We've also provided a list of resources and websites mentioned throughout the book where you can find further information.

Extras

Throughout the book, you'll see notes called out in the text and in the margins of the book:

Hazard

Pitfalls to watch out for in implementing green business practices.

def•i•ni•tion

We provide definitions to green jargon and technical terms we use along the way.

Going Green

Tips on ways to green up your business.

Enviro-Fact

News, facts, and stats about long-range effects of creating green businesses.

Acknowledgments

It's been a great pleasure to put together this guide to greening your business, and it's been rewarding to work with many professionals who shared their tips for creating sustainable businesses, and with others who kindly shared their photos, writing, and research skills. Thanks to all who've helped bring this book from idea to useful tool. I'd like to thank my friend and colleague, author David Kohn, who alerted me that Alpha was seeking an environmental journalist to write this book. He put me in touch with acquisitions editor Paul Dinas, who has been a great pleasure to work with. Paul wanted me to work with an expert in green business to prepare the book, so I contacted Heather Gadonniex, a green business consultant whom I'd met through our mutual business interests and with whom I had already discussed co-authoring just such a book. She agreed this opportunity was perfect for us. Thanks to Heather for agreeing to collaborate! Heather and I turned to many experts to gather the best information available. Our thanks go to Patti Roth, a south Florida environmental journalist, for her contribution on greening office systems and working with green partners; and to James Steele, organic grower and owner of The Herb Garden in Melrose, Florida, for his contribution to greening landscapes. Many thanks to all of you, whose help in bringing this book to fruition was indispensable. I'd also like to thank my son Bud and my daughter Rachel, whose support is unconditional and always precious to me; James, for his patience and comfort throughout the process;

and my two little supervisors, Stella and Teddi, who keep me company during the long days and nights of writing.
—Trish Riley

Working on this project has been an amazing experience. Living in San Francisco, I am so very fortunate to be surrounded by industry experts, some wonderful friends and mentors who have let me pick their brains and talk through complex ideas surrounding the issues of sustainability. Thank you to those who worked so hard during the beginning of this movement. These thought leaders, many of them mentioned in the text of this book, laid the groundwork for what we know as sustainable or green business. We would not be here today if it were not for their tenacity, dedication, and commitment to shifting the current paradigm. Many years of working to merge industry, environmentalism, and social justice are finally paying off! Trish and Paul, thank you for giving me the opportunity to coalesce my thoughts and put them on paper and to contribute to a project that will help start small- to medium-size enterprises on their journey toward sustainability. A few personal notes of thanks go to Rob Sinclair, founder of Conscious Brands, for his expertise and contribution to Chapters 4 and 19; and to Oliver Ferrari, founder of Marian Eco, for his contribution on carbon footprinting in Chapter 6. Thanks to the folks at BBMG and Mind Click for sharing their market research and to the team at Sustainable Industries for always being a fantastic resource and providing cutting-edge sustainability news. Thank you to Dan Geiger, executive director of the northern California chapter of the USGBC, for powering through the draft version of this book in order to write the foreword. A big hug to Miriam Karell, founder of Three Point Vision, who is not only a friend but also an amazing colleague; she helped me remain grounded and provided invaluable ideas for the text of this book. She also contributed to Chapter 3, "Steps to Make It Happen." Thank you to Courtney, Mary, and Brian. Last but not least, thank you to my family for always believing in me. The look on my father's face when I told him I was going to focus my core studies on environmental studies and sustainability and only minor in business was priceless, but I guess in the end he knew exactly where I would end up.
—Heather Gadonniex

We'd like to extend a special thank you to our colleagues, whose generous help and expertise were so valuable to us.

Oliver Ferrari is managing partner of MarionEco, LLC, a sustainability consulting firm that helps organizations establish effective environmental programs that reduce costs and conserve resources. He specializes in quantitative analysis of green projects. Oliver is a LEED-accredited professional, and he holds a Master of Environmental Management degree in Business and Environment from Duke University.

Miriam Karell and Rob Sinclair are co-founders of Equanimi (www.equanimi.com), a consultancy that awakens inspiration, innovation, and interconnection in organizations. A core component of their work is to collaboratively engage stakeholders to make decisions and to take actions that move individuals, teams, and companies toward sustainability. Miriam designs sustainability strategies that lead to profound changes in organizations and has been trained in The Natural Step, Integral Theory, systems thinking, strategic business management, and environmental engineering. Rob's philosophy is, "How you do anything is how you do everything." He's an expert on doing business sustainably.

Patti Roth, a freelance journalist, writes for newspapers, magazines, and websites about environmental topics, architecture, and animals. Her work has been published in the Fort Lauderdale *Sun-Sentinel*, the *Miami Herald, E/The Environmental Magazine,* and *Dog Fancy.*

James Steele is the owner of The Herb Garden (www.steelesherbgarden.com), a wholesale/retail nursery specializing in herbs that grow well in Florida's unique climate. With 38 years of experience growing herbs in Florida, James shares his knowledge of herbs and sustainable gardening through classes and lectures. "Herbs are amazing plants. Growing them and using them for all these years and sharing that information with others has brought me immeasurable reward." James is co-founder (with author Trish Riley) of www.GoGreenAlternatives.com, a green community networking site to help promote green thoughts, activities, businesses, jobs, and growth.

Trademarks

All terms mentioned in this book that are known to be or are suspected of being trademarks or service marks have been appropriately capitalized. Alpha Books and Penguin Group (USA) Inc. cannot attest to the accuracy of this information. Use of a term in this book should not be regarded as affecting the validity of any trademark or service mark.

Part 1

Greening Your Business: Why It's the Way to Go

Greening your business can be a win-win scenario for your business, your bottom line, and the planet. In this part, we explain why it's a great idea to make your business a sustainable enterprise and give you the knowledge you need to develop your plans and help your stakeholders understand why this is the best way to move your business into the future. We recap the issues our planet is facing with global warming and other effects from our reliance on petroleum, such as the contamination of our waterways, air, and soil with synthetic chemicals.

Welcome to the Green Revolution

In This Chapter

- ◆ Benefits for the planet
- ◆ Benefits for people
- ◆ Benefits for your bottom line
- ◆ Benefits for the economy

I (Trish) have been reporting on environmental issues for the past two decades, and both Heather and I have attended and presented at many conferences around the country, dealing with environmental topics from water and waste issues to green building and eco-tourism. For years the scenario was always the same: some academics reporting the dire scientific data they'd uncovered after years of study along with some nature-loving hippies, and everyone wringing their hands, unsure of solutions that could be viable in the fast-paced, business-friendly world.

Then in 2007, I attended a climate change summit in Miami convened by Governor Charlie Crist, a business-friendly Republican who, along with a growing contingent of business people and politicians, realized that without a healthy environment, business would be crippled. Suddenly the academics and hippies had an attentive audience of suits, and for the first time, I saw the two traditionally oppositional groups eagerly working together, respecting one another's positions. There they were, rubbing their hands together as if they'd seen the emerald light.

Business people were starting to realize the importance of protecting the environment and recognized the potential of making money at the same time. Many business opportunities exist in the new green economy, and forward-thinking entrepreneurs as well as savvy traditional business owners and executives are taking advantage of these new avenues for money-making. Green has become gold.

The Bottom Lines

Consumers are demanding greener products and asking questions about the companies producing these products. Going green has become much more than a trend. It is a market force that has the ability to create new jobs, restore our economy, and revive our natural environment. Sure, some of this green speak can be confusing. Common questions include: What is a carbon footprint? How do we calculate it? What is *greenwashing?* And more important, what is the overarching issue of *sustainable development?* We're excited that in this book we can offer step-by-step assistance for any small business owner who wants to join the lead to improve our planet and our lifestyles. We can turn the tide!

def•i•ni•tion

Greenwashing is marketing a product or practice as environmentally friendly when it isn't really as sound as it seems. When in doubt, ask questions to make sure you're getting the full story.

Sustainable development is development that meets the needs of the present without compromising the ability of future generations to meet their own needs, according to The Brundtland Commission, formally known as The World Commission on Environment and Development (1987).

In sustainable business jargon, going green creates an integrated bottom line for businesses: it's good for the planet, good for the people, and good for finances. According to L. Hunter Lovins, sustainability guru, co-author of *Natural Capitalism,* and founder of the consulting firm Natural Capital Solutions, the *integrated bottom line* was built off the concept of the *triple bottom line*. In a September 2008 interview with *Sustainable Industries*, Lovins stresses that when looking at the triple bottom line, businesses should always consider social and environmental factors as well as profits. Lovins said, "with the triple bottom line, you've got these two other areas—social and environmental—that become costs and drag down profit. Now those things are integrated into the sustainable business model, and they provide cost reductions and better management, which positively affect a company's bottom line."

def•i•ni•tion

The **integrated bottom line** relates to the **triple bottom line** concept. Both concepts suggest that business operations should consider the environment, society, and economy. The integrated bottom line goes a step further than the triple bottom line by suggesting that all three topics (environment, society, and economy) should be joined together as a single bottom line.

Business Is Key to Success

Business is not only a driving force that can restore our ecosystems and tackle tough societal issues, it is also a force that can add to the success of our overall organization. Looking at a business from a systemic, holistic perspective, or a "lens of sustainability," leads to myriad improvements, from decreased operational costs to improved brand advantage. In short, incorporating sustainability into our everyday operations is just good business.

Interface Inc., a carpet manufacturer located in Georgia, is well-known in the green business world. Back in 1994, after 21 years in the carpet industry, Interface's CEO, Ray Anderson, was asked to give an inspirational speech to a newly formed Environmental Task Force. Coming up short on what he wanted to say, he turned to Paul Hawken's book, *The Ecology of Commerce* (Collins Business, 1994), when he found it on his desk. This book inspired him to transform his organization from plunderer of natural resources to restorer. From 1995 to 1996, Interface's sales increased by $200 million, although the amount of materials they extracted from the earth was no more than the previous year.

Now Anderson travels the country giving inspirational speeches about looking at industry through a lens of sustainability. When interviewed for the movie *The Corporation*, Anderson stated, "The largest institution on Earth, the wealthiest, the most powerful, the most pervasive, the most influential, is the institution of business and industry—the corporation, which also is the current present day instrument of destruction. It must change."

Enviro-Fact
Business is the only mechanism on the planet today powerful enough to produce the changes necessary to reverse global, environmental, and social degradation. —Paul Hawken, green business author of *Natural Capitalism: Creating the Next Industrial Revolution,* and *Blessed Unrest: How the Largest Movement in the World Came into Being and Why No One Saw It Coming*

Business Drives Our Economy

Businesses make up the backbone of our economic system. Built on capitalism, this system thrives by assigning dollar values to both tangible and intangible resources. Since the Industrial Revolution, though, economists have ignored the economic values associated with systemic ecosystem services such as watersheds and water systems; carbon systems, which maintain the global carbon cycle; and general overall processes that maintain planetary balance.

An excellent overview of how our consumer economy developed and how consumers have become essential slaves to the unceasing push for increasing business profits can be viewed at www.storyofstuff.com, a video created by Annie Leonard for the Tides Foundation & Funders Workgroup for Sustainable Production and Consumption.

In addition, human economic indicators such as employee happiness, well-being, and health were also not figured into the capitalists' equations.

def•i•ni•tion

An **externality** is the side effect on an individual or entity due to the actions of another individual or entity.

This mindset creates economic *externalities*. An economic externality exists when a person makes a choice that affects other people not accounted for in the marketplace. Externalities can be both positive and negative. For example, if a factory is spewing pollution into the atmosphere, it creates unhealthy air quality. Children living and playing near the factory may develop asthma and consequently, miss school because of health problems. The societal cost associated with disadvantaged learning and productivity would be a negative externality caused by environmental pollution. Another example is water pollution. When a factory discharges unclean effluent into a river, it pollutes the river. Local residents bear the cost of the pollution in the form of health costs and water purification costs. Residents also cannot fish, swim, or play in the river.

An example of a positive externality would be the effect a community garden has on an area. People participating in the project benefit from increased health and develop a sense of pride in their community. Increased community involvement brings neighbors closer together; decreases crime; and restores areas of the environment by changing unsightly, unusable, and unsafe areas to green space.

Sustainable Economy Thrives

"Going green" enables businesses to factor in these economic externalities. Accounting for monetary costs that may otherwise be overlooked often builds a more profitable enterprise. Sustainability is key to building a burgeoning, stable economic system that will thrive during resource fluctuation. Healthier environments equal more productive and healthier people, which in turn lead to increased social equity and a stronger economy for our country.

New Green Industries

Developing new energy resources and more efficient transportation modes means that we'll be developing new industries as a result of creating a greener world. Solar energy, wind energy, alternative fuels, and mass transit growth all represent opportunities for new businesses to develop to meet the needs of an environmentally friendly era.

Small business owner Sharon Rowe developed a green niche for herself by selling products that meet a need for the green-conscious consumer. Her company, Eco-Bags of Ossining, New York, produces and sells cloth bags to replace disposable bags, which have become a bane to the environment by creating massive amounts of waste, filling landfills and threatening wildlife when not properly disposed of. Rowe recognized this growing need in 1989, and has since grown to boast sales of $2.2 million in 2007, according to *Time* magazine (July 23, 2008).

As you read through this book, we'll provide many other examples of businesses that have found ways to go green.

Green-Collar Jobs

With the creation of new, innovative industries comes the need for employees, from assembly-line workers to CEOs. As demand for green products and services increases, more jobs will be created. In an on-air interview with NPR, Jerome Ringo, President of the Apollo Alliance, stated that green-collar jobs are projected to create three to five million new jobs and promote $300 billion in investment over the next 10 years.

The introduction of environmentally friendly products or services into the economy has created green-collar employment opportunities. Solar panel installation, waste water reclamation, green building and retrofitting, organic foods, material reuse and recycling, wind power generation, and green product manufacturing are all examples of sectors that create green-collar jobs.

Van Jones is the co-founder of the Ella Baker Center, founder of Green for All, and pioneer for green-collar jobs. In a 2007 interview with *The New York Times*, Jones said, "The green economy has the power to deliver new sources of work, wealth, and health to low-income people while honoring the Earth. If you can do that, you just wiped out a whole bunch of problems."

Recently, Jones was instrumental in launching the nation's first "Green Jobs Corps." Starting with $250,000 seed money from the Oakland City Council, this pilot project will create job training programs for at-risk youth, the formerly incarcerated, the underemployed, and low-income residents of Oakland, California. A collaboration of community organizations, private entities, and city government, the Green Jobs Corps strives to be a catalyst for enabling people from all backgrounds to participate in the burgeoning sustainable economy.

Enviro-Fact

The Ella Baker Center for Human Rights (www.ellabakercenter.org) is a strategy and action center working for justice, opportunity, and peace in urban America. Based in Oakland, California, they promote positive alternatives to violence and incarceration.

Green For All (www.greenforall.org) is a national organization dedicated to building green economy strong enough to lift people out of poverty. By advocating for local, state, and federal commitment to job creation, job training, and entrepreneurial opportunities in the emerging green economy—especially for people from disadvantaged communities—Green For All fights both poverty and pollution at the same time.

A Worldwatch Institute study, *Jobs in Renewable Energy Expanding* by Michael Renner, reports that the renewable energy field employs 2.3 million people around the world today. More people are employed in countries where their government supports renewable development. Renner reports that renewable energy fields employ more people in labor-related jobs, while the coal and oil industries rely more on equipment that reduces the labor force. He says that hundreds of thousands of jobs have been lost in the coal mining industries in the United States, China, Germany, the United Kingdom, and South Africa over the past two decades. However, in those countries which strongly support renewable energies, such as Spain, jobs have increased by nearly 200,000. As jobs decrease in the fossil fuel industries, jobs are increasing in the renewable energy fields, especially in countries whose governments are supporting the development of renewable energies, such as solar and wind energies.

Renner found 1 million *biomass* and *biofuel* jobs, 624,000 solar thermal jobs, 170,000 solar photovoltaic jobs, and 300,000 wind jobs. These numbers are bound to grow as renewable energy industries grow. Projections suggest there will be 2.1 million wind industry jobs and 6.3 million solar industry jobs by 2030.

def•i•ni•tion

Biomass is an organic, nonfossil material that is available on a renewable basis. Biomass includes all biological organisms, dead or alive, and their metabolic by-products that have not been transformed by geological processes into substances, such as coal or petroleum.

Biofuel is any fuel derived from an organic material that is not fossilized like coal or petroleum. Common sources of biofuel grown for the U.S. and European markets are corn, soybeans, flaxseed, and rapeseed. Biofuel can appear in solid, liquid, or gas form.

It's clear that our growing renewable energy industry will contribute greatly to our economy as it continues to develop with our support.

Benefiting Your Business's Bottom Line

Although going green is often derided as too expensive to pursue, innovative business owners and others are discovering that becoming stewards of their environment is actually helping them save money in many ways. When we use less energy, we pay less for energy. When we reduce our waste, we either buy fewer unnecessary materials or make better use of our resources, both of which save money. When we create healthier work environments and happier employees, we increase employee productivity and innovation.

For example, according to the United States Environmental Protection Agency Energy Star Program, Thomas Mott Homestead Bed and Breakfast in Alburgh, Vermont, reduced its energy costs by $10,000 annually, saved over 140,000 kWh, and prevented 240,000 pounds of greenhouse gas pollution from entering the atmosphere. The list of ways to save money by making smarter environmental choices goes on and on. You'll learn more about specific changes you can make at your place of business in the following chapters.

Good for the Planet

Going green is good for the planet in many ways. Reducing and modifying business inputs such as water, energy, and material use will result in a reduction of our overall environmental impact. Perhaps the biggest area that environmentally responsible businesses can impact is in regard to fossil fuels. Scrutinizing supply chains and changing our buying habits to reduce energy spent transporting goods, choosing products that were manufactured using green or lean manufacturing techniques, and procuring materials composed of eco-friendly materials are all more sustainable practices than business has traditionally employed. We'll show you how to make these changes at your business, and by implementing them, you'll be helping protect our environment for future generations.

Going Green

Green manufacturing is a method for manufacturing that minimizes waste and pollution achieved through product and process design. Overall, green manufacturing reduces costs, improves process efficiency, and stimulates product innovation.

Reduce Our Dependence on Oil

Because energy is essential to all aspects of business, from manufacturing and product distribution to running offices and facilities, finding new means of powering your business with less oil can make a dramatic difference to the planet. Current scientific studies indicate the burning of fossil fuels is causing the majority of anthropogenic climate change. Our efforts to conserve energy through efficiency methods can make substantial decreases in our energy usage. Finding alternative energy sources for the remaining demand further reduces our drain and dependence on oil, gas, and fossil fuel products.

Simple things such as switching our conventional incandescent light bulbs to compact fluorescent bulbs can cut carbon emissions by an average of 560 kg per bulb. According to the web resource EnvironmentalChemistry.com, this switch will also save an average of $88.63 over the life of the bulb. When making the switch to compact fluorescent, remember to properly dispose of the bulb when its useful life is over. Compact fluorescents contain small amounts of mercury and must be disposed of at a designated hazardous household waste facility. Check with your local municipal trash service for specific instructions. Replacing traditional bulbs with light-emitting diode (LED) bulbs is a cost-effective way to reduce energy consumption.

Reduce Greenhouse Gas Emissions

Greenhouse gases create a blanket effect in our atmosphere that traps heat and keeps it from escaping, creating the *greenhouse effect.* This process occurs naturally and is essential for maintaining the temperature of the earth. When human activity releases extra greenhouse gases into the atmosphere, this natural blanket becomes thicker and *global warming* results. Water vapor, carbon dioxide, methane, nitrous oxide, ozone, and fluorinated gases are all greenhouse gases. Since the Industrial Revolution, the concentration of greenhouse gases in the atmosphere has increased dramatically due to human action. This creates a planetary imbalance caused mainly by the burning of fossil fuels.

All greenhouse gases have damaging health effects. Scientists have overwhelmingly confirmed in the Intercontinental Panel on Climate Change Report (2007) as well as many other scientific studies that these gases are proliferating into our atmosphere at an unprecedented rate because of the modern industrial dependence on petroleum products. The less oil we burn, the fewer greenhouse gases we spew into the atmosphere.

def•i•ni•tion

A **greenhouse gas** traps heat in the atmosphere.

The **greenhouse effect** is the rise in temperature that the earth experiences because certain gases in the atmosphere (water vapor, carbon dioxide, nitrous oxide, and methane, for example) trap energy from the sun. Without these gases, heat would escape into space, and Earth's average temperature would be about 60°F colder. Because of how they warm our world, we refer to these gases as greenhouse gases.

Global warming is an increase in the global average surface temperature due to natural or anthropogenic (human-induced) climate change.

Good for People

Businesses and individuals are finding that as they adopt more environmentally friendly practices, customers and workers are benefiting from healthier environments, both in the immediate vicinity of the business and wherever the products they produce end up. These benefits are reaching beyond the usual scope of business practices, and employees and customers are responding to the positive change.

Employees Are Attracted to Environmentally Responsible Employers

For decades, the American business climate was based on the idea that employees would work for the company for most of their adult lives, and, in turn, the company provided retirement benefits to protect employees and their families in old age. However, in recent years, that model has gone by the wayside. Employers have provided fewer retirement benefits, and, in many cases, pensions have evaporated after years of dedication and contributions from the employees.

Today's workforce doesn't forget seeing family members and friends cut off from the golden futures they anticipated. Younger workers count among their values the importance of finding a company that demonstrates responsible behavior and actions toward its employees, the community, and the planet. The new green economy brings with it a renewed interest among employees to work in ways that are meaningful to them and which fulfill their values beyond the paycheck. Sustainable businesses strive to provide employment that helps workers achieve greater balance between work and the rest of their lives.

Recent results from a survey conducted by Internet employment resource MonsterTRAK.com show that an outstanding number of young workers want to work for a green company. Eighty percent of survey participants said they are interested in a job that has a positive impact on the environment, and a colossal 92 percent would choose to work for an environmentally friendly company over a nongreen company.

Another study conducted by Kenexa Research Institute shows that employees who work at companies with clear corporate social environmental responsibility (CSER) platforms are most satisfied. The study also showed that employees of these organizations are more likely to stay at their jobs for a greater duration of time, are more committed to their work, and are happier with senior management and executives.

Green Policies Benefit Families and Lifestyles

Employers are finding that adopting environmentally friendly policies is resulting in better employee retention and productivity rates. Employees who feel good about the company they work for and the work they're doing perform better and feel better about themselves. Feeling better mentally and emotionally has a direct impact on our physical health, and happier individuals who feel better about themselves are likely to be more effective parents whose positive attitudes reflect in their children, relationships, and lives. In addition, improved social employee policies, such as flexible hours, provide workers the opportunity to better balance their personal lives and their work lives. This benefits both the employee and the employer.

Environmental policies benefit worker's lifestyles just as much as social policies. For example, implementing a carbon footprint reduction strategy by looking at employee transportation results in "ride your bike to work" programs and carpool programs. The former enables employees to work an exercise routine into their busy schedules, improving mental productivity and overall health. Carpool programs save employees money on gas and road tolls and provide employees with time to get to know their fellow workers. Both contribute to the reduction of greenhouse gas emissions and global warming.

Impact of Healthy Industries on Life

Air pollution caused by burning petroleum products to produce energy, such as with coal plants, diesel-fueled trains, and gasoline-powered autos, contribute to lung disease, asthma, and respiratory problems. Technologies such as alternative energy and hybrid cars that use less petroleum products and produce fewer emissions help us to have cleaner air with fewer disease-causing pollutants.

Water pollution from synthetic petrochemicals and human and animal waste has been linked to several twentieth-century diseases, including cancer, autism, brain damage, and developmental disorders. For example, burning coal releases mercury into the air where it settles in water bodies, contaminating the water and the fish that live there. The mercury is passed along to those who eat the fish and can cause irreparable damage to developing fetuses and young children.

Agricultural run-off contaminates water with farming chemicals, such as fertilizers and pesticides, as well as waste products from livestock. These pollute waterways, causing overgrowth of algae and other plants which choke sunlight from waterways and kill the natural plants that feed fish and amphibians. The lack of plants causes lower oxygen levels, which also kills water-based life. The synthetic petrochemicals used in farming are also dangerous for sea life because many are endocrine disrupters, which mimic estrogen and cause the feminization of amphibians and alligators in waterways. This effect is likely to be more widespread than scientifically proven thus far, which is indicated by statistics showing a decrease in male birth rates and in sperm counts among males worldwide.

Many industries and municipalities flush partially treated wastewater into public rivers and oceans, and small quantities of contaminants are approved by the government. However, in recent years, as water resources become scarce and as we learn more about the dangers of chemical contamination, we are realizing that some chemicals are more dangerous than once recognized—even in the smallest quantities—and that cleaning our waterways is much more expensive than preventing contamination. In some cases, we have not even developed clean-up technologies. Finding ways to avoid contaminating air, water, and soil instead of cleaning up after the damage is done is better for our environment and better for our budgets.

The Least You Need to Know

- ◆ Businesses have a big impact on the planet.
- ◆ Business owners can make choices to limit their environmental footprint.
- ◆ Green businesses can create more jobs and improve the economy.
- ◆ Greening your business can save money and increase profits.

Green Is Gold

In This Chapter

- ◆ Sustainable versus unsustainable business practices
- ◆ The value of sustainable resources: cost-benefit analysis
- ◆ Bottom-line benefits for business
- ◆ Enhanced public image through corporate social responsibility

News stories about companies going green are popping up every day in papers and magazines around the country. Companies debuting case studies on how they are saving money by realizing the value in commitment to environmental and social issues is a common trend and a welcome change from the days when environmental groups and corporations did not see eye to eye. And it's not just big companies that are scrambling to implement sustainability tactics into their business models—small- to medium-size businesses are making the transition to a more sustainable way of "doing business for good" as well.

Cost-Benefit Analysis of Going Green

One of the first things you need to do when considering changing your business from traditional to sustainable practices and policies is conduct a cost-benefit analysis. You'll want to weigh the costs of doing business as usual against the costs of keeping the environment in mind when conducting business. Also consider the social implications of implementing a sustainability program into your organization and how your bottom line will benefit from that aspect.

We'll help by providing checklists to use for making the comparisons in many of the following chapters. You'll find myriad ways to save money through conservation, efficiency, and employee and community engagement. We'll provide information on creative ways to incorporate accounting tactics that track your sustainability progress. This is also known as triple bottom line accounting, which you will learn more about as the book goes on.

Save Energy, Save Money

The Environmental Protection Agency (EPA) estimates that if manufacturers can cut back their energy use by just 10 percent, they'd save nearly $10.4 billion overall in a year, with enough power left over to run almost 10 billion homes for one year. In April 2008, the EPA and the National Association of Manufacturers (NAM) issued a challenge to the U.S. manufacturing industry—14,000 companies—to meet that goal.

> **Going Green**
>
> The EPA Energy Star Program provides a guide for small businesses called Putting Energy into Profits. Find out more at www.energystar.gov/index.cfm?c=sb_guidebook.sb_guidebook.

In 2007, the EPA Energy Star program recognized just eight small businesses that applied energy conservation methods that reduced their consumption by 25 percent, together saving an estimated $1.2 billion and reducing emissions equivalent to taking 1,600 cars off the road.

Reducing energy use through conservation and efficiency can take a huge chunk of energy costs and emission output off the table, saving considerable amounts of money and protecting our atmosphere at the same time.

Reduce Waste, Transportation Expenses, and Supply Costs

Businesses are finding that by reducing waste products, they're reducing the costs of processing waste and getting more from the resources used at the same time. They are also avoiding the sometimes high costs of transporting that waste.

A small company can experience the same kinds of relative expense reduction by following the lead of the companies that are making the effort to reduce waste.

Selecting materials and supplies for business is also an area that can benefit from a sustainability assessment. For example, it might be possible to replace exotic materials with products that come from local sources. Cutting back on remote sourcing—by finding local resources instead of materials from far away—can save energy and reduce costs, too.

Going Green _____

Find out how your business can reduce energy output and join the NAM and EPA Challenge to Save Energy at www.energystar.gov/index.cfm?c=industry.bus_industry.

All these suggested reductions can result in lower expenses, which translates into increased profits. Any business person can see the beauty of that, even if he's not an eco-badge-wearing tree hugger.

Sustainable Business Practices

Economists are well aware that our Garden of Eden is a limited bounty of natural resources, and environmentalists urge us to nourish and protect our air, soil, and water as we use these treasures and enjoy their benefits. Both schools of thought are reaching the same conclusion: creating sustainable business practices is good for the economy and good for the environment.

You can apply sustainable practices to your business in many ways. Let's take a look at why that's important and why you'll want to begin the process of making your business a green business.

What Is Sustainability?

What is all this buzz around green anyway? Some choose to think of "green" only in terms of the environment. However, we encourage you to think beyond green and incorporate a social dimension into your green initiatives. This merging of environment, society, and economy brings us to the idea of sustainability. According to Webster's Dictionary, _sustainable_ means "capable of being sustained." When we take this definition and apply it to the environment and society, sustainability can mean a multitude of things. We can use it to describe resources used in a way that does not take more from the earth than can be replenished or to describe a company that empowers workers to be innovative and balanced. Sustainability can also describe a society or business that energizes people to be productive contributors to their communities. In short, sustainability is about balancing the intricate cyclic systems of ecology, economy, and society.

By applying the same cyclical approach to our business systems, we can help ensure that we will have a continuous supply of resources, rather than eating them up and leaving nothing but waste. Instead of devouring resources and leaving nothing useful afterward, we want to return those resources to the cycle so they can continue to be productive. For example, when we use water, instead of polluting it with waste products so that it is no longer usable, we want to be aware of what we mix into our water supply and clean it before we put it back into the system. Instead of cutting down a tree and burning it for fuel, producing a waste product that pollutes our air, we use the wood in a way that it can continue to contribute to the life cycle of wood. For example, we might salvage wood and create a new product when its product life has ended and return wood, sawdust, or shavings to the earth, where they can feed and nourish the soil from which new trees will grow. We can replicate this idea with any resource we use. Producing energy from clean, renewable resources such as the sun and wind provides a nonpolluting alternative to conventional burning of fossil fuels and coal, which produces much toxic waste.

The World Watch Institute, much like the Brundtland Commission definition mentioned in Chapter 1, defines sustainability as the ability to meet our needs without compromising the ability of future generations to meet theirs. For the benefit of our children and grandchildren, we can adopt systems and policies that nourish our planet, protect our natural resources, and create thriving societies so they can continue to provide for generations to come. We can incorporate this business practice into our daily routines to ensure we'll have adequate resources in the future.

Why Sustainability Is Important

Business has thrived for the past 150 years by feeding natural resources such as water, oil, coal, and agricultural products into our economy. However, the process of retrieving those elements from the earth has often created waste products and pollution. In addition, human life and education have been devalued, contributing to increasing societal and health issues. Today, we are beginning to see the real cost of depleting our natural resources and discarding the by-products, and we realize we must develop a new cycle or we'll soon have destroyed the bounty we've been enjoying for so long. Giving back to the earth in proportion to what we use is the foundation of sustainability.

Ray Anderson, CEO of Interface, Inc., a company that is a leader in sustainable business practices, realized more than a decade ago that his industry was using a lot of our natural resources, and when his product's life ended after just a few years, the old carpets sent to landfills consumed too much space in the landscape. So Anderson went to work retooling his company's waste practices, and in the process he set standards for his industry to use less of our precious limited natural resources in the production of carpet and flooring products and to put far less of them into landfills. Anderson's company takes back used flooring materials and reuses them to recreate new products.

Today's global population is estimated to be just over 6.7 billion people. Over the last two centuries, the global population has skyrocketed, and global trends show that it will continue to rise at a rapid rate. To put that into perspective, according to NOVA science programming, the population of the earth in 1927 was around 2 billion.

Until around 1950, the population growth rate remained steady at around 1 percent per year. About this time, advances in public health, including the use of antibiotics, allowed for longer life spans, adding to the population issue. By 1960, the global population reached roughly 3 billion. In the past 50 years, the global population has increased by almost 4 billion people, and by the year 2050, it is expected to hit 9 billion. Our planet and societal systems will have to provide for nearly 3 billion more people than they do now—3 billion more people who want to live without resource restriction.

Enviro-Fact
A Swedish oncologist named Dr. Karl-Henrik Robert developed The Natural Step Framework in 1989. Based on systems thinking, it is a valuable tool for business to incorporate sustainability into their organizations. Learn more about The Natural Step Framework at www.thenaturalstep.org.

The Natural Step's Resource Funnel is a well-known diagram used to illustrate this concept of finite resource availability. Imagine a funnel viewed from the side. The walls of this funnel represent declining resources and increased demand for those resources used to produce the goods and services we utilize every day. In order to reach sustainability, we need to determine how to balance the supply and demand of resources to create a sustainable future.

Taking strides to move toward more sustainable systems will move us all in a direction that will enable us to thrive as a collective society.

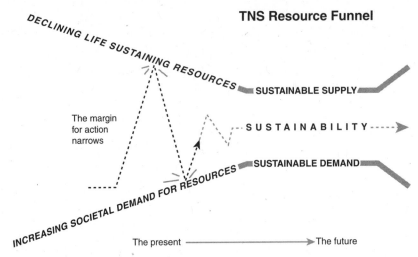

The Natural Step's Resource Funnel.

Enhance Stakeholder Relations

Implementing sustainability into a business model is not just about making an impact on society and the planet. Following sustainable frameworks enhances the relations of all the stakeholders in an organization. Stakeholder value is a different concept than shareholder value. In short, shareholder value considers the interest of business shareholders first and foremost, whereas stakeholder value takes into consideration a broader base of parties that the business affects. These can include shareholders, nonprofits, suppliers, government agencies, customers, employees, and anyone else associated with an organization. According to Mark J. Epstein, author of *Making Sustainability Work: Best Practices in Managing and Measuring Corporate Social, Environmental, and Economic Impacts,* there are two types of stakeholders: core stakeholders and fringe stakeholders. In his book he states, "Core stakeholders are those that are visible and are able to impact corporate decisions due to their power or legitimacy. Fringe stakeholders, on the other hand, are disconnected from the company because they are remote, weak, or currently disinterested."

Improving stakeholder relationships can have a profound impact on your bottom line. Having a better relationship with your customers enables you to understand what they want and how they want you to deliver your goods or services. Creating an open dialogue for discussion gives you an open door for engagement. This theory also holds true for government organizations and nonprofits. Creating a relationship with a nonprofit previously seen as an adversary enables dialogue that encourages collaboration over conflict, and having an open dialogue with government gives you the ability to stay one step ahead of impending regulations. Thus you could save thousands of dollars by avoiding controversy and miscommunication. Enhancing the importance of employees as stakeholders improves the image of your organization and the morale of your workforce. If employees feel they are invested in your organization for more than just a paycheck, they are more inclined to work harder and remain loyal.

Going Green

According to Walker and Marr (2001), the evolution of stakeholder relationships contains four steps:

1. Awareness
2. Knowledge
3. Admiration
4. Action

Showing your stakeholders—customers, employees, and investors—that you're fulfilling a commitment to the environment will produce a payoff that goes beyond the stock report and is sure to result in financial benefits over the long term. Your stakeholders will thank you for recognizing the importance of protecting the environment through your business practices.

Improve Brand Value

The consensus is in: green is the hot new branding technique. It is more important than ever to back up your green story with a sustainability program that produces a credible back story and provable, verifiable data. Greenwashing—claiming you are greener than you actually are—is a term an increasing number of people are becoming familiar with (and more and more companies want to avoid).

According to BBMG, a New York–based marketing agency that brings conscious consumers together with forward-thinking brands, five values drive the *conscious consumer:*

def•i•ni•tion

Conscious consumers purchase on the basis of environmental or social criteria. They often purchase products that have a reduced environmental impact and/or a positive social impact, and they support responsible companies.

- ◆ Health and safety
- ◆ Honesty
- ◆ Convenience
- ◆ Relationships
- ◆ Good deeds

More and more consumers are looking to identify with brands that they can feel good about—brands that can deliver a product and a feeling.

Implementing sustainability into your business model helps you develop a credible green story, increasing your brand value and your corporate image for both your internal and external messaging. After all, your employees can be your most trusted brand angels. Giving them the tools and resources to understand your sustainability initiatives enables them to tout your efforts in a transparent, credible manner. From blogs to social networks, let your employees spread the good word about the positive impact your company is making. We touch more on green marketing and branding in Part 5 of this book. Stay tuned!

Improve Employee Relations and Productivity

Healthier employees make happier employees, and when employees feel good about their work, they are more inclined to give 110 percent each day. Embarking on a journey toward sustainability can make your organization stable in volatile economic times, giving employees a greater sense of job security. This reduces stress and nervousness, which in turn increases productivity. Increased productivity adds to financial gains, which in turn makes your company more stable. Are you beginning to see a trend here?

Talented workers are looking for more meaning from their everyday jobs. They want to be a part of something greater than the company they work for and contribute their productivity to a positive agenda. Outlining a clear vision for sustainability and a well-defined sustainability action plan serves as a magnet for dedicated, talented workers.

To reap the benefits of implementing a full sustainability program, all employees must be on board. Top company executives and management need to embrace and embody sustainability not only to set an example for all employees, but also to maintain integrity in their organizations. Espousing this commitment throughout your organization makes a world of difference in the outcome of your sustainability initiatives. After your organization is committed to the initiatives, open the lines of communication to all employees in your organization. This will strengthen all employee relations.

The Least You Need to Know

- Business has traditionally taken from the environment without reimbursement.

- Preserving resources through sustainability promises continuous value.

- Your cost-benefit analysis will show that sustainability can lead to stronger employee relations and increased profits through reduced costs for energy, water, and waste.

- Shareholders, customers, and employees appreciate responsible sustainable performance.

Part 2

Getting Started on the Green Path

As you begin the greening process, we provide step-by-step instructions to set you on the road to making your business a sustainable entity that contributes positively to the environment rather than damaging the earth by using resources that can't be replenished.

Using this guide, you can better assess your environmental impact, find ways to stop wasting natural resources, and begin to save money while helping the planet become a healthier place for you, your customers, and the children of the future.

Steps to Make It Happen

In This Chapter

- ◆ Develop a sustainability vision
- ◆ Develop sustainability goals
- ◆ Understand how to undertake a strategic process
- ◆ Assess your current operations
- ◆ Put together a strategic plan

This chapter will help you to develop a plan to make your business sustainable.

Visioning Your Green Business Reality

Now that you have the basic understanding of what sustainability means, why it is important, and what changes are arising in the marketplace, you need to determine how you want to integrate these concepts into your business. The first step in executing any sustainability initiative or program is to determine where you want to go. Create your vision and define your goals.

Starting with your vision ensures that you take a strategic approach in the design of your program as well as implement a *backcasting* process.

Normally, we use *forecasting* to plan by examining what has worked well in the past and building future strategies based on those concepts. Backcasting takes the opposite approach by determining what you want to create first and building your strategies based on achieving your vision. This is an important distinction for creating a green business because if you want to see real changes in the current system, you must think and design in new ways. Based on the plethora of statistics outlining the distresses on our shared socio-ecological systems, we already know that if we keep designing based on the current ideologies and frameworks, we may not reach a sustainable society in time.

def•i•ni•tion

Backcasting is a reverse-forecasting technique that starts with a specific future outcome and then works backward to the present conditions. It is a tool with which to connect desirable long-term future scenarios to the present situation by means of a participatory process.

Forecasting is the process of analyzing current and historical data to determine future trends. This planning tool helps management cope with the uncertainty of the future. It starts with certain assumptions based on the management's experience, knowledge, and judgment.

(Source: Online Business and Financial Dictionaries and European Commission Joint Research Centre Online Foresight Guide)

The Natural Step's funnel diagram from Chapter 2 is a good depiction of why it is important to first set a vision and then backcast to redesign based on new thinking. The vision helps us as business leaders and community members move through the funnel to a brighter future. If the vision is based only on actions from the past, our new reality may not be different from our current reality. However, if we base the vision on future ideas, where we have put aside our doubts, fears, and assumptions, our new reality has the potential to be vastly different from our current reality.

The following diagram illustrates the step-by-step process for creating a sustainability initiative or program in an organization, which includes these steps:

1. Determine your vision.

2. Backcast from the future state of your vision to the current reality of your business.

3. Examine your current operations (inputs and outputs).

4. Develop your strategies (sustainability strategic plan) to help you move from where you are to where you want to be.

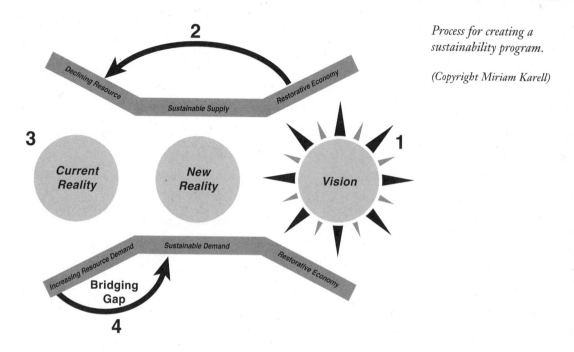

Process for creating a sustainability program.

(Copyright Miriam Karell)

Now let's explore how you actually create your vision. This is where the fun begins, so be creative and future-oriented.

Gather a Team from Your Business

According to Peter Senge, author of *The Fifth Discipline* (Doubleday Business, 1994) and a thought leader in organizational learning, an organizational vision is most effective for all persons in a company if they share it and it is a reflection of each person's own individual vision. Senge writes that it "provides the focus and energy for learning," enabling employees to feel a sense of commonality, exhilaration, courage, aspiration, and the ability to take risks and experiment with new approaches. It is used as a guiding force so when difficulties, challenges, and unexpected turns in the business arise, people still have a fundamental understanding of the company and the long-term strategy for the future.

A shared vision helps everyone in an organization understand how he or she individually and collectively contributes to the success of that company. This can greatly impact the effectiveness of external communication to clients and customers by creating a coherent and congruent message.

Therefore, when you begin the process of developing your sustainability vision, gather a team that represents different levels and departments in your organization, which will help you create a message that will resonate with the majority of your employees.

These tips will help you gather a team for an effective visioning session:

- Find people who have an interest in sustainability or are already integrating sustainability into their work or home activities.

- Gather people from different departments and with different positions in the organization; have a mix of ages, skill sets, mindsets, and titles.

- Get support from management, and have a few members from upper management present for the visioning session.

- Convene only 8 to 10 people for the session—too many people lead to less productivity.

- Visioning is best done in person and away from the day-to-day work environment; the face-to-face contact enhances the creative process and leads to a more successful shared vision. Therefore, whenever possible, organize an off-site, facilitated one- or two-day retreat to develop your sustainability vision and goals.

Define What Sustainability Means to Your Business

Sustainability is a value-based term. No definition can possibly encompass all cultures, nationalities, world views, races, businesses, and so on. We all have different boundaries, so what may be true for me may not be true for you. For example, Company X may place high emphasis on transportation and be comfortable giving employees bonuses for taking public transit to work. Company Y may believe that providing healthy snack options in the kitchen is most important for their employees, so they would not be willing to give bonuses based on transportation choices. Both companies are choosing their strategies based on how they define sustainability and what is important for them, and both choices are valid depending on the culture, the structure, and the management of each company.

Most organizations use the Brundtland definition (see Chapter 1) in defining sustainability for their businesses. However, when you break down the definition, consider what is meant by "needs" and how long into the future you are planning for. The more clarity you have in understanding sustainability for yourself and your business, the better positioned you will be in the market.

Think about your own boundaries and what is important for you in relation to these three questions:

1. Who are you working for—your community, family, shareholders, stakeholders, all species, animals, and so on?

2. What would you like to sustain or achieve?

3. How long would you like to provide benefit and make an impact in the world?

Another key aspect in defining sustainability is to determine your core values. Build these values into your vision and messaging to give authenticity to your statements and better connect to your stakeholders.

Before entering the visioning session, have each person determine their top five core values. Sharing core values enables you to determine what gets people out of bed in the morning and why they are passionate to work in your organization. Once you have all the values, write them on a board and see where there are overlaps and differences. This will help you determine what excites and motivates everyone, and how to incorporate that language into your message.

Next, narrow your list of values to a total of five or six. These will be the values that you work from as you build your vision and goals. Five good questions to assist in this process are:

- ◆ What would your organization look like if it encouraged employees to live up to these values?

- ◆ How would your organization be different if these values were prominent and practiced?

- ◆ As a leader in your organization, what does it mean for you to champion sustainability?

- ◆ How do you show you are walking the talk and inspiring others?

- ◆ How are you integrating sustainability into your personal and work life?

Depending on your answers to these questions, you may want to adjust your values and choose values that will help your organization embrace a different culture or new practices. These are important discussions, so take time to have these values conversations.

Determine Your Green Mission Statement and Priorities

The following are two ways to develop a green mission statement:

♦ Use your existing vision and values as a starting point for your green statement.

♦ Start anew and create something different than your existing company vision.

The choice you make depends on how your company is structured and how you view sustainability.

For instance, if you desire to integrate sustainability into every aspect of your organization, it makes sense to rewrite your company vision to include sustainability. However, if you plan to start with a green team or separate department and build your program step-by-step to spread throughout the company, it's best to start with a new statement and build it into a broader vision later.

Either way, when thinking about your business and your own sustainability vision or guiding principles/values, think systemically (for instance, how your business interacts with different systems and what influence you have on those systems). To create a vision or statement that will hold true for a long period of time and lead to real change, it is important to consider how your choices affect other systems (society, environment, economy) and what it means for you to take an integrated bottom-line approach (see Chapter 1).

One way to start thinking of your business from a systemic perspective is to answer the following list of questions. Because you are visioning, answer the questions as if you are already in the future and have obtained your goals for your company. Push aside limiting beliefs, assumptions, and negative thoughts. Imagine what you will create and how you will feel as part of your future organization.

Purpose

♦ Why does your organization exist?

♦ What is the value of your work?

♦ What benefit does your work bring to society?

Stakeholders

♦ How does your organization relate to people, community, shareholders, customers, and so on?

♦ How does your organization help people meet their needs?

Organizational Structure and Culture

◆ What words do people use to describe the culture of your business?

◆ What is the structure of your organization?

Internal and External Practices

◆ How does your organization determine who to work with, where to get materials from, and how to function on a day-to-day basis?

Relationship to Natural Environment

◆ How does your organization interact with the local ecosystems?

◆ How does your organization utilize different materials and resources from the natural environment?

◆ What does your organization do with its waste?

After you answer these questions, find the key words and/or phrases within your answers that inspire, excite, and motivate you. Then use this language and your core values to build your green mission statement.

Going Green

The following are examples of green mission/vision statements:

Guayaki works directly with growers to deliver unique and beneficial products that enhance personal health and well-being. Our goal is to create economic models that drive reforestation while employing a living wage. (www.guayaki.com)

At Arketype, we believe that architecture is a means by which lives can be enriched, individuals can be inspired, and futures sustained. We achieve these benefits with our clients by basing our work on a set of values. (www.arketypearchitects.com)

Assessing Your Current Operations

Assessing your current operations is critical for understanding how to move forward with greening your business. If you do not know where you are in terms of material use, energy use, water use, waste consumption, and the receptivity of personnel in your organization to change, it is difficult to set realistic goals and metrics to track your goals.

An assessment helps identify the different systems in your organization and clarify how these systems function. For example, a few systems you may identify are purchasing, building management regulations, transportation norms, employee communication norms, recycling and waste norms, and energy and water usage. The assessment helps you evaluate each of these systems and determines if they are functioning optimally or if you need to change them.

When doing your assessment, keep in mind that a green business accomplishes the following:

- Saves energy
- Conserves water
- Reduces waste
- Minimizes travel
- Buys green
- Builds community
- Increases employee engagement and leadership

Take some time to consider how you would examine your organization based on the previous seven categories. What are the important questions to ask?

These three basic questions are good for looking at how you use everything within your organization:

- Where does it come from?
- How do we use it?
- What happens when we are finished using it?

Chapters 4, 5, and 6 give an in-depth review of how to do a sustainability assessment of your organization.

Creating Your Green Goals

After you write your vision and assess your current operations, you can create your green goals. Both the vision and the assessment can help you determine your targets and what will be important to evaluate and change in your organization. Before writing down any goals, reread your vision and review the results of your assessment.

Every goal you create should be in alignment with your vision, helping you move from where you currently are to where you want to be. You may want to categorize your findings from your assessment so you can determine theme areas for your goals. For example, if you find that your janitorial staff throws your recyclables into the trash or your employees do not understand what is recyclable and throw batteries away, you might develop a theme category around waste reduction. You can then develop a few goals underneath that category.

When determining your goals, be realistic. There's no point in making goals that are unattainable; this only leads to frustration and less support for your green initiatives as you begin to implement them.

Also keep your goals to a short list. Write down only the goals you can attain in your allocated timeframe. It's easy to get carried away and end up with 50 goals to achieve, so narrow your list to the 6 to 10 most important goals.

Think of your goals as commitments. You are committing to do some activity as an organization by a specified time. The clearer you are with defining your goals and keeping your commitments, the easier it is to be transparent and accountable for your actions and to involve more people in the implementation process.

What Would You Like to Achieve in Six Months?

Sit down with your team and discuss what you realistically can achieve in six months. To begin the process, use a whiteboard to brainstorm ideas and divide the board into two columns: one for six months and one for one to three years. When thinking of your goals, remember to accurately factor in how much time you will allot to individuals who will be working on these tasks so your goals are achievable. For instance, if one of your goals is to reduce your waste outputs by 5 percent, take into consideration, at a high level, who will be in charge of this task, what effort it will take, and if six months is a reasonable timeframe. If, after talking through the goal at a high level, you determine that it would be hard to achieve in six months, move it to your one- to three-year category.

When writing your goals, keep these questions in mind:

- Is this goal in alignment with our vision?

- Does this goal help us move from where we currently are to where we want to be?

- Does this goal support our definition of sustainability and our values?

- Does this goal help us turn our weaknesses into strengths?

Repeat this process every six months so you stay on track to achieve your long-term goals.

What Would You Like to Achieve in One to Three Years?

By now, you probably have a few goals listed in your one- to three-year column. These goals can be broader and bigger in scope because you have more time to complete them.

Here are some questions to think about:

♦ If you begin implementing your six-month goals, what changes will you see in your organization?

♦ What will you be willing to commit to in the next six months or a year?

♦ How ready is your organization for larger and more complex changes?

♦ What is the best way to move you closer to your vision?

The following table is an example of a brainstorm around goals:

Theme Category	6-Month Goals	1- to 3-Year Goals
Waste Reduction	Educate staff on recycling	10% waste reduction
	Determine current recycling system	Install a composting system
	Clearly mark recycle and garbage receptacles	No disposables in office
Employee Engagement	Create a green board in common area	Train all staff on sustainability
	Form a green team	Build an incentive program to encourage employees to contribute to green efforts
	Create a green blog	
Water Usage	Track water usage	Install low-flow toilets
	Conduct a water audit	Install waterless urinals
		Install low-flow aerators on sinks

Cost-Benefit Analysis of Green Goals

Before beginning your strategic plan, look at the *cost-benefit analysis* of your goals. This will help you prioritize your goals and see what will be your "low-hanging fruit," the least costly goals you can implement right away. To determine the costs and benefits, use a model or program that quantifies each item or simply write a list of the positive and negative factors. Either way, subtracting the negative from the positive will indicate the viability and feasibility of the goal. The real trick in performing a good cost-benefit analysis is to determine all the costs and all the benefits and properly quantify or label them.

In your analysis, you can also include the environmental factors as an indicator for the benefits (termed *environmental cost-benefit analysis*). That is, look at how your goal will enhance local communities and save natural resources and then rate the quality of that benefit to society.

def•i•ni•tion

According to the Online Business Dictionary, **cost-benefit analysis** is a technique designed to determine the feasibility of a project or plan by quantifying its costs (the total money, time, and resources associated with an activity) and benefits (value or usefulness).

Environmental cost-benefit analysis is the evaluation and comparison of capital and environmental costs of a project to estimate its relative merits and demerits.

Another reason to conduct a cost-benefit analysis is that you can determine the amount of payback from your programs. For instance, if you were to install low-flow toilets and low-flow aerators on sinks, you can calculate how much time it will take to break even from the changeover. This greatly helps in determining the feasibility of certain goals.

Establishing Environmentally Friendly Policies

From your goals and your assessment, you can start developing your green or *environmental policies*, which further assist in maintaining alignment with your vision. Green policies can help you better communicate your green messages internally (employee handbook guidelines) and externally (proof that you are taking actions to be green). They can also assist you in getting buy-in for your green efforts if they are collaboratively written.

def•i•ni•tion

According to the Online Business Dictionary, an **environmental policy** is a public statement of an organization's philosophy, intentions, and objectives regarding the environment.

We cover development of environmentally friendly policies further in Chapter 4.

Creating a Strategic Plan

Your vision, assessment, and goals are the backbone for developing a plan to move you forward and keep you on track. A strategic plan helps you document, track, and monitor the different sustainability initiatives rolled out in a fiscal year and assists you in communicating to and getting buy-in from your staff.

The four steps to a plan are:

1. Prioritize your goals.

2. Develop strategies to achieve your goals.

3. Create a timeline for achieving your goals.

4. Determine roles and responsibilities.

Let's examine each of these steps in more detail.

Prioritize Green Goals

Prioritization is essential for a strategic plan because it helps you develop your flow and narrow your focus. A long list of goals may be overwhelming; therefore, breaking down the list into smaller pieces gives momentum to the plan.

Take your goals table and prioritize the goals in your six-month column first. Is there a logical order for accomplishing the goals? For instance, will achieving one goal help you accomplish another goal faster?

After you prioritize your six-month goals, start on your one- to three-year goals. It may be helpful to create a spreadsheet to start tracking your goals and how you will accomplish them.

THREE POINT VISION

Syntony Quest™

WORKSHEET 9: ACTION PLAN FOR SPECIFIC GOAL

No:	Goal:	Purpose of Goal:

Steps to Achieve Goal	How will you measure progress towards achieving your goal? (Indicators of Success)	Who's Responsible? (Leader and Team)	Due Date
1.			
2.			
3.			
4.			
5.			
6.			

Championing Sustainability

www.syntonyquest.org
www.threepointvision.com

Worksheet #9
© Copyright 2007: Laszlo & Karell

Action Plan for Specific Goal worksheet.
(Courtesy Miriam Karell)

Develop Strategies to Achieve Green Goals

The key in developing strategies to achieve your goals is to know how to measure your progress. That is, for each goal, determine the method in which you will know if you are on track with your targets. For example, if you have a goal to educate all employees on your recycling system, how will you determine you have succeeded? One way you can determine success is by sending out a survey to assess whether people understand the recycling system. Another way may be to monitor how many people use the recycling receptacles in the office. Whatever method of measurement you choose, you need to define it from the beginning.

Another aspect to consider when determining your strategies is to think about how you will involve your staff in the implementation process. This is crucial to the success of your initiatives. The more your employees feel included and valued throughout the process, the easier you will accomplish your goals.

For instance, Company A has a green team that is taking the lead on getting the organization to make more sustainable purchasing decisions. One idea is to switch the snacks in the break room from candy and cookies to only organic fruits and nuts. If the green team suddenly makes the switch without warning the staff, there is a greater likelihood their initiative will be met with complaints and attacks. But if before rolling out the initiative they invite all employees to a dialogue about what changes they would like to see and if they would eat fruit and nuts, the green team will have an easier time making the switch.

In general, people resist change, and no one likes to be told what to do or forced to do something without an explanation. Often, changes in organizations come from top management. A sustainable approach is to make the process as inclusive as possible and help management communicate the message in an inviting, educational, and participatory way.

When developing your strategies, you might use the preceding figure to help organize the information and structure the flow. Think about all the tasks you must accomplish in order to complete the goal. Write down all the tasks, even if some seem obvious. It is best not to make assumptions and then later discover a key piece is missing.

Develop a Timeline for Achievement of Green Goals

Developing a timeline can be as simple as filling in a due date, as outlined in the previous figure, or you can use a project management program to produce a chart.

Whatever method you use, it is important to factor in preparation time, meeting time, communication time, follow-up time, and the actual time it takes to work on the item. It is always better to overestimate than underestimate.

If multiple people will be working on one strategy, make it clear who is responsible for what component of the task and how much time you anticipate it will take.

Establish Roles and Responsibility

When determining roles and responsibility, encourage people to volunteer for what excites or intrigues them. This will make for a smoother progression and help everyone remain accountable for his or her tasks.

Accountability is essential for achieving your goals. According to Doug McKenzie-Mohr, a pioneer and leader in the field of community-based social marketing and author of *Fostering Sustainable Behavior: An Introduction to Community-Based Social Marketing* (New Society Publishers, 1999), the most effective way to make a commitment is in a group and in written form. Therefore, the best way to ensure that you establish appropriate roles and responsibilities is have people write out the tasks they will accomplish as well as state the commitments to the group.

Another way to make sure everyone stays on track is to have bi-weekly or monthly update meetings where the employees involved present the status of their tasks.

As you begin to implement your goals, remember to celebrate your successes along the way. Whether it's in the form of a thank-you note, a party, a high-five, or simply a smile, we all like to feel that we contributed to something meaningful and significant.

The Least You Need to Know

- Before beginning any sustainability program or initiative, define sustainability for your business.
- The first step in becoming a green business is to set your vision so you know where you want to go.
- As you develop strategies to achieve your goals, factor in how you will engage your employees and include them in the implementation process.
- Taking a strategic approach to becoming a green business helps you prioritize your goals, develop strategies, create a timeline, and determine roles and responsibilities.

Chapter 4

How Does Your Business Impact the Environment?

In This Chapter

- Assess energy, water, and fuel usage
- Measure waste output
- Develop better efficiencies of resource usage
- Cut costs and increase profits

Everything we do has an impact, a cause and effect, on the environment. Everything on a store shelf has a story. Actually one might say that each product has two stories: the marketing story and the backstory.

What's the backstory? In literature, the backstory is everything that happened leading up to the situation in which the characters find themselves at the beginning of the narrative. In commerce, the backstory is everything that has happened to the product before we buy it.

In this chapter, we look at the backstory of each of these impact areas to further understand how your business impacts the environment.

A great example is food: Who raised it? Where was it grown and on what kind of land? Did the farmer use fertilizers and pesticides or integrated pest management? Antibiotics or free-range grazing? Was the soil conserved, or is it eroding and depleted? By what mode of transportation did it reach us? How was the money we spent on it split up and were the people involved in the processing paid fairly for their efforts?

The 3 Ts (trust, transparency, and traceability) are important areas of the supply chain focus. So the first area we focus on in understanding how your business impacts the environment is sustainability. In Chapter 19, we discuss a sustainability report, so we won't go into that here. However, we do explore sustainability assessment and auditing.

Sustainability Audit and Assessment

Before we look at the function of a sustainability audit and assessment, let's revisit the definition of sustainability.

In basic terms, we should live our lives and do business in a way that meets our needs and allows for success but doesn't inhibit the ability of people in the future to do the same. It is a simple humanistic concept in its essence.

Enviro-Fact
According to Envirowise.com, 93 percent of production materials are never used in the final product, and 80 percent of those products are discarded after a single use.

In the business community, sustainability is referred to as the triple bottom line or the integrated bottom line and is often accompanied by the motto "People, Planet, and Profit."

When we look at doing an audit and assessment, the key is to understand our organizational boundaries and the operational boundaries, including the social and environmental.

Environmental and Social Indicators

A performance indicator is a point of data that enables an individual to monitor and measure an aspect of his business. It describes organizational performance in a clear, balanced, and unbiased way, which is one of the major challenges of effective sustainability reporting.

An environmental indicator is a measurement, statistic, or value that provides a gauge for or evidence of the effects of environmental management programs on the environment. Because we touch on sustainability, we have also included a list of social indicators to help you benchmark your social performance. Quantifying the baseline of your environmental and social performance will help you clearly define areas for improvement, give you a clear idea of where you can reap the greatest amount of financial benefit, and serve as a credible background when creating any green marketing messages.

As we stated earlier, everything we do has an impact. Benchmarking is a key step in creating any green business or sustainability program.

The Key Performance Indicators (KPIs) listed were designed with company sustainability reporting in mind. When you are deciding which KPIs to measure, make use of information that companies in your industry routinely collect. This way, you can start with industry baselines for measuring and monitoring your environmental, social, and financial performance. Talk to your industry association(s) to see if a program or framework exists; if not, develop a task force with in your industry to create a set standard for sustainability reporting specific to your industry.

Example Environmental and Social Indicators

Environmental (impacts on living and nonliving natural systems)	Social (impacts on the social systems and communities in which an organization operates)
Emissions to air	**Labor practices**
Greenhouse gases and so on	Fair trade
Volatile organic compounds	Human rights and so on
Emissions to water	
Includes anything that is discharged into a water source, including sinks, floor drains, streams, lakes, and so on	
Emissions to land	**Workplace diversity**
Waste—landfill, incinerated recyclables, compostables, and so on	Ethnic and gender diversity, particularly relating to management roles
Pesticides, fertilizers, and so on	Pay broken out by role, by gender
	Age diversity
Resource use	**Community impacts**
Natural gas	Volunteering
Water use and abstraction	Purchases that are local and so on
Minerals and so on	Community donations

continues

Example Environmental and Social Indicators (continued)

Environmental (impacts on living and nonliving natural systems)	Social (impacts on the social systems and communities in which an organization operates
Product responsibility	
Design for Environment (DfE)	
Take-back policy for end-of-life disposal	
Considering environmental and social impacts throughout the product's life cycle	

Remember these things when deciding which performance indicators to choose:

♦ Select appropriate and meaningful indicators. Are they manageable and modifiable?

♦ Select indicators that make sense to your business and your stakeholders. Always check in with your vision and the feedback from your stakeholders. Many companies take their indicators to the stakeholders for review before using them internally. This is also a requirement under the AA1000 sustainability reporting assurance framework. For more information, go to www.accountability21.net.

♦ Find out where the data for your indicators is stored and how easy it is to collect. If you have an indicator that requires five steps in the data collection process, make sure it's being collected regularly (and on time) so it is measured accurately.

♦ Review what you are currently measuring and decide if you can dovetail it into the sustainability indicators.

We tried to cover some general areas without being too specific. Don't get overwhelmed trying to cover everything all at once. Just start, and don't try to do everything. Remember quality over quantity.

Creating indicators may seem like a daunting task and a fairly dull part of the whole sustainability program, but it is well worth the upfront investment for any successful organization.

Water

Many regions are experiencing water scarcities due to drought, floods, or water pollution. As we experience climate change, further shortages will occur in regions where summer water supplies are dependent on winter snowfall. In many parts, we are using water faster than nature can renew it, and we need to reduce our wasteful water habits.

According to the Organization for Economic Cooperation and Development, the United States has the highest water consumption rates in the world, which is why more and more businesses are increasing their awareness of water use by conducting audits to better understand their use and to establish more efficient routines. This makes us vulnerable to higher water costs as water scarcity becomes an issue. Reducing your water consumption now will decrease immediate costs and will lead to an increase in future profits.

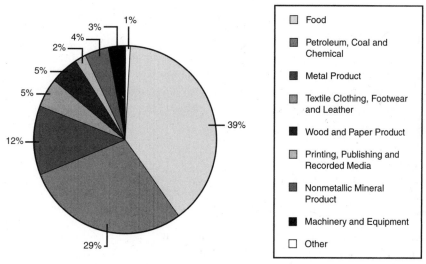

Water Consumption by Manufacturing Sector

Legend:
- Food
- Petroleum, Coal and Chemical
- Metal Product
- Textile Clothing, Footwear and Leather
- Wood and Paper Product
- Printing, Publishing and Recorded Media
- Nonmetallic Mineral Product
- Machinery and Equipment
- Other

Values: 1%, 3%, 4%, 2%, 5%, 5%, 12%, 29%, 39%

Water consumption graph.

(Courtesy Energy in Australia, 2006 ABARE.)

An organization should ask itself a few key questions as it starts to look at risks, related impact, and opportunities around a water sustainability initiative.

- What is our water footprint? How much are we using and what are the related impacts of the water resources?

- Are there water-related risks to our organization? Is the quality and availability of water adequate to meet the current and future needs of our organization? How do stakeholders view our use of and impacts on water resources?

- Are there opportunities present through water for our company? How can we save money, enhance reputation, and reduce risk through changing our water usage habits, such as helping to improve water quality and access to those who need it?

- How does the water-use practice tie in with our overarching sustainability vision? Is this consistent with the rest of our sustainability initiatives? Are we leaders, followers, or collaborators?

> **Going Green** _____
>
> The H$_2$O Conserve Water Calculator is an interactive tool designed to help you figure out how much water you use, how you use it, and how you can use less. You can find it at www.h2oconserve.org/wc_disclaimer.php?pd=ca.

- How can we set realistic goals? We need to have conservative targets so everyone can measure the gains and benchmark our goals against key indicators, such as kilolitres per square meter of space.

- How can we develop a reduction strategy that follows the principles of avoid, reduce, reuse, recycle, and rethink?

- How can we best involve our employees? Behavioral change will lead to water savings. Engaging staff will also empower them to find potential areas that we might not have thought of.

Doing a full water assessment can be more work than your organization has the resource for, so start reducing your usage by looking at the low-hanging fruit. Here are a few easy and inexpensive places to make changes:

- Fix leaky taps. One drop per second wastes about 2,500 gallons a year.

- Install a low-flow faucet aerator, which adds air to a water stream and can reduce water consumption as much as 50 percent.

- Use lever or mixer taps (with a single lever or knob), which lets staff find the right water temperature quickly.

- When cleaning, get staff to use a bucket to wash and rinse where possible, instead of running the taps or hose.

◆ Check for leaks in taps, pipes, and hoses. Remember, one leaking tap can waste more than 500 gallons a month!

◆ Regularly clean the lint filter on washing machines, and use a sink strainer when you pull the plug out of tubs. What you put down the drain can cause blockages and pollute our environment.

◆ Provide incentives for staff to save water by linking water conservation to staff performance reviews.

◆ Use visual tools like charts and graphs to highlight water savings to employees.

◆ Mention water conservation plans and progress in staff meetings.

◆ Include water conservation policies and procedures in staff training programs.

> **Enviro-Fact**
>
> According to the U.S. Global Change Research Program (www.usgcrp.com), receding winter snow pack levels will leave less snow to melt, which will cause the summer water supply to decrease.

Measuring Your Inputs

One of the more acceptable tools for measuring your water input is through the website of the World Business Council for Sustainable Development (www.wbcsd.org). The Global Water Tool (www.wbcsd.org/web/watertool.htm) enables companies and organizations to map their water use and assess risks relative to their operations and supply chain. The tool has two parts: an input sheet (a downloadable Excel spreadsheet) and an online map. The input sheet contains the company's site location and water use information. After you enter your company's water use figures, the sheet automatically provides outputs, including water indicators compatible with the Global Reporting Initiative requirements and downloadable metrics charts that demonstrate the company's data combined with both the country and watershed figures.

Assess Water Quality

Preparing an assessment of water quality is a detailed and time-consuming process, depending on the size of your organization and its constraints regarding people and budget. Anytime you start doing a water assessment, you should contact your local water works agency because of the many considerations you may not be aware of. For larger-scoped projects, you may even want to consider an outside expert who understands the water systems in the area of your assessment.

We have outlined six easy-to-follow steps, which should act as guidelines in performing your assessment:

1. Identify the assessment's scope and motivation (drivers). Is it strategic? Tactical? Are there sensitivities you need to address?

2. Select the area or region where you will be conducting the assessment. Focus on areas where your operations have the greatest impact of the local water catchment.

3. Seek collaboration (partners). Other organizations may have interest in the same area, so see if you can share resources and set common objectives and goals.

4. Assess the water catchment. Look at it from lenses of an integrated approach involving social, environmental, and economic factors.

5. Prepare and implement an action plan. Where are the areas of improvement? What is the timeline? Who is involved?

6. Share the results. Create a report for the interested stakeholders, a press release, a section in your Corporate Social Responsibility report, or a new operating policy.

In general, most businesses (particularly manufacturers) can save water by reusing water from an appropriate source. To do this, they will most likely need to undertake a risk assessment of the water source and its intended uses and conduct trials to make sure the treatment process and its management works well and complies with guidelines and requirements.

Reusing wastewater can be an excellent way to reduce potable water use, but it can also be a costly and complicated process, so start your water conservation program with basic efficiency gains before exploring reuse projects.

Energy

When calculating your environmental impact, it's essential to factor in your energy usage. Most processes rely on energy flowing freely each day to fuel machinery, lights, heating and air conditioning, and transportation of products and raw materials. Where do you get your energy? Are you relying on the burning of fossil fuels, or have you found a renewable energy resource such as wind or solar? Moving in that direction will help reduce your carbon footprint.

How Much Electricity Does Your Company Use?

Calculating electricity usage is a straightforward process for organizations that own the building and facilities where they operate their business and for companies whose utilities are metered separately. For either case, create a spreadsheet and enter the data off your monthly utility statements; find the emissions factor for your utilities from the Environmental Protection Agency (EPA) E-Grid database at www.epa.gov/cleanenergy/energy-resources/egrid/index.html. The International Energy Agency (www.iea.org) and the United National Environmental Programme (UNEP) (www.unep.org) provide country-level electricity emission factors. If your organization does not own or occupy a whole building or you sublet or lease your space (without individual energy meters), you need to estimate your electricity usage based on information you can obtain from your property manager. The following are involved:

◆ The total area of the building

◆ The total area your organization occupies

◆ The total building energy use in kWh (kilowatt-hours)

Use this formula to calculate your organization's electricity usage:

Area of your organization's space ÷ total building area × Total building usage of electricity = Approximate kWh used by your organization

As you can see with the example, this is only an approximate usage of electricity of your organization and will probably be lower than the actual number you calculate. What you will most likely achieve in sharing the process with your building's management company is an awareness of electricity usage, which will hopefully inspire other organizations in your building to follow your lead.

Perhaps you can see if the management company will help fund an electricity reduction program for the building. Why not ask? It will help everyone involved. Be the environmental champion in your building!

Survey Technology Usage

To know where you are going, you need to know where you are. Your office technology is no exception.

The following is a quick list of things to review and a suggested format of collecting data when you do an office inventory of technology usage.

When you have the data, you might want to look at formalizing some kind of environmental policy around shutting computers down before going home for the night and so on (see Chapters 8 and 15).

Item (categories suggested below)	Energy Star (yes or no)	Serial number	Average hours used daily	Workstation environmental policy	Planned replacement date
Computers					
Copiers					
Printers					
Fax machines					
Scanners					

Here are a couple of informal environmental best practices you can share (or post) by each equipment category:

♦ Computers—Turn off computer when not in use for 30 minutes and after office hours, or install software to switch off computers automatically.

♦ Copiers—Think twice about copying; copy double-sided; turn off copier when not in use if the warm up takes less than 10 seconds; turn off copier after office hours; set the power level to the lowest power needed.

♦ Printers—Send documents electronically rather than snail mail; print double-sided (for small-volume printers, print odd pages first then feed those pages again and print even pages on the other side); use print preview rather than printing a test copy; set default time for sleep mode to the lowest convenient setting; turn off printers when not in use after 10 minutes and at the end of the work day, or install software for automatic switch off.

♦ Fax machines—Set default time for sleep mode/standby mode to the lowest convenient setting, especially for fax machines, as they are in standby mode most of the time; make sure the fax machine has toner and ink saving modes; if you have more than one fax machine, divert calls after hours to a few units and turn the rest off; use scratch paper for the fax machine whenever possible; do use stick-on labels with the recipient name, date, and number of pages sent rather than a separate cover sheet; do not use status reports or individual transmission pages.

♦ Scanners—Because scanners aren't a regularly used item in most offices, turn on only when needed; and turn the scanner off rather than use sleep mode.

Waste

Everything that leaves our business that isn't for sale or gifted is waste. The concept of waste is not only from an environmental perspective but also from the perspective of economics. Every business spends money on the items it throws out. Surewood Forest Products, a stair parts manufacturer and distributor, implemented a cardboard recycling program at their Youngwood, Pennsylvania, warehouse. Each month, they saved an average of $600 per month on hauling costs. That is a total of roughly $7,200 per year!

With that rationale, the more we reduce what we throw out, the more costs we will reduce. Right?

Sometimes we can't avoid waste, but having an inventory of what we throw out can give us a starting place to reducing those costs. Here are three easy steps in preparing a waste audit:

♦ Obtain your waste disposal records.

Either go to accounting or contact your trash collector to obtain your monthly disposal services invoices, which can help you answer the following questions: How are you being charged, by the pull or by weight? How much are you paying each month? How much are you throwing away?

♦ Walk through your facility.

A walkthrough of your facility is necessary to learn where trash is coming from and where it ends up. A walkthrough can also help you determine what material is being thrown away and identify reduction opportunities and potential savings. Plan the walkthrough when garbage bins and dumpsters are full. Contact your building maintenance staff for assistance, and ask when a good time would be.

So roll up those sleeves, put on the rubber gloves, and go on a diving expedition that would make Jacques Cousteau jealous. Of course, your dive will be in the dumpsters around your office and facility.

The more people in your organization you can involve in your waste audit, the better the results. Look at everyone from the corner office to the usual suspects.

Tools needed:

♦ Small reusable tarp (for laying out the contents of waste paper baskets—look for anything that could be put into the recycling containers)

♦ Digital camera (for taking those vacation shots)

♦ Rubber gloves

♦ Paper and pen (note taking is usually a good thing)

♦ The waste audit worksheet

♦ A good sense of humor!

The following is a worksheet for your waste audit.

Department:

Date:

Time:

Auditor(s):

No. of bins in office:

Size of bins in office:

Period of accumulation:

Waste Type	Approx Volume	% Waste Stream	Recycling Potential	Comments/ Type
Paper/soiled paper				
Cardboard				
Aluminum cans				
Liquid paper board (milk/ juice cartons)				

Waste Type	Approx Volume	% Waste Stream	Recycling Potential	Comments/ Type
Glass				
Plastics coded R, 1, 2, 3, 4, 5, 6, 7				
Uncoded plastics (i.e., packaging)				
Polystyrene (i.e., coffee cups, packaging)				
Food				
Other (specify)				

After you have done your assessment, summarize your findings on a spreadsheet and start looking for areas in which to reduce. Share your findings with staff, implement your waste reduction plan, and conduct another assessment to see how much you have improved.

Fuel

Depending on your organization and what type of industry you are in, fuel may have a huge or limited impact on your overall environmental footprint. For car-based emissions, the emission factors are based on fuel use. Use your fuel receipts rather than estimate the fuel efficiency. However, if you are just starting to record your impacts, you may not have systems set up to calculate your exact fuel usage. In this case, you can visit a fuel efficiency reference guide such as one from the EPA, which you can find at www.epa.gov/greenvehicles/Index.do.

If you are not currently tracking your fuel use, create a spreadsheet to quantify the amount of fuel you use for each company-owned vehicle. This will help you gauge how much you spend on fuel per month and serve as a resource when calculating the carbon footprint generated from your business fleet. We will dive into carbon footprinting in Chapter 6.

Once you know how much fuel you are using, you can create a plan for use reduction. This will reduce your operating costs, increase profits, and reduce your environmental footprint.

Green Business Programs

There are several green business programs that can help you meet your sustainability goals. Here are a few examples:

- The Energy Star Small Business Program is designed collaboratively for and with small business to help reduce energy costs, while helping protect the environment. Go to www.energystar.gov/index.cfm?c=small_business.sb_index to discover more.

- The National Institute of Standards and Technology has a nationwide network of specialists that help small- and medium-size manufacturers through the Manufacturing Extension Partnerships program that combines environmental practices with "lean" manufacturing. Visit its website at www.mep.nist.gov.

- The EPA's Climate Change Site offers comprehensive information on the issue of climate change in a way that is accessible and meaningful to all parts of society—communities, individuals, business, states and localities, and governments. Go to www.epa.gov/climatechange/index.html.

- Use the WRI's GHG Protocol 9-to-5 program to help set boundaries and calculate your company's total greenhouse gas emissions. You can find this at www.wri.org/publication/working-9-5-climate-change-office-guide.

- The TeleCommuter Hire Savings Calculator is an online tool that shows the employee cost savings in getting cars off the road. Go to www.tjobs.com/hiresavings.shtml.

- Zerofootprint.net contains information and a Personal Carbon Manager that enables you to measure, track, and manage your carbon emissions. You can find these tools at goblue.zerofootprint.net/?language=en.

As you can see, many tools are available to help you develop a reasonable assessment of your business's impact on the environment. Using these measures will help you develop a plan to reduce your energy and water usage and waste output and to increase efficiency for your business. Taking a hard look at the figures you develop might encourage you to consider taking the step to install renewable energy sources, such as solar panels or a wind turbine, if appropriate. Cutting costs in these areas will help you save money and increase profits overall.

The Least You Need to Know

- ◆ You can measure your resource usage.
- ◆ Understanding your usage patterns involving water and electricity can help you increase resource efficiencies.
- ◆ Reducing waste can save you money.
- ◆ Developing efficient policies will increase profits.

Chapter 5

Implementing Your Plan

In This Chapter

◆ Follow your green policies

◆ Develop better efficiencies of resource usage

◆ Establish your sustainable supply chain

◆ Cut costs and increase profits

Now that you have learned how to develop your vision, goals, and strategic sustainability plan and how to benchmark and gauge your organization's current environmental and social impacts, it's time to combine this knowledge and use it to implement your strategic sustainability action plan. This chapter outlines areas to focus on as you implement your plan and gives concrete examples of each focus area.

Establish Environmentally Friendly Policies

One way to start writing your policies is to review the questions you answered in the assessment and base your policies on what changes you want to see happen in your organization. For instance, if you investigated your purchasing processes and found you need to make several changes, you can write a green purchasing policy. Write your policy so anyone making purchasing decisions will understand what he needs to do based on the organization's principles on sustainability. A good policy outlines the high-level issue you are addressing and gives a method for how to execute the solution.

For example, your policy might be to purchase copy paper and other paper products—including envelopes, post-it pads, folders, toilet paper, paper towels, scratch pads, and so on—at minimum 35 percent *post-consumer recycled content*.

def•i•ni•tion

Post-consumer recycled content is material that has been used directly by a consumer and then recovered. Any green purchasing policy should outline purchasing requirements for at least 30 percent post-consumer recycled paper products.

Following is a list of other items to consider when outlining an environmentally friendly paper purchasing policy:

- Chlorine-free paper

- Tree-free paper, such as products at www. ecopaper.com

- Products produced by a company with a stated commitment to minimizing ecological impacts and ensuring long-term, sustainable production

Go through all your practices as you determine your policies based on what you need to change, how you can best educate your staff about the changes, and how to assist them in executing the changes. After you have a draft document, get feedback from all your staff or a select group that represents the staff. This will help you recognize which policies will be difficult to implement and where your staff might need some training.

Even though this section is about establishing environmentally friendly policies, remember to think about social policies you can include that go beyond green by incorporating both social and environmental initiatives into your organization.

The following are examples of high-level policies:

- "We will provide all associates with a safe, friendly work environment and will treat each of them with respect, openness, honesty, and fairness. We will solicit and respond to the ideas of our associates and reward their meaningful contributions to our success. We will provide a *living wage* to all Timbron employees, including comprehensive health benefits to full-time employees."

- "We will minimize waste pollution and develop and operate environmentally sound waste management procedures."

◆ "We value America's diversity, so we will strive to reflect that diversity in our workforce, the companies with which we do business, and the customers we serve."

◆ "We will engage with suppliers and employers to reduce the life cycle impacts of our operations and products."

def•i•ni•tion

A **living wage** is the minimum hourly wage necessary for a person to achieve a specific reasonable standard of living. In developed countries such as the United Kingdom or Switzerland, this standard generally means that a person working 40 hours a week, with no additional income, can afford a specified quality or quantity of housing, food, utilities, transport, health care, and recreation.

This concept differs from the minimum wage in that the latter is set by law and may fail to meet the requirements of a living wage. It differs somewhat from basic needs in that the basic needs model usually measures a minimum level of consumption, without regard for the source of the income.

Office Practices

Greening your office space is a major part of implementing any sustainability plan. Not only will greening your office space help your overall organization reduce its environmental footprint, but it will also get employees engaged in your sustainability initiatives. Making green changes to the work environment of those who are in the office every day and getting them involved in footprint reduction will ingrain environmental values into your organization. Refer to Chapter 4 for detailed suggestions and instructions on how to reduce your office's environmental footprint.

It is useful to create a green office guide customized to your organization that describes in detail environmental policies that relate to your general office space so all your employees understand them and know how to implement them. Also give employees an explanation for why you have chosen to implement the policies you have developed and why they are important to your organization. Make the guide as engaging and user-friendly as possible. Use Chapter 4 as a resources for creating your customized green office guide.

Sustainable Supply Chain

Your organization's supply chain refers to the network of retailers, distributors, transporters, storage facilities, and suppliers that participate in the sale, delivery, and production of a particular product. In short, a supply chain is comprised of every person, company, and resource involved with the manufacturing of a product from beginning to end. When looking at your organization from a lens of sustainability, incorporate a systemic approach when thinking about this supply chain. Your supply chain is connected to the rest of your organization and is an inherent component in the creation of your sustainability program. If your organization produces products, read Chapter 10 for detailed information on how to make your products more sustainable.

Going Green

When implementing your sustainability action plan, don't forget to include your products and manufacturing processes into the equation. After all, what you produce is not only integral to the success of your organization, but is also often the greatest contributor to an organization's environmental and social impact.

If you are a product producer, your supply chain is an area where your organization will have the greatest environmental impact, so it is important that you understand the magnitude of this impact. You can do this by conducting a life-cycle assessment for your products. This life-cycle assessment analyzes the environmental impact of a product from "cradle to grave," or from raw materials extraction through end-of-life disposal (see Chapter 10).

After you understand the impacts of your supply chain, create policies and plans to improve them. These policies will cover what you need to do to reduce the impacts of your supply chain. Perhaps you would like to reduce your transportation footprint. You would then create a policy that outlines your goal of transportation footprint reduction and outline a detailed plan of how to reach that goal. Another example might be improving the social impact of your supply chain. Perhaps you would like to ensure that the people actually making your product work in humane conditions. To achieve this goal, you outline a *"no sweatshop" rule* and develop ways to enforce it to ensure all your products are produced in humane work environments. Each organization's environmental and social policies will be different depending on the needs of that organization.

def•i•ni•tion

A **"no sweatshop" rule** outlines a policy by which manufacturers and product producers will not purchase materials from sweatshops. This encourages local labor reform, living wage, and more humane working conditions for employees in both developed and developing nations.

Create Checklists

A productive way to keep your organization on track when implementing your strategic sustainability action plan is to create checklists that will help employees remember the action items necessary to achieve your sustainability goals. Checklists keep people engaged in your plan and provide tangible, actionable items that each employee can accomplish. If you use the suggestion mentioned earlier and develop a green office guide, you can include the checklists in that document. If you are creating PDF checklists, be sure to design forms that can be filled out on the computer. Using electronic checklists such as PDFs will reduce your organization's paper consumption.

Steps to Reduce Emissions

Most scientists agree that global climate change is exacerbated by human impact, so reducing your company's greenhouse gas emissions and carbon footprint should be part of your action plan. When you understand what your impacts are, you can determine the most efficient ways of reducing them. Learn more about calculating your carbon footprint in Chapter 6, or work with a sustainability consulting firm to assess your carbon footprint and to help you develop a Climate Action Plan.

After you've developed your baseline carbon footprint, it's time to reduce your emissions. Remember that every reduction you make in energy use will result in reduced costs. In addition to the suggestions given in Chapter 4 for energy reduction, take the following tips suggested by the Environmental Protection Agency (EPA) into consideration when implementing your emissions reduction plan:

◆ Manage office equipment energy use better—this includes personal work stations and company-wide IT servers.

◆ Look for Energy Star–qualified products for the office.

◆ Ask your office building manager if your office building has earned Energy Star certification or if energy efficiency upgrades have been implemented in the building.

◆ Use less energy for your commute and product transportation.

◆ Reduce, reuse, and recycle.

For more tools and resources on how to reduce your emissions and implement a Climate Action Plan, visit www.epa.gov/climatechange/wycd/stateandlocalgov/tools_resources.html.

Steps to Reduce Water Usage

Fresh water constitutes only 3 percent of the available water supply on Earth. With an increase in population and increasing growth, water demand and consumption also increases. To protect your business from increasing water costs and water use regulations, create and implement a water use reduction plan as soon as possible.

As you did with your plan to reduce emissions, refer to the information in Chapter 4 for suggestions on what initiatives to include when implementing your water reduction plan. You may want to categorize your water reduction plan into two segments: engineering practices and behavioral practices. Engineering practices include reductions based on modifications in equipment, plumbing systems, or water supply operating procedures. Behavioral practices include changes in personal water consumption habits.

Include the following actions in your water reduction plan:

- Install low-flow faucet aerators and shower heads.

- Install low-flow toilets or utilize a toilet dam system.

- Use water-conserving ice machines.

- Fix leaks on all sinks, toilets, and other water sources.

- Reuse and recirculate water when possible. This is particularly important in manufacturing operations.

- Treat and reclaim water when possible.

- Use nonpotable water when possible and look into installing a *greywater* system.

- If you have the ability, use water cisterns to store rainwater for later use. This is particularly useful for landscaping.

- Design operational processes that consume less water.

def•i•ni•tion

Greywater is nonindustrial wastewater generated from everyday household activities such as washing dishes, doing laundry, and bathing. It comprises 50 to 80 percent of residential wastewater. Greywater can be reused for many purposes, including flushing toilets and landscaping.

Steps to Reduce Waste

Make waste reduction the center of any sustainability program. When you think about reducing your waste, think beyond the recycling bins, composting bins, and garbage cans to your entire operation. Your goal should be to see your entire operation through the idea of *zero waste*.

When you implement your waste reduction plan, be sure to give employees the resources necessary to carry out your goals. Your plan may include the use of composting and recycling bins in your facility to improve diversion rates, so make it easy for your employees to reduce waste by placing waste disposal stations in convenient locations. Make sure each employee has a paper-recycling bin at his or her workstation and is in close proximity to composting and

def•i•ni•tion

According to the Zero Waste International Alliance, **zero waste** means designing and managing products and processes to reduce the volume and toxicity of waste, conserving and recovering all resources, and not burning or burying materials.

additional recycling. Also create recycling centers for batteries, compact fluorescent light bulbs, and other types of hazardous wastes so your employees won't throw them in the trash. Clearly label these areas and mark each container with the type of material that is to be put into it. To further encourage employee participation, hold a brief training session explaining the new waste diversion system. Highlight each new waste receptacle and the material that is to be disposed in it.

Remember, waste is a result of inefficient business processes. The more efficient you make your operations, the less waste you generate and the more money you save!

Strive for Continuous Improvement

Although you should feel a sense of accomplishment for reaching milestones you've laid out in your sustainability action plan, remember to strive for continuous improvement.

As you implement your sustainability action plan, reduce your environmental footprint, and improve your social performance, be sure to track your progress. This serves as vital data for measuring the effectiveness of your program, determines areas for improvement, helps you measure your return on investment (ROI), and serves as the backbone to many of your green marketing initiatives that we will cover more in depth in Chapters 20, 21, and 22.

Small Changes Reap Big Gains

Every small change a business makes to reduce its environmental footprint and improve its social impact adds up. Starting small is a great way to ease into implementing your sustainability plan and to see how your new initiatives benefit your bottom line.

Heather's friend Anna works at a large environmental consulting firm in Concord, California. When Anna took the initiative to be the green champion in her office building, she used the Bay Area Green Business Program's guidelines and started making small changes to her office space, such as increasing recycling programs. Upper management was happy Anna was taking an interest in the company, but she felt it did not fully support her or the greening program she was trying to initiate. One day, as Anna was assessing the facility's water use, she realized that the firm had been watering its neighbor's lawn for over five years, costing them over $17,000 in increased water costs. When Anna pointed this out to her superiors, they were ecstatic about her findings and the cost savings associated with them. After this, Anna was encouraged to continue with her greening initiatives, including creating a water use reduction plan for the facility, and was even allowed to take an afternoon off work to attend the Bay Area Green Business recognition day.

This is just one example that shows how paying attention to details can result in large cost savings. As you implement your green program, remember that cost savings will add up over time. You might not see an ROI right away, but eventually your organization will become more efficient, save money, and operate through a lens of sustainability!

Each Step Moves You Forward

Although achieving sustainability may seem overwhelming at the outset, you'll find that each small step you take—whether improving your waste management practices or increasing efficiency of water and energy use—will move you closer to your goals. As you make these small steps forward, you'll likely find that the habits are easy to adopt. And you'll soon find even more ways to reduce your environmental footprint as well as your costs.

The Least You Need to Know

- Creating a strategic sustainability action plan is key to your success.
- Sticking to a well-planned implementation timeline will make executing your plan easier for you.
- Establishing energy, waste, and water reduction programs will help employees fulfill your plan.
- Implementing specific plans will result in increased savings for your business.

Chapter 6

Calculating and Reducing Your Carbon Footprint

In This Chapter

- ◆ The business case for carbon footprinting
- ◆ Calculate your carbon footprint
- ◆ The key carbon accounting tools and organizations
- ◆ Carbon offsets and their uses

One of the most important steps in making your business greener is to figure out how much and in what ways you're contributing to greenhouse gases. Because the size of your footprint is mostly an indicator of how much energy you're using, opportunities to reduce your footprint are opportunities to reduce or hedge against rising energy costs. This chapter explains what a carbon footprint is and shows you how to calculate yours so you can figure out how to reduce your business's environmental impact on the earth.

What's Your Carbon Footprint?

Television ads speak to everyday folks about their *carbon footprints*. And the *New Oxford American Dictionary* has named the term *carbon neutral* its Word of the Year. An explosion of websites offer to help individuals and businesses calculate and offset the greenhouse gas emissions caused by their activities. Things have gotten quite complicated, which is why steps by national and global institutions to standardize principles and calculations have been particularly welcome.

def•i•ni•tion

A **carbon footprint** is the amount of greenhouse gases (those gases that trap infrared heat in our atmosphere, causing global temperatures to rise) emitted from some defined activity or set of activities. Though called a *carbon footprint*, the term includes other greenhouse gases such as methane.

Carbon neutral describes a product, organization, person, or any other entity that contributes no net greenhouse gases to the atmosphere. Usually the term implies that emissions from one source—like energy use—have been neutralized or balanced out through the purchase of "carbon offsets," or reductions taking place elsewhere.

A Basic Calculation

Let's calculate the carbon footprint of a 4.5-mile roundtrip drive to the grocery store. Imagine we drive a 1979 station wagon that gets 16 miles per gallon in city driving. This trip consumes $9/16$ gallon, or 0.56 gallons, of gas. Doing some online research, we see that combusting a gallon of gasoline (breaking the gasoline's chemical bonds to create carbon-oxygen bonds) creates 19.4 pounds of carbon dioxide, the main greenhouse gas. So we can calculate that the carbon footprint of this drive creates $0.56 \times 19.4 = 10.9$ pounds of carbon dioxide (CO_2).

Enviro-Fact
Oftentimes when businesses talk about their carbon footprint reductions, they talk in terms of "cars off the road for a year." What does this mean? A pickup truck that carries its driver every day on an 80-mile roundtrip commute will have different annual carbon emissions than a sub-compact car that does the occasional city trip. Usually this equivalency of "cars off the road for a year" assumes the average passenger vehicle gets 19.7 miles per gallon and travels 11,856 miles in a year. These numbers come from research done by various government agencies and are compiled by the Environmental Protection Agency (EPA).

What about some of the other emissions not accounted for in that calculation? For example, a small fraction of that gasoline did not combust properly (especially in such an old clunker!) and was emitted into the atmosphere as methane—a greenhouse gas with more than 20 times the global warming power of CO_2! Not to mention manufacturing that 1979 station wagon required huge amounts of energy in the form of natural gas, electricity, and more, all of which created greenhouse gases. So is 10.9 pounds of CO_2 the real carbon footprint?

While technical debates continue, national and international standards have emerged and continue to emerge to help guide us through these issues.

If you think determining the carbon footprint of a car trip to the grocery store is difficult, you can imagine how challenging it could be to determine a company's carbon footprint. Thankfully, some wise folks got together in 1998 to give the world's companies a consistent standard and guidance on calculating their carbon footprints. The World Resources Institute (WRI), an environmental think-tank based in Washington, D.C., and the World Business Council for Sustainable Development (WBCSD), a Swiss organization made up of businesses committed to sustainability, developed the Greenhouse Gas (GHG) Protocol, which has become the foundation of nearly all business carbon footprinting.

Before discussing how to measure greenhouse gases, it is worth asking these questions: Why conduct an emissions inventory? Why should a business care about its carbon footprint? Without getting into anything too philosophical, we do have a good business case for conducting an emissions inventory. Boiled down, this business case is simple: reduce costs, sell more, and manage risk.

To the first point, GHG reduction investments are often great business investments. This is not theory; it is documented fact. For example, Johnson & Johnson disseminates energy efficiency best practices throughout its hundreds of facilities and requires retrofits with simple paybacks of less than five years to be implemented. It uses a $40 million annual rotating fund to help facilities finance retrofits with longer paybacks. It has seen an average return on investment (ROI) of 16 percent on these GHG reduction investments. Taking a proactive stance toward measuring and managing their carbon footprint has allowed Johnson & Johnson to reduce costs while growing sales.

Learning from the sustainability initiatives of larger corporations is a great way for small- and medium-size businesses to shape their own sustainability programs.

Hazard

Don't think you have to start with a giant capital investment in a solar array or all-new manufacturing equipment to green your business. It's a mistake to start anywhere other than the "low-hanging fruit"—this means no-cost or low-cost measures like behavioral and housekeeping changes, or hardware store fixes like lavatory faucet aerators. Building efficiency into your business from the bottom-up will be the most cost-effective and lasting approach.

The recent explosion of green products in the marketplace is evidence that product manufacturers are seeing genuine consumer interest in buying climate-friendly items. And major retailers, most notably Wal-Mart, are starting to recognize efforts from supply chain companies to reduce emissions. Wal-Mart's packaging scorecard, a tool for measuring the environmental impact of product packaging, takes into account the greenhouse gas emissions required to produce a product's packaging. Small- and medium-size businesses that make up Wal-Mart's supply chain are now being held accountable for their product packaging decisions.

As new climate policies take force in the United States and throughout the world, emitting greenhouse gases is quickly going from free to pricey. Companies or supply chains with large greenhouse gas emissions are facing a risk of cost increases. Early action to measure your carbon footprint and assess this risk makes a whole lot of sense both for the environment and your bottom line.

The GHG Protocol

The GHG Protocol Corporate Standard, first published in 2001, tells businesses how to measure their carbon footprints or "greenhouse gas emissions inventory." Because this standard is comprehensive and versatile, both small businesses with a bit of leased office space and large corporate behemoths with complex operations in 50 countries can use it. The folks at the GHG Protocol Initiative have written extensive guidance documents meant to assist users of this standard. Even better, they have made public a handful of spreadsheet-based tools that any business can use free of charge. Most are general, but some are specific to select industries (such as cement manufacturing). Simply punch in your numbers, and out comes a carbon footprint. These tools can be downloaded from the GHG Protocol website: www.ghgprotocol.org.

The GHG Protocol has formed the basis of most other greenhouse gas accounting standards. It helps businesses answer the same types of questions we were facing with the car trip to the grocery store example. As a business, how do you choose which emissions to include and which to omit in your greenhouse gas inventory? Do you have to include that joint venture where you own only 40 percent of the operation? If you have 10 employees commuting to work each day from 25 miles away, does your company take responsibility for all those emissions, or do they belong to your workers?

The GHG Protocol answers these "what's in, what's out" questions. For companies with many different operations, the GHG Protocol Standard helps users set what it calls "organizational boundaries." In dealing with operations and enterprises for which the company does not have full ownership and control, it can choose whether to take a proportion of the emissions commensurate with its ownership percentage, or it can choose to take on only emissions from operations where it has financial or operational control. Whichever route your company chooses, it must be consistent.

More relevant to smaller organizations, the GHG Protocol also tells users what activities they need to account for in their inventory—so-called "operational boundaries." With all the different operations and activities in a business that create greenhouse gas emissions, this is where things get really interesting!

The Example of Little Red Wagon, Inc.

To help us along, let's imagine a mid-size company, Little Red Wagon, Inc. (LRW), that has a single industrial facility with some office space. When a manager at LRW sits down to calculate her company's carbon footprint, she ponders all the different emissions sources:

- The natural gas to heat the space and provide hot water
- The electricity to run equipment, lights, and air conditioning
- Business flights to meet with customers
- Propane to operate the forklifts
- Each worker's daily commute to and from the facility
- The LRW vans used by the sales team
- The daily shipments of wagons all across the country by the third-party trucking company

The LRW manager first needs to decide what types of emissions she wants to include in her calculations. In the parlance of the GHG Protocol, she has to decide what emissions "scopes" she wants to inventory. There are three scopes:

- Scope 1 emissions are greenhouse gases.

- Scope 2 emissions are purchased electricity.

- Scope 3 emissions are a catch-all category.

Generally the first two scopes are required for most reporting protocols, while the third is optional. This is fortunate, as scope 1 and scope 2 emissions are vastly easier to quantify than scope 3.

Scope 1 emissions are greenhouse gases that actually exit from your company's property. Called "direct" emissions, these come mostly from the combustion of fuels, although they can include other types of emissions. In the case of LRW, this includes its natural gas usage to heat space and water, as well as the propane to run forklifts and emissions from those company-owned LRW vans. In all these cases, fuel in the forms of propane, natural gas, and gasoline is entering company property, and the greenhouse gas CO_2 is leaving company property.

Going Green

Lighting is a huge energy user in industrial facilities, particularly those with fixtures using hundreds of watts each. When considering lighting, remember that what you need is a certain amount of illumination on the work surface—not a certain quantity of light fixtures. Think of the most efficient way to meet your target illumination beginning with free natural light, which has been shown to benefit productivity.

Sometimes greenhouse gases other than CO_2 from fuel combustion leave a company's property. For example, during LRW's annual air conditioner servicing, its units require a recharge of 1 pound of hydro fluorocarbon (HFC) refrigerant. These so-called fugitive emissions should be included in the scope 1 inventory. These can be important: 1 pound of a particular type of HFC packs the global warming potential of 14,800 pounds of CO_2!

LRW's electricity use produces no on-site greenhouse gas emissions, but surely somewhere a power plant is supplying energy for their needs. In fact, generating electric power to run our homes and businesses is an enormous source of greenhouse gas emissions. According to the U.S. Energy Information Administration, electricity generation produces 40 percent of total U.S. greenhouse gas emissions.

The GHG Protocol dedicates scope 2 to purchased electricity. The GHG Protocol authors write, "For many companies, purchased electricity represents one of the largest sources of GHG emissions and the most significant opportunity to reduce these emissions."

So how can LRW figure its carbon footprint resulting from electricity use? Of course this depends on how much electricity it consumes, but it also depends on where LRW is located. We can generate electricity in many ways, some of which create no greenhouse gas emissions (such as Wyoming wind turbines) and some of which create a lot of emissions (such as Wyoming coal). The EPA, using its database of virtually every power plant in the country, publishes the greenhouse gas intensity (pounds of CO_2/megawatt-hour) for each region. This is why most greenhouse gas calculators ask you where your facility is located.

Scope 3 emissions are a catch-all category, as the GHG Protocol authors describe them as "optional," and they are seldom included in emissions inventories in any kind of systematic way. In LRW's case, business flights, employee commuting, and shipping products via a third-party vendor would all be treated as optional scope 3 emissions. Other noteworthy sources of scope 3 emissions include emissions from the creation of purchased materials (like emissions from making steel and paint in the case of LRW), use of products by consumers, and emissions resulting from waste disposal.

Creating Your Greenhouse Gas Emissions Inventory

Measuring a business's carbon footprint can be quite complicated for a large multinational organization, but fortunately for small- and medium-size enterprises, the task is fairly straightforward. The most important criteria of a good emissions inventory are that it is comprehensive in its coverage and transparent in its assumptions. After a company answers the question, "Why are we measuring our carbon footprint?", it should determine what its carbon footprint assessment is going to include. In most cases, businesses look at their scope 1 and scope 2 emissions, which include direct fuel consumption, special emissions (if any), and electricity purchases. Create a comprehensive list of these scope 1 and 2 emissions sources at the outset.

The time period over which you will measure emissions is also critical. The GHG Protocol provides guidance on this topic, but for most small- and medium-size companies, you can use the last full year for which all the necessary data is available.

Data gathering often starts with accounts payable. Natural gas bills contain the total quantity of natural gas purchased either in energy terms (usually therms) or in volume terms (often hundreds of cubic feet). Similarly, electricity bills contain the quantity of electricity purchased, generally in units of kilowatt-hours. Always contact customer service at your major utilities to ask for what is already organized into monthly usage; in some cases, utilities can even provide carbon footprint information for consumption of their energy on your site. Propane, fuel oil, and other fuel invoices should contain mass or volume information. You may need to aggregate company fleet fuel receipts to determine how much gasoline and diesel was purchased to run company-owned vehicles.

Hazard

Include only fuel use or miles traveled for company-owned vehicles in a scope 1 and scope 2 inventory. Fuel use from employee commuting and business travel may be worth calculating and taking action on, but it should be treated in the separate category of scope 3 emissions.

After you list each fuel type and other emissions sources and tally the amount consumed during the measurement year, you need an emissions factor. These emissions factors are at the heart of carbon footprinting because they convert the raw number associated with an emissions source—for example, kilowatt-hours of electricity in Macon, Georgia; pounds of fuel oil; or therms of natural gas—into kilograms of carbon dioxide equivalents. The term is "carbon dioxide equivalents" rather than just "carbon dioxide" because sometimes an emissions source creates multiple types of emissions. (Remember our station wagon that produced CO_2 and a bit of methane?) Again, the GHG Protocol is our one-stop shop for emissions factors, as it offers emissions factors for every fuel imaginable as well as electricity throughout the United States and the world.

If you enter the term "carbon footprint" into any online search engine, you'll see loads of online calculators that help compute carbon footprints. Unfortunately, these calculators often lack consistency and rarely give the same result. A University of Washington study found unacceptable levels of variation (a single household's footprint calculators varied by 32,800 pounds of CO_2!) when using 10 online calculators to assess a carbon footprint.

Some online calculators include some GHG Protocol scope 3 emissions like business travel, employee commuting, and even materials management. Most companies willing to invest a bit of time (or hire a consultant) can calculate their carbon footprint on their own using the GHG Protocol guidance and tools. Others choose to hire a consultant to help them. Going through the process of gathering data internally is highly educational and revelatory. It is during the information-gathering process that opportunities for GHG reductions may come to light.

Hazard

Before using the GHG Protocol's emissions factors, users may have to do a bit of unit conversion. Your invoices may give propane use in pounds, whereas the GHG Protocol gives an emissions factor in metric tons. Use an online unit conversion tool such as www.onlineconversion.com to get all your units consistent with the GHG Protocol's.

Greenhouse Gas Reporting Standards

One motivation for a company to conduct a greenhouse gas emissions inventory is the ability to report its inventory with a recognized reporting agency and get recognition for early action and reductions. This improves public image and provides a "trial run" for mandatory greenhouse gas reporting. In some countries and some types of businesses, reporting is mandatory because country-wide greenhouse gas emissions are capped and certain businesses are given a set quantity of allowed emissions. These types of businesses generally include only the major emitting industries, such as power generation, petroleum refining, and other heavy manufacturing.

Presently in the United States, companies can report to several reporting agencies or registries and gain recognition. Some of these are through federal or state government, and others are through nonprofit organizations. The two major voluntary federal registries are the EPA's Climate Leaders and the Department of Energy's Voluntary Reporting of Greenhouse Gases Program (usually referred to as "1605(b)" after the section in the law that created it). Climate Leaders uses its own inventory protocol. Each Climate Leaders "partner" conducts an inventory and then pledges to make a voluntary reduction, which the EPA makes public on its website. Partners range from Fortune 100 companies to small service-sector businesses.

A key benefit of registries, especially to major GHG emitters in presently unregulated areas (such as the United States), is for companies to gain comfort with the inventory process and the other entities involved. This is based on the assumption that greenhouse gas regulations are coming to the United States, and we need to be prepared.

The Chicago Climate Exchange (CCX) is one registry that has gotten significant response. Companies that join the CCX either measure emissions directly—for example, through emission measuring equipment on a smokestack—or they use the GHG Protocol. After they join, members of the CCX face legally binding GHG reduction targets. They can meet these reduction targets by making real emissions reductions through efficiency, fuel switching, renewable energy, and so on; trading emissions reductions with other members; or by purchasing offsets from participating offset providers. CCX is something like a mock-up of what a broad mandatory federal system would look like, and members are gaining knowledge every day about how they will operate under such a system.

Other noteworthy registries include the California Climate Action Registry (CCAR) and The Climate Registry, both of which base their reporting standards on the GHG Protocol. For the CCAR, reporting companies can provide their California-based emissions or total U.S. operations emissions. The Climate Registry—which now boasts membership from 39 states, 11 Canadian Provinces, and 6 Mexican states—asks for the reporting company's operations in the United States, Canada, and Mexico. Again, the so-called scope 1 and scope 2 emissions must be reported, whereas the scope 3 emissions are optional.

Product Carbon Footprinting

Did you notice that when we computed the carbon footprint of that station wagon trip to the grocery store, we did not consider the footprint of the car's manufacture? And remember that LRW must purchase steel to make its wagons. Surely manufacturing and shipping that steel had a huge carbon footprint somewhere!

The WRI and WBCSD teams lumped product and supply chain emissions into that catch-all category called scope 3 emissions in the GHG Protocol. Because calculating emissions in a supply chain is so challenging that it requires its own standard, WRI and WBCSD are developing a new standard for what's called "product carbon footprinting." According to The Carbon Trust, the basic definition of a product carbon footprint is as follows: "the total emission of greenhouse gases in carbon equivalents from a product across its life cycle from the production of raw material used in its manufacture, to disposal of the finished product (excluding in-use emissions)." When a consumer buys a Little Red Wagon, her wagon is carrying a product carbon footprint that includes all the emissions that result from:

- Extraction of raw materials—in this case, iron ore for steel and petroleum for the paints

- Transportation of raw materials to initial refining

- Refining of ore and petroleum into ready-to-use materials

- Manufacturing of the finished product (this is LRW's footprint)

- Transportation of the finished product to the distributor and retailer

- Trucking and disposal of the used product to a landfill or recycling center

In practice, the process is simplified so companies can get decent results without spending too much time.

For major retailers and product manufacturers, an efficient and cost-controlled supply chain is critical. So let's consider Little Red Wagon, Inc. again. Imagine LRW sources the steel for its wagons from two major suppliers, one in the United States and the other in China. They stack up about equal as suppliers; the U.S. supplier is more expensive, but the quality is better and the shipment arrival is more predictable. If LRW conducts a product carbon footprint analysis of its wagon, it needs to include emissions from both suppliers: these suppliers turn raw material into inputs for LRW's operations. The results of this process give LRW quite a bit to work with:

- **They now know the basic efficiency with which both plants operate.** If the American facility has a significantly lower carbon footprint per unit of steel produced, then it knows the Chinese supplier has room for efficiency improvements and cost reductions.

- **They now know what cost risk they are facing if the countries enact greenhouse gas regulations that increase the cost of energy.** Since the United States is likely to have regulations in place before China, this risk of cost increases for their U.S. supplier can be seen from farther away, giving them more time for preparation.

- **They now have an impressive story to tell to the major retailers to whom they sell.** LRW can share the carbon footprint of its product, helping those retailers compute their own scope 3 emissions.

As mentioned previously, the WRI and WBCSD are only beginning to develop a GHG Protocol Standard for calculating product footprints. However, in the United Kingdom two organizations are already leading the way. The Carbon Trust worked with the British Standards Institute to develop a standard and methods for calculating product carbon footprints called the Publicly Available Standard (PAS) 2050. This standard will be applied internationally. They have pilot-tested their standard and method with several companies, and on some of these goods they have printed "carbon labels" which are in essence a product packaging label that displays the product's carbon footprint number in grams of carbon dioxide equivalents. The consumer value and market uptake of these carbon labels is still very uncertain. Similarly, the online offset retailer Carbonfund.org has begun offering "Carbonfree" certification for products that conduct greenhouse-gas life-cycle assessments using their standard and purchase offsets in an amount equal to the total carbon emitted during the product's life cycle.

Carbon Offsets

In essence, all *carbon offsets* are instruments that represent reductions in greenhouse gases.

def•i•ni•tion

> According to the David Suzuki Foundation, a **carbon offset** is an emission reduction credit from another organization's project that results in less CO_2 or other greenhouse gases in the atmosphere than would otherwise occur. Carbon offsets are typically measured in tons of CO_2-equivalents (or CO_2e) and are bought and sold through a number of international brokers, online retailers, and trading platforms.

About Carbon Offsets

The theory behind carbon offsets relies on simple atmospheric science and economics. First, atmospheric science tells us that carbon dioxide is a well-mixed gas, meaning emitting a pound in Shanghai is not much different than emitting it in San Francisco. In the end, greenhouse gas emissions will have the same effect—raising global temperatures—wherever they are emitted on Earth. Second, economics tells us that the polluter who wants to pollute less is not always the polluter who can most cost-effectively pollute less. Each polluter has its own marginal cost of abatement, which is a fancy way of saying its own cost of polluting less. Economics says that if it does not matter where the pollution occurs, then those polluters wishing to pollute less should pay the polluter who has the lowest marginal cost of abatement to do so.

This is a mouthful, so let's think about it in terms of LRW. Suppose LRW decides it wants to have zero direct contribution to climate change. It has already conducted its greenhouse gas inventory, so it knows exactly where and how much it emits. One way for LRW to lower its greenhouse gas emissions is to start getting efficient. It could replace high-intensity discharge lights with fluorescent bays, replace old motors with premium efficiency models, and so on. At some point, options to cut carbon emissions are going to get expensive. It could line its rooftop with solar panels, but given that LRW is in a pretty cloudy region of the country, this hardly seems efficient.

LRW might turn to carbon offsets to get itself from carbon efficient to carbon neutral. To do this, it would need to find a credible offset retailer. Thankfully myriad web-based retailers are happy to sell offsets to businesses and individuals. So where are the retailers getting these carbon reductions that they are selling to LRW? Dozens of different carbon projects around the world are selling carbon credits to retailers, brokers, and other middlemen. Carbon project developers have come up with all sorts of methods of cost-effectively abating or sequestering CO_2, including:

- Reforestation of degraded land to capture CO_2 in biomass

- Large renewable energy systems to offset conventional polluting power sources

- No-till farming to capture CO_2 in soils

- Fugitive methane capture and power generation from dairies, coal mining operations, and more

- Capture and destruction of high-potency greenhouse gases such as fluorocarbons from industrial operations

When you buy an offset, you are buying the greenhouse gas reduction benefits of these projects. Standards for projects vary widely, especially in the so-called "Wild West" voluntary market in the United States. The Voluntary Carbon Standard is emerging as the go-to standard for assessing the quality of voluntary offsets. In areas where greenhouse gas limits are mandatory, offsets are generally conducted through the United Nations' Clean Development Mechanism, which has its own project standards.

Are Carbon Offsets Sustainable?

Depending on whom you ask, carbon offsets are either a critical piece in solving global warming or the modern-day equivalent of medieval "indulgences," payments to the church so one could keep on sinning. Obviously, the first step in reducing one's impact on global warming is to first reduce one's own carbon footprint.

When purchasing offsets, it's critical that they come from a green project that meets the basic standard of "additionality" and that the resulting offsets are measured and verified properly. Measurements are critical, commonsense requirements for any green project hoping to sell carbon offsets. If a project developer is selling 1 million metric tons of offset CO_2, then the developer should be able to show that they actually measured this quantity using accurate methods and that a competent third party verified their measurements.

Additionality is a more subtle requirement. A carbon offset project is deemed "additional" if the emissions reductions it creates would not otherwise have occurred without the purchase of the carbon offsets. A lot of work has gone into defining this, but the basic case is clear. For example, a farmer who has a giant lagoon of swine waste, which through decomposition emits the powerful greenhouse gas methane, is obligated only to abide by local regulations in dealing with that waste. Suppose a carbon offset project developer approaches the farmer with an offer to pay for the equipment to capture the methane from the lagoon and generate power with it. Without the carbon offset money, the farmer would go on, business as usual, allowing the methane to escape. Thanks to the offset money, the greenhouse gas reductions occur, and the project is deemed additional.

With the emergence of well-accepted offset standards and the astounding growth in the carbon offset market, it appears that offsets are here to stay. Whether they are a good option for business investment is another matter entirely. If a business is going to purchase offsets, this investment should fit into a comprehensive environmental plan. An environmental plan that aggressively takes on a business's energy use and greenhouse gas footprint should first look for cost-effective internal reductions, like replacing inefficient equipment, changing building occupant behaviors, and instituting new operational controls. If the company is further committed to balancing out the emissions it can't eliminate through internal reductions, it may turn to offsets as part of its greenhouse gas strategy. Offsets cost money, so investing in them should show some financial return. Businesses that sell to consumers with a particular interest in climate change may find this financial benefit in increased customer loyalty and positive public perception.

Other Greenhouse Gases to Consider

Carbon footprints, carbon offsets, and all other things carbon are generally talked about in units of metric tons of carbon dioxide equivalent. As mentioned previously, the word "equivalent" is used because there are greenhouse gases other than CO_2. Thankfully, the folks at the Intergovernmental Panel on Climate Change have come up with a way of putting any quantity of the greenhouse gases in units of CO_2, based on their lifetime in the atmosphere and their capacity to trap heat.

The so-called "six Kyoto gases", named after the Kyoto Protocol, include carbon dioxide as well as the following. Note that the number in brackets following each gas is the *global warming potential* (*GWP*) of 1 pound of each respective gas compared to 1 pound of CO_2.

◆ Methane [25]

◆ Nitrous Oxide [298]

◆ Hydrofluorocarbons (HFCs) [vary, up to 14,800]

◆ Perfluorocarbons (PFCs) [vary, up to 9,200]

◆ Sulphur hexafluoride [22,800]

def•i•ni•tion

Global warming potential (GWP) represents the ability of a greenhouse gas to trap heat in Earth's atmosphere over a certain time horizon. Gases such as commercial refrigerants have large GWPs because they have long lives in the atmosphere—they don't get sucked up into trees or destroyed by ultraviolet light very quickly. Usually when someone gives a number for a gas's global warming potential, he is referring to its ability to warm the planet as compared to carbon dioxide over a 100-year time horizon.

Clearly, many gases are leaking into our atmosphere and causing havoc on the planet. The process of figuring out how to cut back on your own production of these gases is complicated, but the benefits to the world are great.

The Least You Need to Know

◆ You can calculate your business's carbon footprint using the GHG Protocol tools.

◆ Use your carbon footprint as a guide to saving energy and reducing costs.

◆ Explore the carbon footprints of your purchased materials and supply chain to track supplier progress and manage risk.

◆ Use offsets only after exploiting all energy efficiency options and only as part of a strategic environmental plan.

Part 3

Your Business Environment and Operations

This part provides you with the knowledge to create a sustainable workplace and a sustainable product. Whether you're a manufacturer, a retailer, or even a restaurant owner, we give you ideas about how to cut costs and save the environment at the same time. You can easily change many traditional practices and building configurations to create healthier environments. And you'll be pleased to discover that some changes are cost-effective and can save you money in the process!

Chapter 7

Greening Your Space

In This Chapter

- ◆ Creating a green building for health and efficiency
- ◆ Renovating an existing building
- ◆ Selecting green building materials to reduce costs
- ◆ Improving waste management to reduce costs

Greening your place of business can help you save energy and water, protect your indoor air quality, and reduce expenses while reducing your business's carbon footprint. In many cases, renovating your existing facility can be more cost-effective than building a new office, shop, or manufacturing facility.

In this chapter, you learn how to create a greener space for you and your colleagues to enjoy.

The Benefits of Green Construction and Renovation

Would you like to have a space that is more comfortable, healthy, and energy-efficient? By adopting green building strategies, you can maximize both environmental and economic performance. Just think of the impact you can have if you green up your construction and renovation activities. There are many ways you can make your existing building more environmentally friendly and efficient, from small changes like adding awnings over windows to major renovations such as adding insulation or swapping out appliances and equipment. If you're seeking a new space for your business, you can work with contractors to implement green building practices that will save energy and save you money.

Environmental

The overall effect of the buildings on the natural environment is astronomical. According to the United States Green Building Council (USGBC), the commercial building sector produces more than 1 billion metric tons of carbon dioxide (CO_2) per year. That's a 30 percent increase in CO_2 emissions over 1990 levels. Every day, we use nearly 5 billion gallons of water to flush toilets, and a typical building generates about 1.6 pounds of solid waste per day. These statistics show us how important it is to reduce our waste and cut down on our emissions.

Ideally, using a holistic approach to building instead of a piecemeal system is best because it enables architects, designers, urban planners, environmental consultants, landscape architects, and builders to come together to plan for overall environmental footprint reduction. Building green enhances and protects ecosystems and biodiversity, improves air and water quality, reduces waste, and conserves natural resources. From more outdoor open space to greener building materials, the building industry is raising the bar on green construction thanks to the USGBC, which was founded in 1993 to promote green building. Through their efforts, the building industry was one of the first to adopt green principles and is an industry that is much farther along on the greening curve than most.

> **Enviro-Fact**
>
> According to the USGBC, in the United States, buildings alone account for 70 percent of electricity consumption, 39 percent of energy use, 39 percent of all CO_2 emissions, 40 percent of raw material use, 30 percent of waste output (136 million tons annually), and 12 percent of potable water consumption.

Economic

In addition to helping the environment, building green saves money. Green buildings reduce expenses through lower operating costs over the life of the building. More efficient energy and water use reduce overall operational costs. Building green reduces the lifetime operational costs of the building and enhances the value and asset of the property. More and more people want to work in a building that has healthy indoor air quality, natural lighting, and eco-friendly policies. Business owners and employers benefit by attracting and retaining talented employees because they offer amenities in their workspace that other companies do not. Also some benefits to building green are not as easily quantified; improved occupant health, comfort, and productivity all contribute to an improved company bottom line. Healthier, happier employees are more productive, have fewer sick days, and have reduced health-care costs.

In some cases, a green building may cost more up front, but savings over time greatly outweigh the initial costs. Even with a tight budget, many green building measures can be incorporated into a project with minimal upfront costs. In Chapters 4 and 5, we discussed two ways to reduce costs—energy and waste reduction. An initial investment may be required to upgrade to more efficient lighting, but the payback period is short-lived. According to the Environmental Protection Agency (EPA)'s Energy Star program, LeRoy Harvey's company, Urban Options in East Lansing, Michigan, offers guidance and services for managing homes and yards in more energy-efficient, ecologically sound, and healthy ways. By installing compact fluorescent lamps, T-8 fluorescent lamps, improved insulation, a new high-efficiency heating system, and other measures, the organization has lowered its energy bills by an estimated $2,000 a year.

Starting From Scratch

When building a new, green building, the first and most important step is to gather your team early and talk about your project. Envision how you want the end project to look, and develop a plan to achieve that vision. Hold a preliminary meeting with the building owner, architect designer, engineer, contractor, sustainability consultant, and any participant involved in the project. Often referred to as an *eco-charrette*, this meeting will generate green goals for your project and a pathway to accomplish those goals.

During this initial meeting, you may choose to pursue green building certification such

def•i•ni•tion

An **eco-charrette** is an intense meeting, lasting a half day or more, in which all participants in a building project focus on ideas, goals, and strategies for constructing a green building. Eco-charrettes are also referred to as sustainable design charrettes.

as Green Globes (www.greenglobes.com) or the USGBC's Leadership in Energy and Environmental Design (LEED) certification. (See Chapter 22 for more information about selecting the best certification for your project.)

Since its formation in 1993, the USGBC's LEED rating system has grown to encompass over 14,000 projects in the United States and abroad, covering 1.062 billion square feet of development area and certifying over 43,000 people as LEED-accredited professionals. The various LEED rating systems cover homes, neighborhood development, commercial interiors, core and shell, new construction, schools, health care, retail, and existing building operations and maintenance. Each one of these rating systems has four levels of certification: certified, silver, gold, and platinum. These levels can be reached by obtaining points in various categories.

Enviro-Fact
LEED Credit Categories include:
◆ Sustainable sites
◆ Water efficiency
◆ Energy and atmosphere
◆ Indoor environmental quality
◆ Innovative design

Following the outline of a green building rating system such as LEED will give you and your team a template for building green. Even if you choose not to pursue certification, visit the USGBC website for pertinent green building information that will get you started on the right track: www.usgbc.org.

LEED for Existing Buildings: Operations and Maintenance

If you want to certify your existing building as green, check out LEED Existing Buildings Operations and Maintenance (LEED EBOM). This newly revamped rating system is design specifically to aid in the greening of an existing space and provides a benchmark for measuring operations efficiencies, improving indoor air quality, and reducing your overall environmental footprint.

Just like all the LEED rating systems, LEED EBOM breaks down into the following categories: sustainable sites, water efficiency, energy and atmosphere, indoor environmental quality, and innovative design. Emphasis is put on green cleaning, procurement of environmentally preferable materials for everyday office use, increased recycling programs, exterior maintenance and green landscaping, and building optimization and efficiency.

Begin the LEED EBOM process much like you would a new construction project. Hold an eco-charrette with the key project stakeholders, including the facilities manager, procurement manager, building owner, LEED consultant or sustainability manager, and a representative of those occupying the space that you want certified. After you determine project goals and decide you want LEED EBOM certification, go to the USGBC website to register your project. Certification fees vary depending on the size of your space, so visit www.usgbc.org for the most up-to-date certification information.

Enviro-Fact

In early 2009, the USGBC released LEED V.3, of which LEED 2009 is a part. LEED 2009 refers to the actual LEED rating system and LEED credits. LEED 2009 incorporates New Construction, Core and Shell, Commercial Interiors, Existing Buildings: Operations & Maintenance, and Schools. For more information on LEED 2009, visit www.usgbc.org/DisplayPage.aspx?CMSPageID=1849.

Enlightening Your Landlord

The building owner normally makes the final decision when it comes to greening your space. So if you are incorporating green building tactics into your new or existing rented space, you need to get everyone, including the owner, on board. Different selling points will appeal to different building owners depending on the type of building you are working in. The proposition that healthier indoor air quality and increased daylight is proven to heighten employee productivity might convince a business owner, whereas the enticement of a higher lease rate or faster turnaround time might appeal to the commercial property owner, and the promise of lower operating costs will appeal to the property manager. An April 2008 study conducted by the CoStar Group found that tenants are paying an average of $11.24 per square foot over conventional building competitors. Remember that as a renter, you are the landlord's customer, so it is in the landlord's best interest to work with you to make your environment as pleasant and productive as possible.

Before speaking with your landlord or building owner, list all the positives for greening your space that you can think of, paying particular attention to changes that will save the landlord money through a decrease in operational expenses. This is particularly important for tenants whose monthly rent includes utility fees. Be sure to have a clear idea of who will pay for improvements made to your space. If you are covering improvement costs, how will you recapture your investment? This will help you focus your thoughts and develop concise arguments for your landlord to consider. Consult your fellow colleagues when creating this list to get input from your entire team. It may also help to approach the landlord as a unified team. After all, there is strength in numbers.

Commissioning and Retrofitting for Greater Efficiency

Retrofitting your space for greater efficiency not only saves you energy and money but also reduces your overall environmental footprint by lowering your building's carbon footprint. According to the Energy Information Administration, 68 percent of the energy consumed in buildings is utilized for electricity. Paying for this energy can get expensive and makes up a huge part of a building's operational budget.

Begin the retrofitting process by commissioning your existing building. Existing building commissioning checks the performance of all building systems and determines a blueprint for building improvements. Your energy and water systems are checked during building commissioning.

def•i•ni•tion

HVAC is an acronym for heating, ventilating, and air conditioning. It includes systems used to provide thermal comfort and ventilation for building interiors.

Utilizing the results of the commissioning study, develop a plan for resource reduction through improved building efficiency. This could include optimization of your building's *HVAC* system, lighting retrofitting such as replacing incandescent light bulbs with compact fluorescent or LED light bulbs, and the installation of faucet aerators on all sinks to reduce water usage.

Renovating for Savings

Renovating, or reusing, an existing building is the number-one way to reduce a building's environmental impact. By renovating an existing space, you are saving a tremendous amount of resources that a new construction project would normally utilize, including reducing the overall building footprint of a new construction project. Renovating an existing space also preserves open and green space because you are not breaking ground for a new structure. In addition to benefiting the environment, renovating existing buildings can contribute to community development projects by refurbishing decrepit, run-down buildings. Contributing to community revitalization projects rebuilds towns that are in desperate need of maintenance and care, revitalizes neighborhoods, and brings back the concept of "Downtown America." Choosing to renovate a building in an area in need of revitalization can lead to substantial cost savings. Often local, state, and federal governments provide tax incentives to builders for redevelopment of blighted areas, and property is less expensive.

When choosing a building to renovate, make sure the overall structure is sound and intact. Whether you are conducting a minor renovation or a complete overhaul, a strong foundation is the key to any building.

Applying Green Principles

Use the most up-to-date, efficient appliances and products to save the greatest amount of money over the life of your building. When purchasing appliances for your space, look for the Energy Star logo. Energy Star is a joint program of the EPA and the U.S. Department of Energy. According to the EPA, in 2007 Americans saved enough energy to avoid greenhouse gas emissions equivalent to those from 27 million cars and saved over $16 billion on their utility bills by using Energy Star products.

If you are replacing your toilets and faucets, make sure you replace old models with new water-efficient products. Maximizing water efficiency within your building will save money and reduce the burden on potable water supply and wastewater disposal systems. Water conservation also lowers your overall energy use. Look for products that meet the following water use requirements:

- Toilets: 1.60 gallons per flush
- Urinals: 1.00 gallons per flush
- Shower heads: 2.50 gallons per minute
- Sinks: 2.20 gallons per minute

Incorporating salvaged building materials in your renovation can greatly reduce your overall renovation costs and your environmental impact. When you reuse items, you are diverting materials from landfills and reducing the environmental impact of new material production. Try to reuse things from the renovation itself, such as refinished flooring, and visit your local salvage yard for reused pieces that will make your project unique. According to *Environmental Building News*, existing buildings often contain a wealth of material and cultural resources. Highlighting these unique features in your project will make for a classic architectural piece.

When renovating your building, divert as much construction debris from the landfill as possible. If the space you are renovating contains toxins such as lead or asbestos, handle these hazardous materials appropriately. According to the USGBC, construction and demolition waste constitutes 40 percent of the total solid waste stream in the United States. During renovation, create a waste station outside your project to separate recyclables, compostable items, and landfill scrap. Talk with your local municipalities about construction waste diversion programs, and ask product manufacturers if they have a take-back policy and program for recycling the unused portion of their products.

Reduce, reuse, recycle, restore, and rethink are the five R's to follow when designing and renovating a green space. Think about the size of the space you are working with. Can you make it smaller to reduce your overall material consumption and environmental impact? As reusing materials also has a drastic impact on environmental footprint reduction, offer your used building materials to a local builder's recycling resource so others can use what you no longer need.

Local Materials

When specifying materials for your project, use local materials first. When choosing local materials, take into consideration where the raw material for those products was extracted, harvested, or recovered, as well as where the product was manufactured. A good example of a locally manufactured product would be one that recovers a recycled raw material, such as a glass bottle, and makes that item into a finished product.

For example, Vetrazzo, a manufacturer in Oakland, California, collects bottles recycled locally to make building products. Bottles are collected from local manufacturers and transported to their manufacturing facility, where they are transformed into one-of-a-kind slabs that are used to fabricate countertops and other slab surfaces. People purchasing this product in close proximity to Vetrazzo's manufacturing facility are making a local purchase that supports the local economy. Using local materials reduces your overall environmental impact due to reduced shipping distances. Barges, tractor-trailer trucks, and trains all use fossil fuel to operate, and therefore, contribute to air pollution and global warming. Local procurement also supports local economic development, keeps money paid for the materials in the regional economy, and provides jobs for local workers, all of which further fuel a healthy, sustainable economy. While it may not be possible to purchase products that are all extracted, harvested, recovered, and manufactured locally, it is possible to support locally owned and operated businesses. Research locally owned stores in your area and make an effort to support them. Ultimately, this will build your local economy and reduce your environmental impact.

Natural and Rapidly Renewable Materials

The use of natural building materials offers a way to utilize resources that are often renewable and grow in the natural environment. Many of these materials reduce the release of toxins indoors and contribute to healthier indoor air quality. Natural materials consist of building products which are composed of raw materials derived from natural sources and minimally processed.

Examples of natural, *rapidly renewable* materials include wool, bamboo, cotton, wheat board, cork, and linoleum. If you are procuring natural, rapidly renewable wood products, be sure to ask what types of binders or adhesives were used in the manufacturing of the product. Choose products that emit low or no *volatile organic compounds* (*VOCs*) to maintain healthy indoor air quality.

Kirei Board is a good example of an eco-friendly decorative design material. It's made from the waste stalks of the edible sorghum plant, waste fiber that previously was burned or sent to landfill for disposal. Using this rapidly renewable fiber for a building product creates a sustainable use for something that was previously considered waste material, prevents its disposal in landfills, and gives rural farmers a new source of revenue.

Kirei Board, environmentally friendly building material.

(Courtesy Kirei USA)

def•i•ni•tion

A **rapidly renewable** material is an agricultural product, both fiber and animal, that takes 10 years or less to grow 'or raise and to harvest in an ongoing and sustainable fashion.

Volatile organic compounds (VOCs) are toxic substances in gases emitted from caustic chemicals, paints, adhesives, formaldehyde, and many common building materials. If you can't avoid using VOC-containing products, use them in well-ventilated areas.

Maximize Natural Light and Ventilation

Studies show that hot and stuffy work conditions have little appeal to employees. People who work in poorly ventilated environments need to rest more often and have difficulties concentrating. Stuffy environments create cranky, nonproductive people and lead to an increase in absenteeism and sick days.

To ensure you have proper ventilation in your building, utilize an outdoor air delivery monitoring system. For buildings that use a mechanical ventilation system, provide a CO_2 sensor in densely occupied spaces. High CO_2 levels indicate a low air circulation and dilution rate of occupant-related contaminants, leading to an unhealthy workforce. Keeping the indoor CO_2 concentrations relative to those found outdoors creates the best indoor air quality for building occupants. The initial cost of installing a monitoring system will be recouped over time through increased efficiency of your HVAC system, increased employee productivity, and decreased absenteeism.

For naturally ventilated spaces, make sure you have a crossflow of natural air. Open windows as much as possible to ensure proper airflow. It's also a good idea to install an outdoor air delivery monitoring system in naturally ventilated spaces. According to the Natural Institute on Building Sciences Whole Building Design Guide, in favorable climates, buildings with natural ventilation can use an alternative to conventional air conditioning, saving 10 to 30 percent on total energy consumption.

Natural lighting and views have a profound effect on employee productivity and result in an overall reduction of utility costs due to a decreased use of electrical lighting. The Sustainable Buildings Technical Manual estimates that a building well-lit with daylight reduces lighting energy use by 50 to 80 percent. This not only reduces building operational costs but also reduces air pollution impacts and global warming associated with conventional energy production.

Increase natural lighting whenever possible by utilizing all the windows in your space. Remove thick, dark curtains and any other obstructions that would block views and prevent daylight from entering windows. Skylights and *Solatubes* are also fantastic, cost-effective ways to add more daylight to your space without embarking on a complete redesign.

def•i•ni•tion

A **Solatube** is a daylighting system that captures light through a dome on the roof and channels it down through an internal reflective system. At the ceiling level, a diffuser that resembles a recessed light fixture spreads the light evenly through the room.

Of course, you need to work within the parameters available to you, but when you're selecting a business location, if you wish to create a sustainable business, these are some of the things you'll want to take into consideration. You may need to start simply when working in a less-than-ideal space, but you'll have a greater idea of what to look for in the future and what to work toward. Whether you have a strip mall location or a stand-alone building, there are certainly some things you can do to green up your space.

Solar Power and Renewable Energy Credits

According to the American Solar Energy Society, a minute's worth of sunshine provides enough energy to power the earth's needs for a year. Investing in renewable energy systems will lessen your environmental impact and reduce your overall long-term energy costs. The sun provides natural, renewable energy and enables you to create your own miniature power plant directly on your property. As energy prices increase, independent solar will prove to be increasingly cost effective. The three types of solar available in today's market are monocrystal, polycrystal, and thin film. Monocrystal has the highest energy output at the moment. Many solar providers will be happy to discuss your options when going solar. Visit www.lowimpactliving.com/providers/Solar-Power/31# to find a solar provider near you.

When you can't install on-site solar, opt to purchase *renewable energy certificates* (*RECs*). RECs, renewable energy credits, or green tags represent the commodity formed by the environmental attributes of a unit of renewable energy. Under most programs, one REC is equivalent to the environmental

def•i•ni•tion

Renewable energy certificates (RECs) represent the commodity formed by the environmental attributes of a unit of renewable energy.

attributes of 1 megawatt-hour (MWh) of electricity generated from a renewable source. In short, purchasing RECs help you offset your carbon footprint. But only purchase RECs after you have finished energy conservation and reduction measures. Think of them as an avenue to offset what you cannot reduce or manage, not a first resort to reducing your carbon footprint.

Reduce Toxic Materials and Emissions

By using natural materials in your building construction and renovation, you can also reduce your exposure to toxins and the emissions they produce (see Chapter 8). Look for materials that do not emit VOCs and other harmful gasses that affect indoor air quality. VOCs react with sunlight to create ground-level ozone, commonly known as smog. This can cause unfavorable health conditions for workers, such as respiratory problems and eye irritation. Ask product manufacturers if their products emit any VOCs. If they say no, be sure to ask for back-up documentation and testing that proves the products are nonemitting.

Eco-Friendly Waste Disposal

The first step in creating a successful waste reduction program is to contact your local waste hauler and ask if it collects recycling and compost as well as trash. When discussing your options for recycling, be sure to ask what number plastics, 1 through 7, it recycles. Most municipalities that recycle commonly take PETE (#1) and HDPE (#2) plastic, but more areas are broadening the types of plastic they can recycle. If your waste hauler will not take recyclables, seek out alternative options for recycling disposal. A recycler might even pay you for your bottles and cans!

If you have a proper method of disposal for recycling, compost, and trash, you can create a *three stream waste system* in your building, which will enable you to reduce your waste and your garbage bills. A three stream waste system consists of three separate areas designated for trash, recycling, and compost. Provide three different-color bins—green for compost, blue for recycling, and black for trash—in an easily accessible area. Designate a paper bin that is separate from a bottle-and-can recycle bin. Having multiple waste

def·i·ni·tion

A **three stream waste system** provides three separate receptacles for trash, recycling, and compost in one designated waste station area.

stations set up around your facility and providing signage telling occupants what to throw in each bin will improve your waste reduction program. For example:

◆ Compost (green bin)—Organic matter such as vegetables, tea bags, and coffee grounds. Check with your local municipality for acceptance regulations.

◆ Recycling (blue bin)—Plastics, paper, glass bottles, and cans. Check with your local municipality for acceptance regulations. In most areas of the country, you will have to separate paper from plastics.

◆ Trash (black bin)—Anything that can't be recycled or composted.

It is also important to create a disposal area for hazardous materials like batteries, incandescent light bulbs, and electronic waste. Check with your local waste management provider to find hazardous household waste drop-off centers, collection dates, and times.

You must educate and engage your employees on your new waste reduction program to ensure success, so think of creative ways to get your team involved. Give them smaller trash cans at their desks and provide incentives for increased building diversion rates. Holding a brief training session educating all employees on the new waste diversion program will also help increase your diversion rates.

Conserving and Reusing Water

According to the USGBC, approximately 340 billion gallons of fresh water are withdrawn per day from rivers, streams, and reservoirs to support residential, commercial, industrial, agricultural, and recreational activities. Americans extract 3,700 billion gallons of water per year more than they return to lakes, rivers, streams, and underground aquifers. With rising water costs and increased water scarcity and drought, now is the time to conserve water.

When landscaping, planting species native to your area will reduce water consumption, and you can increase water efficiency by watering your lawn pre-dawn. Rainwater harvesting provides a great solution to outdoor watering needs. To set up a harvesting system, place a catchment barrel under your downspout gutter. To prevent infestation of bugs and keep out debris, cover the main opening of the catchment barrel, leaving a hole where the downspout meets the opening. Use this water to water your garden, but do not drink it unless you filter it with a trusted water filter (see Chapter 9).

And remember, faucet aerators are an inexpensive way to reduce energy and water consumption. For as little as a few dollars and a few minutes of time, you can easily retrofit your sink or showerhead with an aerator.

Adding a toilet dam to all the toilets in your building will reduce water consumption. Toilet dams, placed in the tank of a toilet, reduce tank size, which uses less water. Some people put a brick in their tank to reduce water consumption, but this is not recommended, as it could damage your toilet.

> **Enviro-Fact**
>
> Inexpensive and simple to install, low-flow shower heads and faucet aerators can reduce water consumption as much as 50 percent and can reduce your overall water bill.

Check for leaks in sinks, showers, and toilets. Water leaks can cost hundreds to thousands of dollars per year depending on the size of the leak. The best method for determining whether or not a leak exists is to take a water meter reading, which will check the entire internal plumbing system for leaks.

As you can see, there are many ways to create a more efficient, sustainable workplace. Applying some or all of these principles will save you money and resources and help ensure better health for everyone.

The Least You Need to Know

- ◆ Use nontoxic, renewable, and local building materials.
- ◆ Save energy with efficient equipment and design.
- ◆ Reduce water consumption with conservation techniques and efficient plumbing.
- ◆ Reuse and recycle your waste.

Chapter 8

Green Interiors and Indoor Air Quality

In This Chapter

- ◆ Making the interior of your workplace more sustainable
- ◆ Decorating techniques and materials matter
- ◆ Saving energy and water
- ◆ Using healthier products in the workplace

Even though listing current outdoor air quality condition reports in the local news has become common practice, our indoor air quality is often more dangerous than the polluted air outside, thanks to the mixture of synthetic chemicals often used to create the materials and furniture that decorate our homes and offices. Because we spend more time inside, we're likely breathing in more harmful pollutants when at home, school, or work than when we're outside. If you wish to create a sustainable business, creating a sustainable and environmentally healthy workplace is an important part of the task. A good place to start is by tackling the indoor air quality. In this chapter, you'll learn about ways to reduce your exposure to chemical contaminants that pervade your air via building materials and furnishings in your office and business. We'll also take a look at ways you can reduce your energy and water consumption as well as waste.

Indoor Air Quality

The Consumer Products Safety Commission and the Environmental Protection Agency (EPA) have joined forces to create a free public document, "The Inside Story: A Guide to Indoor Air Quality" (CPSC Document#450; www.cpsc.gov/cpscpub/pubs/450.html).

Polluted indoor air can cause a variety of noticeable reactions similar to allergic reactions, such as irritation to the eyes, lungs, nose, throat, and respiratory tract; headaches; dizziness; and fatigue. Such reactions are particularly dangerous in young children, whose lungs and bodies are still developing and are subject to developmental damage, and the elderly, whose bodies may already be compromised by age and/or previous exposure to contaminants.

When such symptoms present themselves, especially if more than one person in the building is experiencing similar conditions, a good preliminary way to test the air quality is to remove the affected people from the environment for a short time. If their symptoms subside, there is reason to begin investigating the indoor air quality to identify the offender, remove it, and eliminate exposure of others to the potential source of toxic chemicals.

Hazard

The EPA reports that since people may spend up to 90 percent more time indoors than outside, the indoor air quality has a very significant effect on our health, perhaps more than polluted outdoor air.

Some indoor air contaminants may also cause serious and sometimes fatal diseases, such as cancer, heart disease, and respiratory illness, that may not present themselves until years after exposure. Eliminating potential toxins from the indoor environment is especially important to avoid such serious consequences.

Dangerous Indoor Air Contaminants

Formaldehyde has been linked to many respiratory illnesses and is a known carcinogen, yet it's commonly used in many furnishings and is used as an additive in many adhesives that are used in flooring materials, carpets, furniture, and wall coverings. Conventional paints contain volatile organic compounds (VOCs) which can cause respiratory irritation.

The EPA reports that air cleaners may help remove particles of some pollutants, such as humidity or smoke, but they're not effective against many airborne gases, such as radon, which can seep into buildings. Radon, a chemical naturally emitted from the earth when uranium breaks down in certain geographic areas, is not visible and has no odor. But it is a leading cause of lung cancer, with estimates from 7,000 to 30,000 related cases per year in the United States. The EPA advises business owners to install radon detectors in all buildings. You can find radon detectors at most hardware stores to place in your business. In the event of a high concentration of radon, professionals can work to seal the building to prevent its continued infiltration.

Using an indoor air cleaner or filter can help to eliminate toxic chemicals from your workplace, but the EPA does not recommend the popular ozone air cleaners because ozone is harmful to our health and can combine with other chemicals in the environment to create even more toxic chemicals.

In your office space, increase ventilation with fans and open windows to help move airborne toxins out of the area, but remember that materials in the environment may cause some toxins to continue to off-gas and cause problems.

There are multiple options available if you choose to conduct an indoor air quality test. You can conduct a "do it yourself" test for under $200.00 using a kit such as the Enviro Check Home Test Kit. According to the manufacturer, this test is suitable for smaller spaces and tests for mold, bacteria, yeast, fungus, and various harmful gasses.

If you do not want to conduct the test yourself, consider hiring a consulting firm to test your indoor air quality. Research indoor air quality specialists in your area to find the organization that best fits your needs. But beware that sometimes conducting toxicological tests on indoor air can be expensive and inconclusive.

Hazard

One method some testing companies apply is to take samples from materials in the environment, such as fabrics or flooring, and contain them separately in a closed jar. After a period of time, they expose a test mouse to the air in the jar. If the mouse exhibits respiratory distress, motor difficulties, or dies, toxicity is suspected. Many people—especially those concerned about the environment and protection of nature—oppose this type of testing on the basis of animal cruelty. A better alternative would be to learn which materials contain potentially toxic substances and remove them from the environment to prevent toxic exposure.

Biological Contaminants

Many biological contaminants, such as mold, mildew, cockroaches, mites, and pollens, can present problems in your indoor environment. However, these are natural potential toxins, and if you've been dusting and cleaning regularly and avoiding or repairing moisture damage, your environment will be safer. You can best deal with pollens by using effective air-conditioning filters—allergists recommend electrostatic high-efficiency particulate air (HEPA) filters. You can avoid vermin by keeping food and water sources unavailable to them. You can also find exterminators who specialize in nontoxic and natural pest control methods. Because synthetic pesticides can be extremely toxic, always avoid using them if possible.

Another concern comes from furnaces and stoves, including those powered by gas, kerosene, or wood. Carbon monoxide (CO) is a potentially fatal yet odorless gas that can be emitted from fuel combustion, so place sensors near the floor in buildings with stoves or furnaces. Nitrogen dioxide (NO_2) is also a colorless, odorless byproduct of combustion. Burning materials can release dangerous miniscule particles into the air that can cause lung disease and cancer. The EPA advises using fuel-burning furnaces and stoves in well-ventilated areas and conducting regular maintenance checks on such equipment to avoid these potentially dangerous emissions.

Although these dangers are familiar and need to be considered, we are more concerned here with the potential toxicity of synthetic materials used to furnish and decorate your office, retail, or manufacturing space. So let's review some of the materials and products you may want to replace or avoid and which items you'll want to select instead.

Paints and Fabrics

Many commonly used paints and fabrics are made with toxic synthetic petrochemicals, including formaldehyde and VOCs. These substances, which are known to release toxic gases into the atmosphere for years, can aggravate asthma, irritate lungs, and have been linked to cancers and other diseases, yet they're everywhere. When purchasing paints, ask the person selling the paint if it is rated low or no VOC.

Formaldehyde

Formaldehyde can cause lung and eye irritation, a burning sensation in the throat, and nausea. The chemical, which is commonly used in adhesives, building materials, and paints, can trigger asthma attacks and cause cancer in animals. The International Agency for Research on Cancer has recognized it as a human carcinogen, and the EPA calls it a probable carcinogen. The EPA reports that some people may develop sensitivity to formaldehyde from increased exposure. Formaldehyde is colorless but does emit a pungent odor and is found to off-gas when it's new, with emissions decreasing over time. Heat and humidity can increase the rate of emission. Healthy interior specialist Debra Lynn Dadd suggests "baking out" chemicals by closing the building and raising the thermostat for a day, then airing out the space with fresh air ventilation. This excessive heat will help release toxic gases from carpets, paints, furnishing, and building materials more rapidly than would naturally occur over time.

Although formaldehyde is approved for use in many applications in the United States, the European Union, which adopted REACH (Registration, Evaluation and Authorization of Chemicals) in 2007, has banned the use of formaldehyde. The European Chemicals Agency (http://echa.europa.eu/home_en.asp) provides a database of chemicals subject to regulation under REACH, requiring much stiffer safety testing and regulation of synthetic chemicals. The regulation is based on the Precautionary Principle, a statement adopted by an international group of scientists and diplomats from 32 countries who developed the Wingspread Statement. This statement deals with the introduction of products into commerce before safety has been established. The group developed a standard that products should not be approved until they can be proven safe to consumers and society, which is in opposition to the method of approval currently accepted in the United States, which allows products on the market until they prove to be toxic or unsafe.

> **Enviro-Fact**
>
> When an activity raises threats of harm to the environment or human health, precautionary measures should be taken even if some cause and effect relationships are not fully established scientifically.
>
> (Source: The Precautionary Principle, a statement issued as a result of The Wingspread Conference in 1998)

The U.S. Department of Labor Occupational Safety and Health Administration suggests limiting employee exposure to formaldehyde as much as possible by using respirators, personal protective equipment, and adequate ventilation when formaldehyde is in use.

> **Hazard**
>
> For more information on the toxicity of formaldehyde, call the EPA Toxic Substance Controls Act (TSCA) office at 202-554-1404, or go to www.osha.gov/SLTC/formaldehyde/.

Interior Fabrics

Synthetic fabrics for curtains and upholstery are often made with petrochemical-based plastics—you should avoid these in your home or office. Another fabric should also be of concern. We often think of cotton as being a healthy, natural fabric—the fabric of choice for the neo-hippies and generations that followed. However, cotton turns out to be one of the most heavily pesticide-sprayed crops in the field. Specifically because farmers don't need to worry about consumers ingesting the product, they've liberally dosed poisons on the plants to keep bugs at bay.

Also beware of the dyes used to color the fabrics. Many dyes are made with petrochemicals and can emit toxic gases, thus being harmful to the puppy or visiting child who decides to taste the stuff.

Nontoxic and Natural Choices

When selecting paints for your office interior, store walls, or manufacturing facilities, look for paints that have no VOCs. Most paint companies offer a line of no-VOC paints with a wide color selection to choose from. Although these products may cost slightly more than conventional paints, you'll notice the difference immediately in the mild odor. And though you may not physically feel the difference, everyone who comes into your office will certainly benefit from this alternative.

> **Hazard**
>
> "No VOC" is not the same as "low VOC" or "no odor" when it comes to labeling paints and fabrics. Low-VOC and no-odor products still contain volatile organic compounds—they're just reduced or covered up with synthetic fragrances, another potential hazard. Choose no-VOC products for the healthiest product.

If cotton is your fabric of choice for curtains and furnishings, look for organic cotton to reduce your and your colleagues' exposure to pesticides. Many other healthy fabrics are on the market today, too, including hemp, which has gained in popularity because it is a fast-growing, inexpensive crop that can be grown successfully without synthetic pesticides, herbicides, or fertilizers. Hemp has many uses, from paper and fabrics to fuel and even health foods. Even though it's in the same family, hemp is not the well-known cannabis and is not a drug, although that's a common misconception.

Because of its relationship to the drug plant, hemp is banned from industrial production in the United States, but the United States is the biggest importer of the material in the world, and that's legal. It's a bit of an absurdity that we have found so many eco-friendly uses for this plant but aren't allowed to grow it in the United States, although its cultivation could be very profitable and help to reduce our dependence on forest products. Address this issue through your legislators. In the meantime, when you choose hemp, remember to factor in transportation considerations—using materials that must travel a long distance to get to you just burns more fuel and causes more greenhouse gas emissions.

Floorings

When it comes to finding sustainable flooring products, you must consider many factors. Again, cast a watchful eye for formaldehyde, which is commonly used in carpeting materials, pressed woods, laminates, and adhesives used to apply any of these flooring choices.

Ask the salesperson to provide you with the manufacturer's statement about the use of formaldehyde in any product you're considering. Avoid any product that uses formaldehyde.

Flooring Options

If you do select conventional carpet and are concerned about off-gassing formaldehyde, ask the installer to open the carpet roll outside or in the warehouse to air it out for a day or two before installation. Also ask the installer to use a low-emitting adhesive or tacking strip instead of a formaldehyde-emitting adhesive. You'll want to open doors and windows for a few days after installation so any fumes can be carried outside.

Many healthier options are available for your flooring needs, and you may wish to consider these because formaldehyde can take years to dissipate from glues and fabrics. Instead of conventional flooring laminates, you might choose a new, greener version of engineered wood flooring such as that created by Goodwin Heartpine, a lumber and flooring company that specializes in River Recovered wood, lumber that tumbled off river barges decades ago and was rescued from river bottoms for use today. Goodwin Heart Pine Company also salvages wood from demolition sites and recycles wood from centuries-old buildings. Either of these wood flooring options provides sustainability as well as beautiful, durable wood floors taken from trees felled more than a century ago instead of today from dwindling forests. Goodwin's engineered wood is different from other laminates in that the wear layer is equivalent to a solid wood floor from these age-old trees, sawn and applied with low formaldehyde-glues to low formaldehyde plywood. The final product has all the beauty and glamour of a heart pine wood floor at only a fraction of the cost and without the emission concerns of conventional laminates. See Appendix B for more information about healthy wood flooring options.

That's not the only way that Goodwin is green. The husband-and-wife team is working to turn their small business into a sustainable business. "All of our wood products are produced sustainably and our business practices are healthy for the environment," says company co-owner Carol Goodwin. A board member of the Florida Green Building Coalition, she devotes her time to helping homeowners, builders, and other businesses learn how they can be green, too. The Florida Green Building Coalition has certified 1,700 homes in the state of Florida since 2003. Many similar organizations exist around the country. You may wish to explore your area for such an organization that can help you find green building alternatives for your business.

"It's so exciting that the balance of our lives has tipped toward green building," says Carol Goodwin. "It is the intelligent choice—the only choice."

Logs often fell from barges as they traveled from forest to lumber mill. Today those logs are recovered and used for sustainable, high-quality wood products.

(Courtesy Goodwin Heart Pine Company)

Reduce Flooring Waste

A major concern with carpeting—beyond its potential for toxicity and for accumulating dirt, dust, and toxic substances that track in from outdoors—is the disposal issue. Carpet generally lasts 10 to 12 years and then needs to be replaced because of wear, tear, and ground-in dirt. Installers rip out and roll up the old rugs, but where does that used carpet go? Most of the time, it goes straight to the dump, where it takes up space and releases all the toxic chemicals that are in it to the surrounding air and soil. Our landfills are filling far too rapidly, and part of creating a sustainable environment means reducing or eliminating our need to cast off waste products for no further purpose or gain to the cycle.

As we mentioned in Chapter 1, Interface Inc. is working to reduce its use of energy and water in the production of carpeting and to reduce toxic emissions in the process. The company creates carpet tiles that are simpler to replace than whole floor coverings, and they take back used carpets and tiles, recycling them into new products for the marketplace instead of adding them to the landfills.

Other carpeting manufacturers are working to create a more sustainable product, too. The Carpet America Recover Effort (CARE; www.carpetrecovery.org) works to help industry representatives divert carpet from landfills to recycling programs.

Milliken and Company was the first carpet company in the United States to replace chlorinated solvents with organic alternatives in 1990 and began using PVC carpet in 1986. Milliken, a founding member of the U.S. Green Building Council (USGBC), operates a zero-waste business and offsets its carbon emissions through investments in forestry and alternative energy.

When it's time for you to consider new flooring for your business, you may wish to look into carpet tiles, recycled wood floors, or other sustainable flooring choices from companies that are working to reduce their environmental impact and waste production. By choosing a sustainable flooring option, you reduce your office space exposure to toxic chemicals and reduce your other environmental impacts, such as energy use, water use, and waste. Ask your flooring professional if they can recycle your old flooring instead of just sending it to the landfill. Although these flooring options should not cost much more than conventional floorings, any extra expense should be recognized as an investment in a healthier future for your business as well as the planet.

Reduce Toxic Exposure

Using natural materials such as stone, tile, and terrazzo is a more direct way to reduce toxic exposure. The concerns to watch out for with these materials are how far the material must travel to reach your business—energy costs associated with shipping tile or stone from far away can negate the environmental benefit of using these materials. Also confirm that the adhesives used to apply stone or tile are nontoxic.

Recent news has brought into question the safety of using granite for flooring and countertops because it has sometimes been found to emit radon and/or radiation, which can be carcinogenic at certain levels. The stone is mined from geological areas rich in uranium, and it has absorbed some of the radiation produced when uranium breaks down—a natural, though toxic, process. If granite is your choice product, be sure to inquire about the origin of the stone and ask that radon tests be conducted on the stone before it comes into your place of business.

Another thing to remember is that stone is procured through a mining process that often takes place in developing countries around the world, where fair labor practices may not apply.

Increase Durability

Terrazzo is a product of ground rock with concrete, applied and polished to a durable and beautiful finish. Popular in the 1950s, the technique has seen a resurgence in the past decade, and newer finishes include products made with recycled glass, which creates a beautiful nontoxic flooring or countertop that endures for decades.

Furnishings

Less expensive furniture is often made with pressed wood products instead of whole wood, and that entails using adhesives that are often made with formaldehyde. Choosing your office furniture is another area that will benefit from judicious discrimination.

Sustainable Materials

When you're purchasing new office equipment, look for furnishings made from natural, sustainable materials, such as metal and whole wood. Don't rule out shopping for used office furnishings—desks, chairs, shelving, and filing cabinets made before synthetic chemicals became popular are much healthier and more durable products. They're also much less expensive than many modern choices, especially those made with natural materials. For sustainable furnishing options, visit www. sustainablefurnishingscouncil.com.

Healthy Choices

When developing a sustainable workplace, the best route is to use natural materials in construction and decorating choices, including furnishings and equipment. Provide adequate ventilation to ensure that fresh air flows throughout the work environment, carrying away toxic airborne substances and bringing in fresh air and oxygen. But don't think blowing the toxic chemicals out of your way is the best solution to establishing a sustainable workplace. Preventing exposure to contamination instead of mitigating it is far more preferable.

Going Green

Call the National Institute for Occupational Safety and Health (NIOSH) for information on obtaining a health hazard evaluation of your office (1-800-35NIOSH), or contact the Occupational Safety and Health Administration: 202-219-8151.

The EPA has created "An Office Building Occupant's Guide to Indoor Air Quality" to help businesses determine the health quality of the workplace (see Appendix B).

Lighting

You can increase your office efficiency overnight by switching out all incandescent lighting for compact fluorescent or LED light bulbs. Although the upfront costs for these light bulb alternatives may be higher than traditional incandescents, the EPA estimates you'll save as much as $60 on electricity for every five CFL bulbs because they use less electricity and last longer than their predecessors.

Compact fluorescent bulbs can last 10 times longer than incandescent bulbs, use 75 percent less energy, and produce 90 percent less heat. For detailed information on lighting options for your commercial building, see Appendix B.

The way you light your work environment can have a surprising impact on your employees' productivity. Not only does artificial light require a constant flow of electricity, but it can also create a somewhat unpleasant artificial atmosphere for workers and sales forces.

Daylight Harvesting

Incorporating windows into the workspace can benefit both your bottom line and the moods of workers and customers. Try to locate workplaces in areas with windows or skylights to capitalize on the reduced need for electric lighting as well as the increased human potentials that can translate into productivity and sales for your business.

The Green Meeting Industry says daylight actually improves sales by up to 40 percent. Not only does daylight help create a more aesthetically pleasing environment, but it also stimulates the human body to beneficial aspects, according to a study conducted by the Lighting Research Center at the Rensselaer Polytechnic Institute in 2003 (see Appendix B).

Thin-film coatings on glass windows can help deflect solar radiation and heat that contribute to your energy costs. Be certain your windows can offer the benefit of lighting without the added cost caused by unwanted heat that will cause your air conditioning system to work overtime.

Motion Detection

A simple way to reduce the expenditure on energy for lighting and heating is to invest in motion-detecting sensors that shut HVAC and lighting systems down automatically when no one occupies a room and switch on again when triggered by body heat. If your business includes rooms that aren't constantly occupied, it may be beneficial to invest in automatic temperature sensors.

Equipment

You'll want to cast a careful eye toward all the equipment that makes your business run effectively to find opportunities to create a sustainable office or workplace.

Energy Conservation

Finding ways to cut your energy costs with the equipment you need to run your business will make a noticeable difference to your bottom line. As many experts are telling us, finding ways to conserve energy—by using your equipment more efficiently—can have a dramatic impact on your energy usage and emission output. So review your office and production processes carefully to determine ways that you can use electric equipment for fewer hours each day.

When you shop for equipment, seek machinery vetted by the Energy Star office of the EPA to ensure that the equipment uses the least amount of energy in the most efficient ways possible. See Appendix B for contact info for the EPA Energy Star office.

Another sustainable approach to increasing efficiency is by considering the possibility of forming cooperative relationships with other businesses in your district. Might you and a neighbor share equipment instead of maintaining duplicate operations? Ask your landlord or join a local business group to see whether cooperative arrangements might be available.

Sustainable Materials

A beautiful alternative to plastic (Formica and Corian) or granite countertops are the stunning new terrazzos being made with recycled glass. Vetrazzo is a California-based company that creates 9'×5' panels of recycled glass terrazzo without using petroleum binders sometimes used in terrazzo mixtures. Your local dealer will help you find a fabricator who can cut the panels to fit your needs and install them. The company is a member of the USGBC, uses only U.S.-based raw materials, and pays its workforce a fair living wage. They apply many sustainable practices at their factory, including using daylight, reducing dust from processing, and recycling water. If you're applying for a LEED certification from the USGBC, you'll earn points by using this product.

See Chapter 14 for more ideas on finding and applying sustainable equipment, materials, and practices in your office, manufacturing facility, or retail space.

Bathrooms

Every office or retail facility must provide facilities for workers and customers to relieve and refresh themselves. Restrooms provide a great opportunity to increase your business's sustainability and reduce your environmental impact.

Efficient Toilets and Sinks

Begin addressing your restroom by finding ways to reduce your water use and waste output. Flushing waste away with clean, treated water seems ludicrous when viewed through the lens of sustainability. However, saving water in the restroom is a responsible way to contribute to saving the planet's water supply.

Choose low-flow toilets that operate with miniscule amounts of water compared to their counterparts of the past 50 or more years. Waterless urinals can save up to 3 gallons per flush. If you need some plumbing work done, it would be a good idea to inquire about the possibility of routing greywater from sinks into the toilets for flushing. For more information, see Appendix B.

You'll also want to use low-flow faucets, which provide aeration to take the place of the missing water but create a full-force flow of water. Faucets that turn off automatically can help save water—and money—lost from faucets that aren't properly closed after use or which develop drips.

Napkins Versus Blowers

If you've managed to increase energy efficiency and established a renewable energy supply through solar, photovoltaic, or wind supplies, electric hand blowers are a good choice for hand drying in the bathroom. Hand towels are another option if traffic is limited and a laundry facility or a laundry service is available. The last choice on the sustainability scale is to offer recycled paper toweling in restrooms. You don't need electric towel dispensers—hand-operated equipment saves energy.

Nontoxic Soaps

Replacing conventional soap products with nontoxic alternatives is an important yet often overlooked way to decrease your company's contribution to synthetic chemical exposure, both to immediate users and to the water supply. Soaps with anti-bacterial properties usually have triclosan as an ingredient, a synthetic petrochemical that's known as an endocrine disrupter and not something you want to be exposed to. Shop for a nonhazardous, nontoxic, biodegradable soap alternative that won't be irritating to users and won't send toxic chemicals into the air or wastewater stream.

An interesting nontoxic natural soap that's been on the market for decades is Dr. Bronner's natural and organic castile soap. Choose organic soaps with tea tree oil, a natural antibacterial, to replace the synthetic antibacterial soaps. Offered in liquid form or bars, the soaps have distinctive labels that can be fun to read (see Appendix B).

Biodegradable and Nontoxic Cleaning Supplies

Although you may think using the cheapest cleaners available is the obvious choice and therfore feel reluctant to spend more for a nontoxic alternative, you may be surprised to learn that using healthier cleaning products will benefit your bottom line. The *Sustainable Industries Green Office Guide* reports that the EPA estimates that poor indoor air quality can result in an 18 percent loss of employee productivity, translating to $60 billion in the United States in just one year. And cleaning products can be a major source of toxic air pollution in the workplace.

Many commercial products have come on the market in response to consumers' desire for less-toxic cleaning products. Your supplier probably has alternative products to offer instead of traditional ammonia and bleach cleaning agents. Although your cleaning staff might resist your efforts to go green when it comes to cleaning—they've been using the "big guns" of stain removal and disinfectant action for a long time and might find it hard to give up these miracle products that make their work so easy. But when you tell your janitors that breathing the fumes of these toxic cleaners every day has been harmful for their lungs and bodies, they should be thanking you. Shop for cleaners that are both nontoxic and biodegradable.

You can even concoct your own natural cleaners with baking soda (a serviceable scouring powder), vinegar (a disinfectant that's recommended for window cleaning and surface cleaning), or a few drops of your favorite essential oil (I like grapefruit or lavender) in a bucket of hot water with a drop or two of natural liquid soap to create a liquid for dusting and mopping that has antimicrobial properties that will combat germs and odors.

Air Fresheners

We've been so misguided on this room freshening issue. We want our workplaces and homes to smell pleasant and inviting; however, instead of the scent of whatever we're working on—whether it's hot presses and reams of paper or soups and pies—we've been led to believe we should eradicate natural smells and replace them with unnatural odors made from synthetic petrochemicals that are supposed to smell like flowers, fruit, or sea breezes. The problem is that the real things smell much better, and the fake smells are made with endocrine-disrupting chemicals that could cause havoc on our hormonal and immune systems. These also are sometimes designed to numb our olfactory senses (and our sense of taste) so we can't detect offensive odors. They're messing with our heads, and we don't need that.

If the air in your workplace smells stale, throw open the windows and doors and flip on a fan or two to replace the used air with fresh oxygen from outside. If the air smells musty, check for water leaks around the building that could be causing mold and mildew problems. Bring in fresh flowers or use a few drops of essential oils in diffusers to help spread a more pleasant and safe natural scent around the space.

As suggested earlier, cleaning with essential oils is an effective way to combat bacterial problems and to infuse the atmosphere with genuine fresh, healthy scents. Using commercial anti-bacterial products can introduce unwanted toxic chemicals into your indoor atmosphere.

The Least You Need to Know

- The indoor air quality of your workplace can be a toxic cloud of pollution.

- Improve air quality by choosing healthier materials and furnishings.

- You can cut back on energy costs and conserve water if you update your office with environmentally friendly products.

- Improved working conditions can lead to increased employee productivity.

Chapter 9

Greening Your Landscape

In This Chapter

- ◆ Benefits of a green landscape
- ◆ Hiring professionals—or not
- ◆ Fundamentals of xeriscaping

Your sustainability initiative extends outside your product line and place of business to include your outside property. And first impressions of your business often come from the aesthetics of your landscape, because a well-landscaped business invites interest and reflects the values of the owners. Whether you're in an office building with a parking lot, a warehouse bay in an industrial zone, a retail strip mall, or a quaint historic house in your town's center, you may also reduce your impact on the environment by tending to your water use, plantings, and tree cover. You can cut landscaping costs; beautify your workplace; and create an inviting presence that customers, colleagues, and staff can enjoy. Creating an inviting landscape that shows an interest and a concern to environmental needs can increase your business traffic.

The Benefits of a Green Landscape

Designing a sustainable outdoor environment has many benefits over conventional lawn and landscape designs. Perhaps the greatest benefit is being part of an environmental solution. As our population continues to increase, placing demands on our natural resources, it will become more important for individuals and businesses to share a desire to use our resources wisely and in a way that is friendly to the planet and to each other.

Self-Maintenance Versus Professional Services

You may not have a green thumb of your own, or even if you do, your time is probably spent attending to other business details. So you may want to hire landscaping professionals to manage your outdoor environment. Let's look at several important factors to consider when making this decision.

Finding Eco-Friendly Lawn Care

One option is to consult your local county extension agent for a referral to someone who can meet your needs. Look for a company that understands and appreciates your desire to be kind to the planet and create a sustainable business.

But before you pick up the phone, remember that an important element of sustainability and the green movement is to create more satisfying lives where we strike a healthier balance between work, family, and creativity. Spending time outdoors and being involved with nature is relaxing and nourishing for our souls. Even if you can't find the time or energy to tackle this job yourself, you might consider whether any of your employees would be interested in taking on this task as part of their routine, giving them the chance to get outside once a week or so and a reason to take pride in the appearance of their business.

Time and Cost Assessment

How much does maintenance of your outdoor environment cost you now? Here are a few things you'll want to factor in to your decision to create a sustainable landscape:

- Do you have to pay for lawn care or area maintenance?

- Does someone sweep and clean a concrete or asphalt yard regularly? How long does it take this person, and how much do you pay him?

♦ Labor is always one of the highest costs of a business. Compare the wages of your own employees to that of a landscaper you might hire.

♦ What will your maintenance savings be?

♦ How much water do you use, and what does that cost?

♦ Do you have to replace plantings or container plants with the seasons? What are the costs involved?

♦ Calculate the costs of replacing your lawn or existing landscape with native plants. What are your savings with a green landscape?

Replace Your Lawn with Native Plants

That lovely all-American green lawn certainly looks great but comes with a high price when considering the maintenance costs and the cost of our natural water resources. Most of our common landscaping plants and lawns are based on hybrids—plants raised in exotic locales or greenhouses that need extra care, water, and chemicals to survive long term after they are planted.

If you've got a swath of green lawn, you might want to consider replacing the high-maintenance grass and hybrid plants with native plantings indigenous to your area, which are basically maintenance free, attractive, and well adapted to local climate fluctuations. Having survived over long periods of time through changes in climate and attacks from insects and diseases, these plants have adapted and built defenses that make them able to continue to survive with minimal input from us. Although any plant benefits from being watered and given a steady dressing of fertilizers, natives survive despite their conditions. By utilizing native plants in a green land-scape, you promote the continued process of survival of these plants as well as the insect and animal life that have survived and developed along with them.

Native plants, used to the water variations in your area, can tolerate the hot summer droughts far better than transplants from more tropical areas, so you'll use less water. Using less water means saving money and also reducing waste because you won't be watching that water wash down the sidewalks and into the gutters.

Xeriscaping reduces maintenance and conserves resources by making use of several basic fundamentals. Once promoted in locales where fresh water supplies were limited, xeriscaping is now widespread and a foundation for conservation-minded landscaping. Herbs are excellent choices for the xeriscape, especially rosemary, sage, thyme, and lavender. These small-leaf herbs are well adapted to hot, sunny climates and with their lower watering needs are low maintenance.

Native planting has become quite popular in the past decade or two as agricultural specialists recognize the dangers of using exotic plants, which can often be invasive in communities. Check with your local agriculture extension office to find a native plant nursery in your area and see Appendix B for tips and resources about xeriscaping from Denver Water.

def•i•ni•tion

Xeriscaping is landscaping based on conserving water. From a combination of the Greek word *xeros* (meaning dry) and landscaping, xeriscaping (pronounced *zîr´-ĭ-skāp-ing*) utilizes a combination of native plants, soil management, and water management to create a landscape that, when established, has a minimal demand on water and maintenance resources. The term xeriscaping was coined in Colorado by Denver's water department.

Plant Placement and Diversity

Plant placement is another key component for the successful green landscape. The design of the landscape should take advantage of the direction of the light source, the size of the plants and trees, the water requirements, and the growth habits. Considering these factors in the design will create an integrated plant environment that will make the best use of the natural characteristics of the plants and their relation to each other—certainly a goal of an environmentally sound landscape.

Plant leaves come in all shapes and sizes. Consider planting larger-leaf, sun-loving varieties so their leaves shade smaller plants that are less tolerant of the sun.

Trees and small shrubs are important sources for filtering light and protecting the soil from the harsh sunlight. Using deciduous trees and shrubs enables the warming sun to reach plants during the cooler weather months and provides valuable organic matter to the soil when the leaves drop.

A green landscape is a diverse landscape. Instead of planting one or two varieties of trees and shrubs, incorporate several varieties as well as different sizes and colors, shapes, and smells. The result is a micro ecosystem that will invite an assortment of wildlife and create a buffer to diseases or insect destruction as well. The varied native landscape acts as its own natural pest control. Not only have individual plants developed natural defenses over time, but, inter-planted with numerous other native species, they enhance their own defenses against disease and insect attacks.

Avoid Synthetic "-Cides"

The positive result of this natural defense system allows you, the business owner, to buy and use fewer harmful pesticides. Remember the "-cide" in pesticides means "to kill." By developing a green landscape and creating a diverse planting scheme, nature manages the landscape with a natural balance. Green landscapes deter overpopulation of destructive insects with a balance of beneficial insects, and this reduces or eliminates the need to use harmful chemicals for their control.

If pests do become a problem, you can buy organic gardening products made from plant materials, or you can easily make natural pest deterrents with simple products such as cayenne pepper, garlic, and vinegar. Keep in mind, however, that just because a product is natural or organic does not necessarily mean it is safe. Some of these natural deterrents are potent; read labels to ensure proper administration and use them with care. The Environmental Protection Agency (EPA) registers pesticides for use and requires manufacturers to put information on the label about when and how to use the pesticide.

Hazard

Some natural and organic pesticides—such as Pyrethrum, Rotenone, and Diatomaceous Earth—can be dangerous when used improperly. Avoid breathing in the dust of these products, and don't use more than you need—overdosing can harm the beneficial insects your organic landscape needs to thrive.

Water Conservation

Saving water is a key purpose in greening your landscape. Our water resources are continually threatened by nature and man. As the population increases, demand for water grows, land is paved for expanded development, fertilizer runoff from farms and lawns gets into our streams and rivers, and droughts seem to be increasing in frequency and duration. Conserving and protecting this natural resource is paramount. Using less water means saving money and reducing waste, so let's look at some ways you can put water conservation to use in your landscape.

Drip Irrigation

Overhead sprinklers result in a lot of wasted water because it either evaporates or runs off, never reaching the plants and soil it's intended for. Water loss estimates due to evaporation are as high as 35 percent—and you're paying for the water that just washes away, as well as the electricity to run the sprinklers and water pump. It's best to run overhead systems early in the morning when evaporation is minimal, but other alternatives are more efficient, can conserve water, and can place water where it is needed. And you'll save with a lower water bill.

Drip irrigation is a system of watering that emphasizes water conservation by delivering water directly to the root zone through a system of tubing, emitters, and soaker hoses perforated with thousands of small holes. Soaker hoses, which can be placed directly on top of the soil or even covered with soil or mulch for aesthetics, put the water in direct contact with the soil and fertilizer, minimizing wasteful evaporation and maximizing the amount of dissolved fertilizer the plant can uptake.

Another benefit of drip irrigation and soaker hoses is a deeper root zone. As roots go deeper, they are less affected by the hot soil above, resulting in plants that can withstand hotter afternoon temperatures. Although watering times may be longer at first to facilitate deeper root zones, the result is that less water is eventually needed. Frequent, shorter watering from overhead irrigation creates a shallow root zone which causes plants to wilt more frequently and landscape maintenance requirements to increase. A great rule of thumb for establishing your plants in the landscape is to water as long as possible to maximize root depth and as infrequently as possible to minimize maintenance. Drip irrigation accomplishes this.

Sprinkler Timers Help Conserve

Irrigation timers are available to fit any business budget and any size landscape. Simple screw-on dial-type timers that connect to outside water faucets can let you dial in a duration period for water flow and then shut off, while more sophisticated programmable timers enable you to choose the duration period.

Collecting Rainwater

If you consider the importance of water conservation, you can easily understand why implementing a rain collection system is not only economical but a wise environmental choice. Water runoff picks up all the pollutants found in our yards, parking lots, and streets on its journey to our waterways. This is called nonsource point pollution and is considered the greatest source of pollution to threaten our waterways. So saving rainwater before it has a chance to become runoff is good common sense.

As a business owner, the opportunity to harvest rainwater for reuse presents a good way to conserve water and save money. The costs involved are minimal and balanced by the reduced cost of water usage. Collecting rainwater can be done on a small or large scale. You can convert food storage barrels, wine barrels, and whiskey barrels into rain barrels or buy water tanks of all sizes for collecting and storing rainwater. The practice of building cisterns for water collection has gone on for centuries out of necessity, and today many use cisterns out of a basic concern for water conservation.

Collecting rainwater for green landscaping does require a little forethought in deciding just how you are going to use the water. Many businesses have large roof surfaces, and the amount of collected water can be quite surprising. Deciding on the size of collection container is also important, as most food-grade barrels average from 50 to 80 gallons of water. Considering that 1 inch of rain on a 1,000 square-foot roof will give you more than 600 gallons of water, it's easy to see that several barrels will be needed to make use of that amount of water.

A rain barrel collects water.

(Courtesy James Steele)

Although many types of barrels and containers are available, it's important to know what they originally held, because some may have contained toxic chemicals. See Appendix B for ideas on finding the best container for your needs.

Getting the collected rain to your landscape is another aspect to consider. In smaller collection systems, gravity is the main force that will get the water to your plants, so you may consider using xeriscape techniques, enabling the water to flow through tubing to irrigate the nearby plants. As the collection containers become larger and perhaps even more permanent as a cistern, you might utilize small pumping devices to send the water where you need it, but this will cost money.

Some basic requirements for your collection system are necessary. Ideally, roofs of tile and metal provide the safest, cleanest surfaces with minimal contamination to the water. You'll need to install and maintain a gutter system, which includes screen filters at the top of the downspout as well as the entry point into the container.

Going Green

If you would like to make your own rain barrel, the city of Bremerton, Washington, provides step-by-step instructions and advice: www.cityofbremerton. com/content/sw_ makeyourownrainbarrel.html.

Screening prevents leaves and other natural substances from entering your barrel and also prevents mosquitoes from laying eggs in your water container. An overflow outlet will be necessary to allow excess water to flow away from the collection container. You can connect several containers with simple overflow tubes to create a larger-capacity system. Water quality is also a concern when using collection containers, but the water will be used for landscape maintenance and not for drinking, unless you install a sanitation filtration system.

A well-planned water collection system is a wise, inexpensive choice for greening your landscape as well as providing water for indoor plants. Rainwater is much more beneficial to plants than treated city water thanks to the natural nitrogen converted by lightning in the atmosphere—a kind of fertilizer from the sky. It makes sense to capture this green rain for your green landscape; it's free, it's recycling, and it's an environmentally wise choice for a green business. You'll invest about $50 for each rain barrel, and you may already have a guttering system to feed into it. If you don't, installing gutters along your roofline isn't cost prohibitive. In the long run, capturing the rainwater to use for irrigation will save you money when compared against using city water for irrigation, and it's just a good idea to make use of the resource that otherwise slips by and runs down into the sewer drains.

Reusing Water for Irrigation

You might want to check building codes and check with your plumber to see whether you can reuse greywater to irrigate your landscape. Greywater from sinks, dishwashers, laundry machines, and showers has been used but is not so contaminated that it can't still be useful and reusable in the landscape.

Terracing

Terracing is an age-old practice of preventing water runoff and soil erosion by turning a sloping area into several flatter levels, creating a series of extended steps. This step effect slows down the water, giving it more time to be absorbed into the soil where it is needed rather than washing away and bringing the soil with it. In the green landscape, terracing becomes an attractive way to turn sloping areas into areas of water conservation.

Soil and Fertilizers

Soil conservation is an important benefit of green landscaping and xeriscaping. Soil is the foundation and support system for our plants and trees and the main holding area for the dissolved fertilizers waiting to be taken into the plant. A healthy soil will produce healthy plants. As a business owner considering green landscaping, talk with your landscaper to make sure the company understands the value of soil conservation. Healthy soils are alive with organic matter, microorganisms, minerals, air, and water. These soils provide the pathway for roots to penetrate and act like sponges to absorb rainfall or drip irrigation. They hold this water, along with dissolved fertilizers, long enough for the plants to absorb them. Healthy organic soils promote root growth and, coupled with organic matter, reduce soil erosion. The key benefit of a healthy soil is a healthy plant or tree, which results in fewer diseases, fewer pests, and less maintenance.

Compost

Soils remain healthy when there is a constant supply of organic matter feeding soil microorganisms. When it comes time to rake leaves, instead of bagging them up and hauling them off, use them around plants and trees as natural mulch and compost the excess. Compost is the single most important soil additive you can place in your landscape, and it's free. It provides a well-balanced helping of carbon, nitrogen, and many other necessary elements plants need for good growth. Compost is easy to make. Many composters are available on the market today in all sizes and shapes to fit your business needs and aesthetics. Often the key ingredients in compost, nitrogen and carbon, are bagged as cut grass and raked leaves and not even used in most landscapes. Save these landscape nutrients by reusing them to create a sustainable landscape.

Collect Yard and Snack Room Scraps

Your interest in developing a green landscape for your business will eventually lead you to composting, and this doesn't have to leave you restricted to using outdoor materials. Consider putting several recycle bins in your food preparation and snack room areas. Not only can you recycle your papers, plastic, and glass, but also consider the wealth of ingredients for your compost pile from leftover food scraps. Coffee grounds are a great source of nutrients for the compost pile, as are any vegetable wastes and eggshells. But don't add any meat or dairy scraps to your compost bins. A diverse compost pile leads to great soil. The resulting compost eliminates the need for synthetic fertilizers, which are costly and created from petrochemicals. We want to avoid adding these to the landscape, soil, and water because of their potential as environmental poisons.

Your compost is alive and dining all the time. Following are the best ways to feed the bacteria that will turn your scraps into rich, fertile soil:

Compost ingredients: A ratio is 3 parts green material to 1 part brown material.

> **Do use:**
>
> Vegetable scraps
>
> Grass clippings, leaves
>
> Fruit, peelings

The previous green materials provide nitrogen for your bacteria.

Brown leaves, dried grass, corn husks, paper, and very small-diameter vines are the brown materials that break down slower but add carbon and trace minerals to your pile.

> **Do not use:**
>
> Meat and dairy products: These break down slowly and actually putrefy, causing bad odors that attract animals and rodents.

Pet and human feces: These contain bacteria that often survive the composting process and may spread disease. Farm animal manure is different due to their grain and grass diet (i.e., chicken manure, horse manure, cow manure, and rabbit manure).

Avoid diseased plants, as the pile may not get hot enough to kill the pathogens and thus you will be spreading the disease back onto your landscape.

Use Natural Fertilizers

Compost is the ideal fertilizer, but sometimes you may need a supplement and the use of natural fertilizers. Synthetic fertilizers are petroleum-based, and the processes to manufacture them require great energy outputs and mining. Synthetic fertilizers on the market today are made for quick results, completely bypassing the natural cycle of interacting with the soil and soil organisms, the heart of organic gardening and green landscaping. Talk to your landscaper about fertilizer to be sure he uses natural fertilizers for your landscape. Bone meal, blood meal, cottonseed meal, fish emulsion, seaweed, manures, and wood ash are all examples of natural fertilizers. These fertilizers are lower in nutrient value than synthetics and break down more slowly, but their interaction with soil bacteria and in building soil nutrition makes them a valuable choice.

Hazard

Some fertilizers are marketed as organic, but they're actually created from sewage sludge—waste left over from our sewer plants when the water has been removed. This waste is in fact human waste and is often contaminated with the pharmaceutical products that humans ingested. These chemicals can be dangerous, and using sewage sludge as fertilizer has been implicated in hormone disorders and illnesses among field animals exposed to such sludge. Check the label when you're buying organic fertilizer and select products that are not related to sewage sludge.

Mulch to Nourish and Retain Moisture

Mulch provides several advantages in creating a greener, maintenance-free landscape by minimizing the growth of weeds, providing a protective blanket over the soil to minimize water evaporation, keeping the soil cooler, and protecting shallow rooted plantings from getting too hot. Natural organic mulches such as pine bark, wood chips, leaves, and pine needles are not only aesthetically pleasing to the eye, but as they break down over time, they also add nutrients, including *humus*, to the soil and improve soil structure.

def•i•ni•tion

In agriculture, **humus** is sometimes used to describe mature compost, or natural compost extracted from a forest or other spontaneous source for use to amend soil. It is also used to describe a topsoil horizon that contains organic matter.

To be effective, organic mulches should be at least 4 inches thick. Over time they will break down and need to be replenished. Other popular mulches are small river rocks and gravel. Although they don't break down to provide nourishment to the soil, they do keep weeds out and maintain moisture, and they don't have to be replaced. Glass nuggets are becoming quite popular and provide a beautiful touch to the landscape while recycling a valuable resource. See Appendix B for information about recycled glass mulch from American Specialty Glass.

The Least You Need to Know

- Green landscaping is a better use of our flora, utilizing native plants and trees acclimated to the local climate and thus putting less demand on water resources.

- Incorporate innovative design techniques that work with nature, and build a better sustainable habitat for both flora and fauna, reducing or eliminating the need for harmful pesticides.

- Water conservation through innovative watering techniques and rainwater harvesting saves hundreds of gallons of water yearly.

- Recycling natural materials for composting and mulching and returning these materials to the landscape eliminates our need for synthetic fertilizers.

Chapter 10

Greening Your Products

In This Chapter

- ◆ Ensuring products are sustainable
- ◆ Patterning products after nature
- ◆ Understanding life-cycle assessment
- ◆ Preventing pollution produces profits

You want to green your products. And with all the hype surrounding green and the purchasing power of green consumers growing stronger every day, why wouldn't you want to take advantage of the green wave? Creation of green products begins at the drawing board and design phase of the production process. By assessing the overall life cycle of your products and utilizing greener product design methods and concepts such as biomimicry, design for environment, and cradle-to-cradle design, you'll be able to understand the environmental impacts of your products and determine the most efficient and effective means to make them greener.

Using Life-Cycle Assessment

Do you ever wonder if the recycled-content paper you're purchasing as part of your green office program really has less of an impact than nonrecycled paper? How about if the fuel-efficient hybrid Prius is really better for the planet than a compact fuel-efficient vehicle? More and more consumers are asking these difficult questions and expecting product manufacturers and marketers to give them accurate answers. But just how do you compare one product or service's environmental impact to another? As consumers become savvier and ask difficult questions about why products are green and how one product is greener than the next, manufacturers must respond with answers based on scientific data.

Addressing Life-Cycle Assessment

Enter *life-cycle assessment* (*LCA*). LCA assesses products and the processes used to create them from a *cradle-to-grave* approach. Cradle to grave begins with the gathering of raw materials either by extraction, harvest, or recovery and ends with the product disposal. This could mean land filling, composting, recycling, reusing, or any other means of product disposal. LCA analyzes all components of a product's life cycle in an interdependent manner so that all the tabulated data relates to each stage of the product's life cycle. This provides a complete picture of the product's environmental impact and the ability to compare multiple product impacts. According to a report published by Science Applications International (SAIC) in conjunction with the Environmental Protection Agency (EPA), the term *life cycle* refers to the major activities in the course of the product's life span from its manufacture, use, and maintenance to its final disposal, including raw material acquisition required to manufacture the product.

def•i•ni•tion

Life-cycle assessment (LCA) helps us understand the environmental and social impacts of a product from materials extraction to end-of-life disposal. LCA is also known as cradle-to-grave analysis.

Cradle to grave refers to the stages of a product's life cycle, from the time natural resources are extracted from the ground and processed through each subsequent stage of manufacturing, transportation, product use, and disposal.

Conducting an LCA for your products or services has myriad benefits. An LCA can help an organization figure out the most efficient and environmentally preferable means of not only producing a product but also creating the most healthy, environmentally preferable products possible by figuring out what product inputs are not good for human or planetary health. Without a comprehensive understanding of your product's impacts, how will you ever determine which changes are necessary to make improvements for both reduction of environmental impact and cost savings? LCA provides a systematic, interconnected picture of a product, enabling decision-makers to see what impact changing one facet of the product's life cycle has on the product as a whole.

According to a document published by the EPA's National Risk Management Research Laboratory (in conjunction with SAIC), the benefits of an LCA include the following:

◆ It develops a systematic evaluation of the environmental consequences associated with a given product.

◆ It analyzes the environmental trade-offs associated with one or more specific products/processes to help gain stakeholder (state, community, and so on) acceptance for a planned action.

◆ It quantifies environmental releases to air, water, and land in relation to each life-cycle stage and/or major contributing process.

◆ It assists in identifying significant shifts in environmental impacts between life-cycle stages and environmental media.

◆ It assesses the human and ecological effects of material consumption and environmental releases to the local community, region, and world.

◆ It compares the health and ecological impacts between two or more rival products/processes or identifies the impacts of a specific product or process.

◆ It identifies impacts to one or more specific environmental areas of concern.

Assessing Environmental Impacts of Materials

When embarking on an LCA for a product or service, you first need to scope out your project and define your goals. Assess the product or service and describe in detail the processes that go into making it. In this initial step, define the boundaries and assumptions you make when conducting your assessment so they will be clear in your final LCA report.

Next, identify and quantify all the inputs that go into making the product or service. These could include—but are not limited to—water, energy, and material use. Remember to include inputs from raw material extraction throughout disposal. Also look at the outputs or environmental releases associated with the process you are assessing. This can include emissions (including greenhouse gases such as carbon dioxide), waste, pollutants, and wastewaster discharge.

Now assess the impacts of these inputs and outputs; include both environmental and human impacts. After you calculate your inputs and outputs and assess both the environmental and human impacts of each, evaluate the results and create a report. You can use this report internally to determine if you can use alternative product inputs or more efficient manufacturing practices to create a more environmentally preferable product or externally to support a green marketing story.

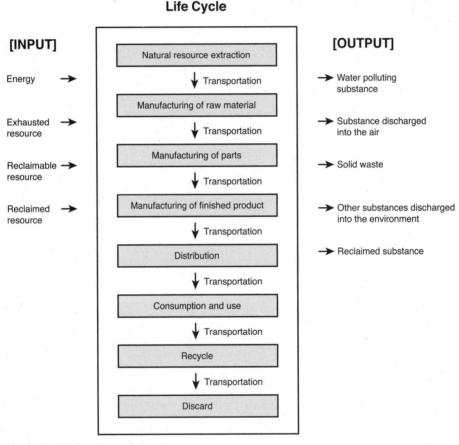

Example of life-cycle analysis.

(Courtesy the Ministry of the Environment, Japan)

Multiple computer programs and input databases can assist you in conducting this life-cycle analysis (see Appendix B).

This is a brief overview of how to generally conduct an LCA. But like many disciplines in the green arena, the subject is still being defined. Entire books are written on LCA, and there are international guidelines and protocols to follow when conducting your own LCA. We encourage you to dig deeper into LCA by conducting further research on the subject or contacting a consulting firm that regularly conducts these assessments to assist you.

The International Organization of Standards (ISO) developed the ISO 14040:2006 protocol for life-cycle assessment with top leaders in the field of LCA. According to ISO, "ISO 14040:2006 describes the principles and framework for life-cycle assessment (LCA), including: definition of the goal and scope of the LCA, the life-cycle inventory analysis (LCI) phase, the life-cycle impact assessment (LCIA) phase, the life-cycle interpretation phase, reporting and critical review of the LCA, limitations of the LCA, the relationship between the LCA phases, and conditions for use of value choices and optional elements." For more information on ISO LCA protocol, visit the International Organization of Standards website at www.iso.org.

Going Green

LCA is a complex subject. If you are looking to conduct a full-product LCA, it may be best to contact a consulting firm that specializes in product quantification and life-cycle analysis.

Green Manufacturing

Green manufacturing provides many cost benefits: reduced cost of exotic materials, reduced waste produced by reusing and recycling materials, and increased health benefits of selecting nontoxic materials. All the measures in this chapter and throughout the book will help you increase efficiency in your manufacturing and business practices and reduce your overall operational costs, which of course leads to increased profits.

Reducing the impacts of manufacturing is an important part of greening your products. Remember, it's important for your overall sustainability initiatives to reduce the impact of all your operations, including manufacturing. Consider developing an environmental management system such as ISO 14000 for your organization. This will help you determine and manage the environmental aspects of products and activities. Also identify lean manufacturing techniques for your industry to help reduce your environmental impact.

Biomimicry

Product designers are turning to nature for inspiration and ideas when designing their products. This mimicking of nature is known as *biomimicry*. After all, not only do ecological systems operate in a symbiotic way that keeps our environment healthy and thriving, but the lessons learned from observing nature can make our products function better and last longer. Understanding and learning from these natural systems and basing human design on them will enable us to better co-exist with the species that surround us and leave less of an impact on the environment.

def•i•ni•tion

> According to Biomimicry.org, **biomimicry** is a new discipline that studies nature's best ideas and then imitates these designs and processes to solve human problems.

Learning from Nature

Biomimicry looks at nature as a model, measure, and mentor. The Biomimicry Guild's website breaks these concepts down further:

- **Nature as a model**—Biomimicry is a new science that studies nature's models and then emulates these forms, process, systems, and strategies, to solve human problems sustainably. The Biomimicry Guild and its collaborators have developed a practical design tool, called the Biomimicry Design Spiral, for using nature as a model.

- **Nature as a measure**—Biomimicry uses an ecological standard to judge the sustainability of our innovations. After 3.8 billion years of evolution, nature has learned what works and what lasts. Nature as measure is captured in life's principles and is embedded in the evaluate step of the Biomimicry Design Spiral.

- **Nature as mentor**—Biomimicry is a new way of viewing and valuing nature. It introduces an era based not on what we can extract from the natural world, but what we can learn from it.

The Biomimicry Design Spiral, a methodology which helps designers work through the ideas and framework of biomimicry when designing new products and systems, breaks down into six sections, each flowing into the other:

- **Identify**—Develop a design brief of the human need. In this phase, identify the problem you need to solve and the function you want your design to accomplish.

- **Translate**—Biologize the question; ask the design brief from nature's perspective. In this phase, ask yourself how nature performs the function you've identified. What would nature do to arrive at a solution to your problem?

- **Observe**—Look for champions in nature who answer/resolve your challenges. Look to nature and find organisms and ecosystems you can learn from.

- **Abstract**—Find the repeating patterns and processes within nature that achieve success. During this process, create a "taxonomy of life's strategies" that best solve the issue you've identified.

- **Apply**—Develop ideas and solutions based on the natural models. Apply the lessons you learned in the previous phases of the spiral to your designs.

- **Evaluate**—How do your ideas compare to the successful principles of nature? To create the most effective designs, we must reevaluate the effectiveness of our success.

- **Identify**—Develop and refine design briefs based on lessons learned from evaluation of life's principles. Implementing what we learn in the evaluation is the key to improving our products. Just as nature evaluates and adapts, we can take this concept into our design processes.

Enviro-Fact

The mission of The Biomimicry Institute is "to nurture and grow a global community of people who are learning from, emulating, and conserving life's genius to create a healthier, more sustainable planet." For more information on this and the Biomimicry Design Spiral, visit www.biomimicryinstitute.org.

Cradle to Cradle

Michael Braungart and William McDonnough published the concept of cradle-to-cradle design in their 2002 book, *Cradle to Cradle: Remaking the Way We Make Things*. Since the debut of the book, cradle-to-cradle design has blossomed into an industry standard for sustainable design and has accompanied the C2C Certification which Braugnart and McDonnough's firm MBDC also developed and administrates.

The basic premise behind cradle to cradle is that products should be designed so they never have to be tossed into a landfill. This is best described by MBDC's "waste equals food" principle, which eliminates the concept of waste all together. All raw material inputs are valuable and can be reused. They are broken down into one of two categories: *biological nutrients* and *technical nutrients.*

def•i•ni•tion

A **biological nutrient** is a biodegradable material posing no immediate or eventual hazard to living systems that can be used for human purposes and can safely return to the environment to feed environmental processes.

A **technical nutrient** is a material that remains in a closed-loop system of manufacture, reuse, and recovery (the technical metabolism), maintaining its value through many product life cycles.

At the end of its useful life, the product would either be recyclable or biodegradable depending on material inputs. Another important piece of the cradle-to-cradle concept is the elimination of hazardous and toxic substances that make up our products. If we follow the "waste equals food" mantra, this concept makes complete sense. Would you want your food contaminated with toxic and hazardous substances? No. So why should it be acceptable for products you utilize every day that will eventually be put back into our ecosystem to contain contaminants? To learn more about cradle-to-cradle design, visit www.mbdc.com.

Choose Green Materials

The LCA will help you understand your product's current environmental impact, and biomimicry and cradle-to-cradle designs will help you green your products "from the inside out." Now let's talk about some practical first steps you can take to make your products greener.

Ask yourself the following:

♦ Where do the inputs used in my products originate? Can I purchase these inputs closer to my manufacturing site? This will help reduce your environmental footprint through transportation reduction.

◆ Are any of my product inputs listed as toxic or hazardous? List your product inputs and research them to determine their impact on human health and the environment. The EPA's Integrated Risk Information System is a great resource to use when determining the health and environmental impacts of materials. Begin phasing out the toxic and hazardous materials you use in your manufacturing processes.

◆ Can I replace any of my product inputs with greener options? Perhaps you can utilize raw materials made from rapidly renewable resources or recycled content. Use the list you made when checking for hazardous materials to research greener, alternative inputs.

◆ Are my products produced using green or lean manufacturing techniques? Is my company practicing sustainability internally? As our good friend Sara Gutterman, CEO of Green Builder Media, says, "You can't produce green products from brown companies." It is imperative, for both cost savings and marketing/branding, that you internalize your green messages.

◆ Can I dispose of my products in an environmentally preferable manner when a consumer is no longer using them? Green products do not just mean green inputs. Remember, you must consider the entire life cycle of the product to make sure it is green.

Answering the previous questions enables you to determine the areas you need to assess and ultimately change to make your products greener. To create the greenest products possible, maximize the green benefits as much as possible.

Minimize Adverse Health Effects

Look at the health issues associated with your product, including negative health impacts resulting from the creation of your product. Are you emitting volatile organic compounds (VOCs) during your manufacturing process that are harming your worker's health or discharging hazardous materials into the environment? Also consider the health impacts of your product once it is sold to consumers. This will protect your reputation as well as your bottom line.

If an ingredient, production process, or final product has questionable health concerns, ditch it. Sustainable production is based on the Precautionary Principle, a statement crafted by an international panel of scientists agreeing to prove the safety of products before they're introduced to the market. The European Union passed this into law in 2007, and sustainable businesses worldwide abide by the premise as a basic tenet of their operations.

Sustainable Supply-Chain Policies

Creating sustainable supply-chain policies that outline your raw material purchasing goals, lean/green manufacturing goals, reduced impact distribution goals, and end-of-life product goals will keep your organization on track when greening its products. See Chapter 3 for detailed descriptions on how to lay out and write your environmental policies.

Local Sourcing

Seeking out raw materials from local sources is beneficial to your business in many ways. You'll reduce the expense of shipping materials, which cuts down on fuel consumption and emission output. At the same time, you'll be supporting local businesses, creating partnerships with your neighbors, and generating more local business for your own business.

Cost Savings and Marketing Benefits

Streamlining your supply chain and detailing your environmental goals in sustainable supply chain policies will improve the efficiency of your operation by reducing costs and environmental impacts associated with wasteful processes. This will also improve your green marketing messages because your organization will have a policy and plan in place to use as a guide.

Maintain Safety, Price, and Performance

Green is not the only selling point that influences a consumer's purchasing decisions. Quality, performance, and price are three main factors consumers take into consideration when they buy a product. Look for creative ways to keep the costs of your products down, even if you end up spending a little bit more money when transitioning to green product options. Incorporating green/lean manufacturing techniques into your manufacturing process will create cost savings that you can use to balance or reduce the price of your products. Often, purchasing green inputs is less expensive than purchasing conventional product inputs. Many manufacturers who are altering their product inputs from toxic to nontoxic raw materials are seeing a decrease in disposal costs because they do not have to spend money disposing of hazardous waste.

Alternatives

Utilizing alternative and less-toxic materials to create your products are both ways to create a greener product. Greening what you put into your product is a surefire way to reduce your product's environmental impact. For example, if your product inputs consist of toxic components that emit VOCs, the end product you produce will not be green. As you learn more about toxic materials, you can ensure that your products are toxin-free and more sustainable.

Seek Recycled Materials

When possible, increase the amount of recycled materials used in the production of your product. Using recycled materials as raw material inputs creates new markets for waste and encourages recycling. If there wasn't a commodity market for that milk jug you are throwing into the recycling bin, would your recycling program exist in the first place? If we do not encourage the use of recycled content in new products by incorporating it into our product manufacturing processes and purchasing goods composed of recycled content, we jeopardize our recycling systems.

> **Going Green**
>
> You can seek eco-label certifications from third-party organizations to provide your customers with "seals of approval." See Chapter 22 for a review of eco-label certifications you may wish to consider applying for.

An example of positive market development through the use of recycled goods is The California Resource Recovery Association's Polystyrene Recycling Market Development Zone program. The California Resource Recovery Board teamed up with local municipalities and Timbron International, a manufacturer of products made from recycled polystyrene, to create a market for recycled polystyrene (or Styrofoam as it is commonly called). This plastic is typically known as a "difficult to recycle" plastic because it's not commonly recycled.

The Association created a pilot recycling project that allowed counties surrounding Timbron's facility to recycle the plastic by organizing a logistical system that delivered the recycled polystyrene to Timbron for reprocessing and new product manufacturing. The end result was that the participating counties decreased the amount of waste they sent to the landfill, and Timbron International made their products greener by increasing the amount of local recycled material in their product. Currently, Timbron International also participates in pilot polystyrene recycling programs with the cities of Los Angeles and San Francisco.

Timbron's story is a prime example of how a business can work with their local government to find solutions to waste problems. The community benefits because its waste is reduced and recycled, and the manufacturer benefits because it receives local and lower-cost materials.

This is just one example of new markets we can generate through the use and creation of recycled products. The ability to create products from recycled content is not limited to plastic; we have seen products composed of recycled glass, aluminum, wood, chewing gum wrappers, tires, blue jeans, and paint.

Pollution Prevention

Preventing pollution during your manufacturing process saves your organization money and further backs up your green story. The first step to pollution reduction is understanding where and how you are polluting. Create an inventory of all pollution points associated with your manufacturing operation. Look at sources of air, water, land, noise, thermal, and light pollution. After you determine all points of pollution, take strides to reduce each source you've located.

Going Green

To learn more on Pollution Prevention, also known as P2, visit www.epa.gov/p2/.

Replace Traditional Solvents with Bio-Based Options

Solvent usage is an essential part of most manufacturing processes. According to SRI Consulting, the annual global consumption of solvents is estimated at 30 billion pounds per year, and consumption in the United States alone is in excess of 8.4 billion pounds per year. Users of petroleum-based solvents are feeling more pressure than ever before from regulators to reduce the environmental impacts associated with solvent use. This includes emission reduction, improper disposal, and reduced use. Swapping petroleum-based solvents with bio-based options is an easy way to reduce the environmental impact of your manufacturing operations and to prepare you for current and future regulatory requirements.

Bio-based solvents are made from a renewable agriculture source such as corn or soybeans and emit less VOCs than petroleum-based solvents. Oftentimes bio-based solvents are biodegradable and are less toxic, creating a healthier workplace for your employees through both improved indoor air quality and reduced contact with toxic chemicals. In addition to environmental and employee health benefits, bio-based solvents often perform better than conventional solvents.

Going Green

According to the Ohio EPA, bio-based solvents have a lower environmental impact—they have low toxicity and high biodegradability. Also, lower VOCs and less pollution are generated during the manufacture of a bio-based product than a petrochemically based product. Increased business advantages of using bio-based solvents include reduced disposal costs, improved worker safety, and the ability to market "green consumerism."

Offset Emissions with Renewable Energy Credits

After you have improved the energy efficiency of your operations and reduced your emissions as much as possible, you can purchase renewable energy credits to offset your remaining emissions if you have first determined your carbon footprint (see Chapter 6).

The Least You Need to Know

◆ Follow product materials from source to disposal to create a sustainable flow.

◆ Look to nature for models of sustainability.

◆ Reuse materials to cut costs.

◆ Check the environmental safety of materials, and do not use them in your product if they pose any risk.

Chapter 11

Greening Retail Operations

In This Chapter

- ◆ Save money with environmentally responsible products and practices
- ◆ Useful tips for a healthy and eco-friendly shop
- ◆ Inspirational examples of retailers reducing energy and waste
- ◆ Educate consumers about environmental topics
- ◆ Sell green products to meet the growing demand of eco-minded shoppers

If you are a retail business, you can create a more environmentally friendly shop to attract customers interested in supporting environmental initiatives. You can also inform others about the importance of your decision to adopt these innovations. As a retailer, you're the connecting point between manufacturer and consumer, and as such, you play an integral role in helping change the shape of consumerism and the habits of consumers.

Creating a Healthy Store

To ensure staff and shoppers enjoy a pleasant and healthy indoor environment, beyond focusing on lighting, temperature, and sounds, put an emphasis on providing healthy air quality. Everyone will appreciate it.

Keeping an indoor environment pollutant-free involves various factors, from the quality of the building's airflow equipment to the type of paint on the walls.

Set up the shop with adequate and well-maintained heating, ventilation, and air conditioning (HVAC) equipment, and investigate efficient appliances when it's time to replace any items.

When selecting paints, furnishings, and cleaning products, evaluate each for its particular effect on air quality. Give preference to those that offer eco-friendly attributes, and avoid products that emit undesirable odors and fumes. Read the content information to determine which products are made with low or no volatile organic compounds (VOC).

The Environmental Protection Agency (EPA) provides other tips for promoting healthy indoor air quality as follows:

- Don't block air vents with furniture, boxes, or other items.

- Avoid using solvents, adhesives, and other materials that may emit bothersome odors or contaminants.

- Toss out garbage promptly.

- When decorating or remodeling, think about alternatives to furniture, flooring, and supplies that emit pollutants. Generally, odors and emissions are highest when furniture and building materials are new.

The EPA suggests, "Ask the designers, suppliers, and manufacturers to provide information on chemical emissions from products and any potential associated respiratory hazards. While emissions information may not yet be available for many products, many product manufacturers are starting to do emissions testing. The more consumers request such information, the sooner it will become widely available."

Going Green

For detailed information on achieving healthy indoor air quality, take advantage of the EPA's various free resources. The Indoor Air Quality (IAQ) Information Clearinghouse phone number is 1-800-438-4318. For the selection of free publications, log on to www.epa.gov/iaq/pubs.

Another resource related to healthy indoor environments is "Building Air Quality, A Guide for Building Owners and Facility Managers." That information, provided by the EPA and National Institute for Occupational Safety and Health (NIOSH), is available online (see Appendix B).

Reducing Supply Costs

Incorporating environmentally responsible practices into a business often offers the extra advantage of reducing expenses. Before automatically replenishing supplies, determine if they're absolutely necessary. Avoiding excess helps maintain an uncluttered shop while reducing expenses. By demanding less stuff, you're reducing the amount of environmental impact related to manufacturing, transporting, and discarding.

Be creative. Take advantage of the eco-preferable principle of reusing and repurposing items. Rather than purchasing standard display racks, think of innovative and interesting ways to use old furniture or pieces from thrift stores to showcase your merchandise and create point-of-purchase displays. The effort will be visually distinctive and delightful to eco-savvy shoppers. Also you can scratch that purchase from the budget and put discards to good use.

Reducing Waste

Eliminating excess of all sorts is a key aspect of an environmentally responsible approach to business. It also saves money.

Just as we have advised for all small businesses in this book, you should look at all facets of your venture with a fresh set of eyes. It's likely you'll be able to reduce waste in various areas—from office supplies to store furnishings to the bags shoppers need to cart home their purchases.

Reducing waste also is accomplished through various techniques and approaches. In enhancing the green attributes of your retail store, it's wise to think about that useful trio: reducing, reusing, and recycling. Reduce the amount of new materials acquired, reuse items already available, and responsibly recycle items not needed.

Some efforts at reducing waste are delightfully simple. For example, skip the printing press and ask shoppers to register for online newsletters. Sending out ads and other store information via e-mail rather than the postal service saves tons of paper—along with printing and postage costs.

Another simple approach is to reuse items rather than toss them out. For example, after opening a package, save the packing filler and recycle it in your outgoing mail.

Recycling Used Products

Using products more than once provides various benefits. In addition to the environmental perks of source reduction and waste reduction, potential economic advantages exist for the business.

A retail store should recycle its own used products. However, plenty of businesses are also approaching recycling in another way by promoting themselves as a convenient drop-off point for items such as computers and portable phones. Offering to serve as a recycling center is a marketing opportunity that showcases a store's environmental responsibility and draws foot traffic.

Other efforts at reducing waste may involve some design innovation and an initial investment, but they're likely well worth it. You might retailor your packaging to be more environmentally friendly, as discussed in Chapter 13, or establish a paperless program for customer feedback.

For office supplies, furnishings, and other items you no longer need or want, look for a school or an organization that might want them. Or recycle through a public or private materials exchange or other practical and convenient trading service available in different regions.

The Alaska Materials Exchange, for example, is a free online service for businesses and organizations wanting to offer and acquire materials. Among the categories are computers and electronics, paints, paper products, office supplies, and furniture (see Appendix B).

Its counterpart on the other side of the country, the Vermont Business Materials Exchange, is also free. In 2007, approximately 57,600 items (weighing approximately 1,000 tons) were traded through this service (see Appendix B).

Some businesses, such as the Pizza Fusion restaurant chain, incorporate waste reduction and other aspects of sustainability into their basic practices and marketing. In fact, waste reduction is a facet of the stores' physical design. Countertops are made from recycled detergent jugs, and floor tiles are fabricated with discarded glass bottles saved from older stores. Water also is a focus at this business—for example, wastewater from the sinks is recycled to the toilets. For a detailed description of Pizza Fusion's sustainability plan, see Appendix B.

Reusable Packaging Materials

Reusable bags are good for the environment—as long as they're responsibly manufactured and used. Many bags are made from recycled plastic, which is better than nonrecycled plastic. For additional eco-friendly options, choose bags made from fabric such as hemp, kenaf, or cotton—preferably organic.

The quality of the bag is an important factor, according to the online business resuablebags.com. If they're given out in abundance and are of a cheaper, less-appealing quality, they're going to pile up and be discarded, defeating the key purpose of waste reduction.

Some factors to consider when looking at various types of reusable shopping bags include durability, safe and nontoxic materials, and whether fair labor and trade standards were adhered to in the manufacturing process.

Hazard

In coastal clean-up projects, plastic bags are among the most common types of debris collected, according to the nonprofit Center for Marine Conservation.

The Minnesota Pollution Control Agency offers a reusable packaging transport directory with an array of resources for different types of shipping and storing packaging and equipment.

The directory also includes tips for businesses who are venturing into reusable transport packaging products. Among these is to ask for suggestions from the various workers and suppliers who handle packaging. "Encourage everyone, including forklift and truck drivers, custodial staff and the boss, to put their ideas into suggestion boxes," the guidelines suggest.

The guidelines state, "Reduced and reusable transport packaging does more than protect and move products with less cost and waste. For many companies, it is improving relationships and communication in the warehouse, on the sales or assembly floor, on the road, with vendors and with the community."

For more tips from the Minnesota Pollution Control Agency related to reusable transport package, see Appendix B.

Reducing Energy and Water Usage

Energy and water efficiency are essential facets of establishing an environmentally responsible retail business. As in other aspects of going green, the more standard electrical power and water you save, the more money you save.

Energy Reduction

Simple efforts, such as manually turning off lights and appliances, are helpful, but some businesses take additional measures, such as investing in energy-efficient equipment. Pearl Pressman Liberty, a commercial print facility in Philadelphia, Pennsylvania, upgraded its lighting equipment and now saves more than $21,000 a year, according to the EPA, who also states the amount of energy saved is equivalent to removing 28 cars from highways. The firm switched its lighting fixtures to florescent and compact florescent bulbs.

The EPA also acknowledges Hand Motors, an auto dealership in Vermont, for using familiar and unconventional approaches to energy efficiency. Among the business's more typical projects were upgrading lighting fixtures and using products that meet the Energy Star efficiency standards. The shop also installed timers and motion detectors, including the vending machines, to automatically turn lights on and off.

In another energy-saving effort, Hand Motors uses motor oil waste and vegetable oil to heat the service shop, which saves the business more than $15,000 a year in heating oil, the EPA states.

While vegetable oil will only be appropriate and efficient for a small number of small businesses, check out Chapter 7 and www.energystar.gov/index.cfm?c=heat_cool for other ways you can be more energy efficient with your heating, cooling, and ventilation.

Water Reduction

Enhancing water efficiency involves a focus on products (such as water-saving plumbing fixtures) and practices (such as repairing leaks). Among trendy products designed to waste less water is the dual-flush toilet, which enables the user to select either a full-tank flush or a half-tank flush.

For those who don't want the expense and hassle of installing new toilets, consider revising standard toilets so they feature dual-flush efficiency. A retrofit valve kit, Flush Choice, is designed to do just that and reduces water waste substantially. The product, sold by retailers and plumbing businesses, is installed in the toilet tank. The user turns the handle to the right for a full-tank flush and to the left for a half-tank flush (see Appendix B).

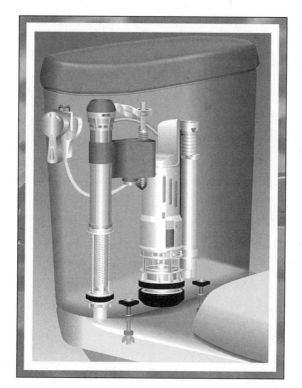

A dual-flush toilet.

(Courtesy Aqua Save Products, Inc.)

For retailers, water conservation tips from the Florida Department of Environmental Protection include the following:

- Wash business vehicles less often and in a facility that uses recycled water.

- If dressing up a storefront with landscaping, use native plants that do well with natural climate and don't require as much watering.

- Install only decorative water features that recycle water, and promote that aspect with signs stating that the water is recycled.

For additional information on techniques to improve water and energy efficiency, check out various resources from the EPA available at www.epa.gov/energy/energy.html and www.epa.gov/watersense.

Streamlining Fuel Expenses

Reduce vehicle travel when possible. For meetings with suppliers, colleagues, and other business partners, try holding a phone conference. When meetings outside the store are required, offer co-workers an incentive to carpool.

For retailers adding to a fleet of store-owned vehicles, take advantage of the automotive industry's fuel-efficient vehicles, such as electric hybrids. Organize delivery schedules to capitalize on each area to reduce travel time and cost.

Reviewing Delivery Practices

We offer many ideas for cutting down on delivery costs through packaging and utilizing fuel-efficient vehicles or shipping services. See Chapter 14 for ideas on moving your product to consumers.

Encouraging Walk/Bike Traffic

Place your retail shop, if possible, in an area that's appealing to pedestrians and bikers. Offer safe bicycle parking facilities and perhaps refreshing beverages to attract those who are thirsty from tooling around town on two pedals or two feet.

If the access to your store isn't particularly designed for bikes and pedestrians, work with area government agencies and other businesses in the neighborhood to add safe bikeways, pedestrian paths, and other appealing amenities for the nonmotoring customers.

Going Green

The city of Oakland, California, encourages shoppers and employees to use their bicycles with facilities and amenities geared specifically for them. The city used grants for its CityRacks Bicycle Parking Program and added more than 900 bike racks and lockers in commercial districts of the city.

Educating Customers

Along with simply selling products, many retailers promote the benefits and approaches to sustainability by giving out information specifically related to the store's green practices and products. Other retailers offer information that focuses on broader environmental topics. Positioning your business as a reliable source of information for customers to learn from can help increase your credibility, the traffic to your website, and your stature in your field.

REI, a retailer that sells outdoor apparel and equipment, uses a specific label (the ecoSensitive label) to showcase products with sustainable attributes. Among those is apparel made with substantial amounts of recycled content, organic fibers, or easily replenished resources.

The retailer's ecoSensitive program also provides customers with additional information about advantages and drawbacks of the particular materials, which include organic cotton, bamboo fabric, hemp, and recycled plastic bottles.

Going Green

The businesses that produce store fixtures and display pieces for the retail market are accommodating the retailers' demands for eco-friendly materials and practices. For example, Barr Display, which sells custom pieces to retail stores, offers a selection of tables, rounders, and other furniture made from reclaimed wood.

The federal government's Energy Star program offers an array of free downloadable materials that businesses are welcome to distribute (see Appendix B).

Selling Green Products

With so much emphasis on green lifestyles, the demand for products with environmentally preferable features is strong. You should meet that demand and incorporate green products in your inventory.

The Least You Need to Know

- Incorporating sustainable products and practices in a retail shop often provides the added bonus of financial savings.

- Offering green products and adhering to environmentally responsible practices appeals to eco-minded shoppers who want to support merchants who adhere to the same principles.

- The sustainable attributes of a retail shop offer potential for marketing and promotional themes.

- Many resources are available to help retailers green their businesses.

Chapter 12

Greening Your Restaurant or Food Supplier

In This Chapter

- ◆ Food's high carbon footprint
- ◆ Reducing energy use and emissions through food service
- ◆ Healthier meal options to customers
- ◆ Increasing profits through savings and premium offerings

One of the dire projections of global warming is that poverty and diminishing natural resources will lead to increased starvation around the world, which in turn will fuel increased poverty, crime, and the black market. Already the shift of using corn for fuel instead of as food for masses of impoverished countries has led to unprecedented hunger worldwide. The World Bank reports the price of corn has gone up by 83 percent in three years. The high cost of food may force as many as 100 million more people into poverty in the near future. Food purveyors can actively change these dire projections into a more positive future by purchasing locally grown, organic foods.

Restaurant owners and food purveyors can make a significant impact on the planet by greening up their shopping habits, cooking techniques, and kitchen maintenance plans.

The Cost Benefit of Organic Foods

Organic foods may seem prohibitively expensive, but if we were to calculate in the cost of synthetic chemicals and their negative effects on our health and the environment where they're grown, organic foods would seem much more reasonable. And as consumers demand more organic produce, prices will drop, which makes this choice even more acceptable against conventional produce.

def•i•ni•tion

Organic foods are foods which are grown or produced without the use of synthetic chemicals or genetic modification.

Organic foods are quickly becoming mainstream as consumers recognize the health benefits of avoiding food that's been grown with potentially dangerous synthetic chemicals. In its report "Natural and Organic Food and Beverage Trends in the U.S.," the market research firm Packaged Facts estimates that 2008 sales of natural and organic food and beverages will reach $32.9 billion, reflecting a double-digit growth—as much as 67.6 percent over the three-year period of 2005 to 2008. Consumers want organic, natural, non-genetically modified foods, and restaurants and food suppliers who provide them are in demand.

Why are consumers so interested in choosing organic foods over conventional foods? Conventional agriculture has been dosing fruits and vegetables with known poisons in the form of pesticides, fertilizers, and herbicides since the mid-twentieth century. Livestock and fowl are injected with hormones to accelerate growth and milk production. All these practices have been found to have potentially hazardous health consequences for those who consume the synthetic petrochemicals used in conventional food production.

In a landmark long-term study of children of farmers in the Yaqui Valley of Mexico, Dr. Elizabeth Guillette, an anthropologist at the University of Florida, determined that children exposed to commonly used agrichemicals showed physical and mental developmental delays that could result in a range of difficulties, including poor health, reduced birth rate, an inability to properly nurse and feed infants, and a reduced intelligence quotient.

In an interview for *E/The Environmental Magazine*, Dr. Guillette told me, "It's been projected that if IQ decreases just five points across a community, you lose roughly two-thirds of your geniuses and increase the number of children who are mentally retarded by two-thirds. This has huge consequences in terms of education, care, and medical needs. Also it's the children of today who are going to be responsible for our communities, nation, and world tomorrow. If we lose them, what are we going to do?"

In addition, organic foods have some proven benefits. Swedish scientists have determined that organic strawberries possess greater breast and colon cancer–fighting qualities than their conventional counterparts. Organic foods also have richer nutrient values—including copper, magnesium, iron, and calcium—thanks to the lack of nitrates and food additives and to soils rich in natural compost and nutrients. Organic tomato crops have been found to be 80 percent higher in flavonoids, beneficial to the heart and in the prevention of cancer and dementia.

The British Journal of Nutrition published a study indicating that mothers on organic diets provide healthier breast milk with more conjugated linoleic and trans-vaccenic acid, fatty acids thought to protect against several diseases, including diabetes and colon cancer.

Another point worth noting is the fact that genetically modified foods are not organic. Many consumers are uncomfortable eating genetically modified foods, so choosing organic foods assures them they're not consuming so-called "franken foods."

Enviro-Fact

The Union of Concerned Scientists released a report indicating that genetically modified foods actually require greater use of pesticides than organic foods. There are other concerns about genetically modified foods. Learn more at www.ucsusa.org/ food_and_agriculture/science_and_impacts/impacts_genetic_engineering/ genetically-engineered-crops.html.

As a restaurant owner, you can reap the benefit of offering organic food. Highlight your switch in a marketing campaign and let customers know that you are working to improve their health by offering organic options. If you are concerned about raising food costs, start by offering a few organic options to test your market. Once people start biting, offer more and more organic options on your menu. Also purchasing locally grown foods whenever possible can lead to reduced food costs and reduced transportation costs.

Food's Impact on the Environment

The organic farming industry—the pioneers at the Rodale Institute—contend that we can make a significant dent in greenhouse gases and thus in the damages of global warming by adopting organic farming techniques. Recent studies from the University of Michigan, the U.S. Department of Agriculture, and the Leopold Center for Sustainable Agriculture have also shown that organic farming leads to increased yields and improved soil.

The Rodale Institute reports that organic farming even helps reduce greenhouse gases and is a good hedge against global warming. In 2008, the Institute released a report stating that converting conventional fields to organic farming could reduce carbon dioxide (CO_2) emissions by as much as 10 percent.

Meat's High Carbon Footprint

Did you know that raising livestock creates more greenhouse gases than our transportation industry? Mass production of meat uses tons of energy and resources and produces huge amounts of pollution. Bringing cattle, pork, and fowl to the table requires massive amounts of grain, even though it's not the natural feed source nor the healthiest for the animals. Grain makes the animals fatter, so consumers pay more per pound. In addition, livestock farming requires a great deal of energy, and livestock waste is a huge polluter, emitting methane and CO_2 into our atmosphere and polluting wide swaths of land and water with problematic nitrogen and petrochemicals.

Enviro-Fact
Dr. Rajendra Pachauri, chair of the United Nations Intergovernmental Panel on Climate Change, which shared the Nobel Peace Prize with Al Gore in 2007, said that individuals can have a positive effect on global warming by having just one meat-free meal each week. He encourages people to continue to reduce meat consumption beyond that modest restriction. The UN's Food and Agriculture Organization estimates that meat production creates nearly one fifth of greenhouse gas emissions worldwide.

Animal rights activists have also released investigative reports of horribly inhumane conditions in meat production facilities detailing torturing and beating of animals bound for the table. Animal activists maintain that by buying meat from production facilities, consumers are condoning maltreatment of animals. A tenet of the new green industry is to create a world that respects life, seeks harmony and sustainability, and does not include cruelty in any form. Restaurants that develop more vegetable-based fare can take the lead in the green food industry and reduce costs by purchasing more vegetables instead of expensive meats.

Even if you're not ready to switch to a vegan, animal-free, or vegetarian lifestyle or restaurant, cutting back on your meat consumption seems wise. Creating meals that celebrate organic vegetables without meat can be good for business and good for your customers, as well as the planet.

Chemicals in Foods

Organic farming and landscaping protect our food, the water supply, and even the air we breathe by keeping synthetic petrochemicals out of the mix.

A landmark study by the Environmental Working Group found that on average, we have up to 200 synthetic chemicals in our bodies. Some are known carcinogens and endocrine disrupters, but most are simply of unknown toxicity.

Tens of thousands of the chemicals approved for use in the United States have not been tested to determine their safety or effects on humans. However, there is evidence that some are dangerous and may cause cancer or hormone disturbances, neurological damage, and lung irritation. Have you heard about the hermaphroditic alligators in lakes and rivers or the male frogs with feminine characteristics? These animals have been traced to areas with high levels of DDT and other agricultural chemical use, which are known endocrine disrupters and have been associated with decreased sperm counts in humans.

However, hope is on the horizon. Studies indicate that when the water is cleaned up, these amphibians begin to reproduce normal offspring again. In another study at the University of Washington, children who had eaten conventional diets and whose blood and urine showed traces of pesticides and other synthetic chemicals showed remarkable reduction of these contaminants after just a few weeks on an organic diet. Many chemicals wash through our bodies rapidly, leaving little damage, but others can cause developmental and even genetic damage that persists for generations.

Although we're exposed to many synthetic chemicals through our food and water, some chemicals also come from the containers food is packaged in. Bisphenol A (BPA), used in the linings of cans and hard plastic containers, has recently been detected in the urine of 93 percent of Americans. An overwhelming majority of these studies show that the chemical is harmful—causing breast cancer, testicular cancer, diabetes, hyperactivity, obesity, low sperm counts, miscarriage, and a host of other reproductive failures in laboratory animals.

Canada and Wal-Mart have both taken steps to restrict BPA in products even though the Food and Drug Administration (FDA) hasn't yet ruled against it.

Phthalates, endocrine disrupters that can cause immune system and hormonal problems, are found in some plastic containers such as water bottles and baby bottles and can leach into the liquids and foods they contain. Wal-Mart and other retailers have agreed to stop selling baby bottles made with plastic containing phthalates.

Hazard _____

When purchasing food, beware of the following: meat and dairy items that are not hormone/antibiotic-free, milk produced from cows treated with bovine growth hormone, nonorganic fruits and vegetables, and foods marketed as "natural."

In response to customer demand, Wal-Mart is also serving up hormone-free milk, even though the FDA has said milk from cows treated with bovine growth hormone poses no risk to human health. Restaurants that follow suit by providing hormone-free dairy products can market that health benefit to customers.

To reduce exposure to synthetic chemicals in any way is a good thing, and restaurant customers understand that as well. Going organic is a great first step.

Transportation Costs of Food

An important consideration in the cost of goods is always the transportation expense and emission output related to getting product to your doorstep. In today's free-trade world, we've become accustomed to enjoying produce, spices, and exotic culinary treasures from around the world all year long. However, this can be a dangerous, as well as an expensive, practice. In recent news, we have heard of many instances of contaminated food and other products entering the country from China, Mexico, and other countries where regulations may not be as strict nor practices as stringent and careful as in the United States. This concern helps reinforce the importance of reducing transportation costs and emissions by sourcing for local supplies.

In addition to producing less pollution in transit, locally grown foods support local farmers. And because local foods get to you much more quickly than those shipped across the country or around the world, they can be organic and preservative-free, an important bonus for buyer and consumer.

Contact your local government agricultural division to locate local organic farms within your area and consider developing working relationships with these farms to utilize their produce and meat and dairy products in your restaurant. Be sure to notify customers that you're working with local farmers, which means you're utilizing fresh resources and supporting the local economy.

Organic Versus Conventional Food Purveyors

The agricultural food industry has become a corporate enterprise. Factory farms have become food production industries that only resemble a distant relative of traditional farming. Synthetic petrochemicals take the place of natural nutrients, sometimes almost entirely replacing the natural foods that plants and animals need to grow normally. Crops are raised in water or stone beds without soil, fed only by injection of chemical nutrients. Added medications compensate for the lack of natural immunity and protection afforded by a rich soil. Scientists have genetically developed modifications that add pesticides to plants or synthetic resistance to natural predators. Some consumers are uncomfortable with this nascent science because we don't fully understand what their effects will be.

Companies developing these genetically modified plants have patented the seeds and affected legislation prohibiting farmers from re-supplying themselves with seeds from their crops. Therefore, farmers unable to reseed their own crops are forced to buy new supplies of seed for each subsequent crop. Some farmers, facing financial difficulty and unable to purchase new seed, have used their own crops to reseed their fields and have been subjected to lawsuits from the seed companies. The validity of being able to control ownership of seeds and the subsequent food supply has come under intense fire from environmentalists and others who believe in the fundamental right of farmers and individuals to perpetuate plants and provide food supply for those dependent on it.

When you buy locally grown, organic foods for your restaurant or food business, you're helping to strengthen the market for healthier products and supporting the local farming industry at the same time. You'll also reduce some expenses related to commercial foods, and you'll add to your reputation and mission as a sustainable business.

Green Restaurant Association Resources

Started in 1990, the nonprofit Green Restaurant Association (GRA; www.dinegreen.com/solutions.asp) was formed to provide food purveyors with knowledge and connections to reduce costs and environmental impact while becoming more sustainable. The GRA claims the world's largest database of environmental solutions and products that meet certification standards for the restaurant industry. The GRA provides assistance and certification to restaurant owners who want to go green, offers educational outreach to consumers, and produces a Certified Green Restaurant Guide to help environmentally conscious consumers find restaurants that meet their standards of responsibility and service. The website lists 177 members as of January 2009.

To learn how to get started greening up your restaurant and food business practices, the GRA provides a set of simple guidelines that give you the points you'll want to consider:

- Energy efficiency and conservation

- Water efficiency and conservation

- Recycling and compost

- Sustainable food

- Pollution prevention

- Recycled, tree-free, biodegradable, and organic products

- Chlorine-free paper products

- Nontoxic cleaning and chemical products

- Green power

- Green building and construction

- Education

Going Green

Restaurant owners curious about their own sustainability and their impact on the environment might begin a self-study by using a simple quiz on the GRA site that reviews energy use, water use, waste practices, and toxicity awareness: www.dinegreen.com/quiz.asp.

Electricity

The GRA website states that restaurants use more electricity than any other business, so making improvements in this area can greatly impact the amount of greenhouse gases produced by the industry. The GRA encourages its members and other food providers to reduce electricity use by installing energy-efficient equipment, replacing incandescent light bulbs with CFLs or LED bulbs, using monitors and other routines that limit the use of electricity to an as-needed basis only, and seeking out renewable sources of energy. Some of these changes may seem costly at the outset, but money saved in reduced energy use will be substantial and should make these expenses cost-effective within a few years.

Water

The GRA says restaurants use up to 300,000 gallons of water annually. It asks members to reduce water consumption by installing low-flow faucets, spray valves, and toilets and by providing water to customers on request instead of automatically.

In the United States, this reduction could save millions of gallons of fresh water each day, and the improvements could save as much as $5,000 in a year. Another way to conserve is to reuse water from sinks, showers, and laundry machines for irrigation of outdoor landscaping and/or for flushing toilets. Check with your code enforcement office before having a plumber redirect your flow pipes.

Waste

Restaurant members of the GRA say they can reduce their waste output by as much as 95 percent by finding ways to recycle paper, plastic, metals, and food waste at waste management companies or on-site facilities and by donating leftover food to homeless shelters and charities.

Here are a few more tips from the GRA:

◆ Instead of packaging take-out meals in Styrofoam or plastic, use cardboard or compostable containers.

◆ Use compostable flatware instead of disposable plastic.

◆ Serve condiments such as ketchup, sugar, and salt in bulk containers instead of individual packets.

◆ Purchase food from local farmers and at local farmers' markets to reduce chemical content and transportation costs and emissions.

◆ If possible, reuse your fryer oil as biodiesel fuel for equipment and delivery vehicles.

A new Boston-based company, Converted Organics, has started a business that collects food waste from restaurants, groceries, and other businesses; composts the waste; and converts it into a liquid fertilizer, which it then sells to farmers and growers seeking a cost-effective organic nutrient for crops. The company reports that 85 percent of its buyers are conventional farmers tired of paying increasingly high prices for conventional petrochemical-based fertilizers. This keeps food from the landfill (the company says that 25 million tons of food waste typically end up in landfills each year) and produces an economically attractive and sustainable solution for the organic food chain.

Pizza Fusion, a Fort Lauderdale–based franchise that has expanded rapidly across the country, channels heat from ovens to heat dining rooms; uses 75 percent organic ingredients for its pizzas, sandwiches, salads, and desserts; and offers organic drinks, including beer and wine. Restaurant founders Michael Gordon and Vaughan Lazar haven't joined the GRA but are members of Green America (a group of certified green businesses), and the business is certified organic by the USDA. The company uses hybrid vehicles and encourages franchisees to develop facilities that meet U.S. Green Building Council (USGBC) LEED certification.

Marketing Your Environmentally Responsible Food Offerings

Education is an important element to success with a sustainable business plan. Engaging staff in the process by empowering them with an understanding of why your business is making these changes helps them carry out new plans. Informing customers of your efforts will increase your business among socially and environmentally responsible consumers and is likely to increase your sales and profits. Post signs wherever you've made a sustainable change to let staff and visitors know what you're doing and how they're helping save water and energy, reduce emissions, and protect the environment. They'll feel good to be part of the solution for the planet, and they might even choose to come back to your place a little more often.

Going Green

Although people may think that going green is more costly than towing the traditional line, the GRA says that some members save thousands of dollars by adopting their green restaurant guidelines. For more info on cost savings, see www.dinegreen.com/sixreasons.asp.

As you can see, the food service industry greatly impacts the environment. By establishing more sustainable business practices in the handling and processing of food and in food retail and restaurant operations, food providers can significantly contribute to greenhouse gas reduction and reduce environmental contamination of soil, water, and air. In the process, increasing sustainability in food service businesses can reduce energy, water use, and waste; save money; and increase profits. Employees, customers, and the planet will benefit from healthier, more nutritious, and less potentially dangerous dining choices.

The Least You Need to Know

- The food industry has a great impact on the environment.
- Reducing energy costs and selecting healthier food choices are key to creating a sustainable restaurant or food business.
- Conscious consumers are drawn to healthier food options.
- Sustainable food practices can greatly improve emissions and expenses.

Packaging Cost Benefits

In This Chapter

- Reduce packing materials
- Select biodegradable packaging
- Develop reuse and recycling plans
- Reduce package size and delivery costs

Because packaging our products consumes a lot of paper, plastic, and energy, it presents an excellent opportunity to reduce resources and cut costs. In the following pages, we'll take a look at how your business can reduce the waste cycle and provide sustainable packaging that will cost less and benefit the environment.

Sustainable Packaging Resources and Information

The Sustainable Packaging Coalition is a project of GreenBlue, a not-for-profit organization working to educate businesses and the public about the importance of creating and utilizing packaging that is sustainable throughout its life cycle. The coalition defines sustainable packaging with these criteria:

- Is beneficial, safe, and healthy for individuals and communities throughout its life cycle

- Meets market criteria for performance and cost

- Is sourced, manufactured, transported, and recycled using renewable energy

- Maximizes the use of renewable or recycled source materials

- Is manufactured using clean production technologies and best practices

- Is made from materials healthy in all probable end-of-life scenarios

- Is physically designed to optimize materials and energy

- Is effectively recovered and utilized in biological and/or industrial cradle-to-cradle cycles

Wal-Mart is making a big difference in its environmental impact. As *Newsweek* reported (September 22, 2008), it has demanded its suppliers cut the cost of importing goods from China and other countries. By asking detergent suppliers to use more concentrated formulas and reduce container size, less petroleum is used and more containers can be shipped per carton. This also reduces cardboard packaging, allowing more containers to be shipped per truck and reducing the amount of fuel needed to bring the product to the retailer.

This kind of position taken by the world's biggest retailer will affect small businesses as suppliers develop packaging standards that become routine procedures that affect the products and supplies you use, too. Be prepared for changes enforced by government and larger corporations by adopting a sustainable packaging strategy now.

Packing Materials

For decades, plastic, cardboard, Styrofoam, and paper have commonly been used as packing materials. In developing more sustainable packaging, the first line of defense is to reduce the amount of materials. By using sustainable materials, we can preserve the packing and shipping resources we use. Developing a sustainable package design at the outset of product development—instead of as an afterthought—can maximize environmental benefit. Remember to consider the energy expense of creating materials and the waste impact of materials to find the best balance of cost-effectiveness and sustainability.

Impacts of Packing Materials

Earth Policy Institute reports that packaging uses 7 percent of the food-related energy produced in the United States, and if you're a food business owner, the cost of that energy is contained in your packaging processes. Packing for other products is also energy intensive. You can reduce this energy expense and its attendance emissions by developing more sustainable packaging for your products and purchasing sustainably packaged supplies.

The Environmental Protection Agency (EPA) reports that corrugated fiber and plastic packaging made up about 25 percent of discarded packaging materials in 2000. In 2006, paper products amounted to 85 million tons of waste, 40 percent of all municipal waste.

Plastic and Styrofoam, both produced using potentially toxic synthetic petrochemicals, contribute greatly to our waste problem because they don't break down but instead pile up in landfills and fill our oceans with dangerous detritus. Fortunately, the plastics industry is beginning to understand the need to develop comprehensive recycling programs for difficult-to-recycle plastics and is educating consumers and producers on the importance of proper end-of-life disposal for all types of plastics. If you choose to use plastic packaging, choose a type of plastic that is easily recyclable in most municipal waste collection streams, such as #1 (PETE) or #2 (HDPE).

Paper-based packing materials, including cardboard, represent a substantial use of trees for materials typically disposed of after a single use. The GreenPostalStore.org, which offers eco-friendly packaging materials, says the United States destroys 200 acres of trees each day for packaging materials and throws 200 tons of plastic packaging away. We can do better than this!

Examples of Biodegradable and Eco-Friendly Packaging Options

Cardboard and paper are biodegradable, but let's not send a good resource to the waste pile before it's fully utilized. Let's find secondary and further uses; simply reusing the packaging helps extend its usefulness.

Many companies are now designing biodegradable packing materials that can be composted into soil without leaving a toxic trace. From packing peanuts to molded recycled fiber containers, you can find ways to pack your product that will lessen its negative environmental impact on the planet.

Sustainability-minded engineers are designing differently shaped liquid containers that take up less space in shipping and often don't require cardboard boxes; they can be loaded directly onto pallets and shrink-wrapped for secure shipping. In the GreenBiz.com e-zine (July 2, 2008), a Wal-Mart milk supplier reported that its new container can accommodate 224 1-gallon jugs in a space that previously carried only 80. The dairy estimates they've cut labor costs in half, decreased water use by more than 60 percent, and reduced deliveries to Sam's Club stores from five times a week to two.

Green Packaging, Inc., a Pennsylvania-based company, specializes in providing sustainable packing materials to replace Styrofoam and plastics. They offer 100 percent recycled and recyclable packaging alternatives to peanuts and bubble wrap. They also carry recycled corrugated cartons, tissue paper, and paper tape. See Appendix B for contact information.

Shipping Cartons

The common practice of tearing down cardboard shipping cartons for recycling is preferable to incinerating them, but it's even better to reuse them.

Many shipping companies provide recycled and recyclable materials for clients. Even the United States Postal Service (USPS) offers eco-friendly packaging through its Priority and Express Mail services, which offer free flat-rate cardboard, envelopes, and boxes that have earned cradle-to-cradle certification for ecologically intelligent design.

Design for Disassembly and Reuse

Designing cartons we can easily disassemble and reassemble for reuse is a simple design change that can help continue the life cycle of the container beyond the recycling bin, saving energy and preventing pollution emissions.

Essential Design, a product design firm based in Boston, has produced an alternative packing carton called Treepac, made with cellulose acetate and designed for continuous reuse many times more than traditional cardboard packaging. The Treepac, which according to its manufacturer can be designed as a biodegradable product so it won't contribute to landfills, won a Silver International Design Excellence Award in the Ecodesign category.

Help Customers Maximize Benefit

Printing instructions for the reuse of containers on the package (in nontoxic ink) can help consumers continue the cycle of sustainability by returning the container and packing to retailers for reuse instead of sending them to the waste system or recycling bin. Ask your packaging supplier if this type of consumer information is available on packaging you purchase to use for your business, or create a stamp, sticker, or package insert that can be applied during the packing process.

Another way to help your customer carry out your sustainability initiative is to provide a system for him to return materials and containers to you for reuse. Again, provide instructions for return in nontoxic ink.

Reduce Plastic

According to the EPA, Americans recycle just 7 percent of the more than 200 billion pounds of plastic produced each year. The Green Postal Store says that 200 tons of plastic packaging materials go to landfills each day. Reducing the amount of plastic used in packaging can help reduce the plastic that goes to the landfills and also reduce toxic emissions from its production and degradation which pollutes our air, water, and soil. Reducing our use of plastic also reduces the amount of energy used to create it.

An alternative, sometimes called bioplastic, is being used for some food products such as coffee packages and water bottles. It is made with PLA (polylactic acid), a plant-based polymer said to be nontoxic and biodegradable. However, sustainability proponents have reservations about the product because it can still take up to 1,000 years to biode-grade and it's often blended with plastic for the final product, reducing its sustainable value. In addition, it can be made from genetically modified plants, which have not received the green light of overall safety from environmentalists or many consumers yet (although genetically modified foods have been federally approved for use).

Going Green

Scientists at Clemson University announced in September 2008 that they'd developed the Earthbottle, a biodegradable bottle made from all-vegetable materials. Their company, Earth Renewable Technologies, is creating the bottle for Gaia Herbs as a container for herbal supplements. A good example of the emerging technologies that will help move us away from to more Earth-friendly packaging, the company says the bottles are stronger, lighter, and cost less to transport than plastic. They weigh about 20 grams each, compared to 115 grams each for the glass bottles the company now uses.

Weigh Your Options: Shrink-Wrap Plastic

Shrink-wrap plastic has become popular as a means of ensuring a package has not been opened or tampered with. But weigh this concern against the environmental cost of producing plastic and disposing of it, and you'll find it is sometimes unnecessary and more sustainable to avoid using shrink-wrap plastic on products. Some companies find that by securing materials to pallets with shrink wrap, they can eliminate excess cardboard boxes. This is certainly an area that will benefit from further development of green technologies and ideas for the best packing practices. Until a truly green choice comes along, you will need to weigh these options to determine the most cost-effective and eco-friendly choice for your company.

Replace Plastic Cases with Biodegradable Cardboard

Plastic cases on packages are usually cut or broken off and disposed of in the trash or recycled as soon as the product makes its way home with the consumer. This represents unnecessary waste and produces piles of trash. Although we have established means for recycling plastic, a small percentage is actually recycled, so it's better to avoid using plastic packaging material in favor of biodegradable or reusable materials whenever possible.

Biodegradable Packing Materials

Molded fiber packaging materials are made with recycled paper products and can be form-fitted to your more sensitive products that need specialized cushioning for shipping. The molded fiber is nontoxic, biodegradable, and recyclable so it can remain in the useful cycle of sustainability. Several companies specialize in creating molded fiber packaging, including EnviroPak of Earth City, Missouri (www.enviropak.com), and UFP Technologies of Georgetown, Massachusetts (www.ufpt.com). You may wish to search out a supplier located near your place of business to reduce transportation cost for the packaging.

Green Peanuts

Biodegradable peanuts, which dissolve in water and are nontoxic, have been developed from corn starch, soy beans, and sorghum. They are lightweight and cost-effective when compared to traditional plastic-based packing peanuts.

Post-Consumer Recycled Paper

According to TreecycleRecycledPaper.com, only a small percentage of used paper is recycled. We need to find more ways to recycle our paper products and to select paper products made from recycled paper whenever possible. Look for the Post-Consumer Waste (PCW) designation on the paper packaging materials you purchase, and make your customers aware of the importance of recycling the paper that comes with your products. Select unbleached paper materials—bleaching serves no functional purpose and yet the process contributes hazardous carcinogenic chemicals to many of our waterways. We can help reduce the impact of using paper products on our environment by choosing natural-colored, unbleached paper products.

TreecycledRecycledPaper.com recommends choosing paper labeled Process Chlorine Free (PCF), which means that it is recycled with no chlorine bleach or chlorine derivatives.

Reducing Package Weight

Some packing materials weigh more than others, and by choosing lighter materials, you'll reduce the package weight and the cost of shipping. Plastic is usually heavier than paper or peanuts.

Using Less Packing Materials

The best solution for reducing your environmental impact through packaging is to reduce your use of paper, plastic, and other materials. By consolidating your package to protect its contents in the smallest possible space, you'll use less packing materials.

Pallets are a staple in shipping products, yet the wooden boards are often left to waste once the product reaches its distributor. Develop a plan to reuse your pallets so this resource can continue to serve your business long into the future; you'll save a considerable amount of money on raw materials. The Rainforest Alliance promotes recycling pallets. Some enterprising businesses collect unwanted pallets, repair or dismantle them, rebuild them to make them sturdy, and then resell them.

Plastic pallets that have come on the scene are touted as more environmentally friendly than wood for two reasons. They are approximately 30 percent lighter than wood and therefore, require less energy to transport and they are recyclable, often being reground and cast into new pallets. As with many newly developed sustainable solutions, you need to weigh the options to find the best solution for your company and keep an eye on new developments that may offer better ideas.

Reducing Package Size

The smaller your package, the less it will cost to ship. By cushioning your package in the most efficient way, you reduce package size and the cost of transporting it. If you can ship smaller packages, you'll reduce the energy expended to get your product to its end destination and thus reduce your product's carbon footprint.

Cost Benefits of Reducing Package Weight

Reducing package weight also reduces shipping costs. By using less packaging, lighter materials, and smaller containers, you'll reduce your shipping expenses overall.

If you're doing your own shipping, you'll benefit from applying sustainable packaging principles to your products. Smaller packages with fewer, lighter-weight materials will make room for more packages in your shipping delivery vehicle, consolidating fuel expense and emissions.

Lighter loads also reduce fuel consumption, and if you consolidate shipping services by using smaller packages, you'll reduce shipping trips and expenditures, as well as shipping emissions.

Reducing your shipping emissions means you'll be reducing your company's contribution to the pollution problem with fewer fuel emissions, less energy expended in the packaging materials and process, and less pollution generated thanks to using sustainable materials.

The Least You Need to Know

- ◆ Evaluating your packing and shipping processes may result in saved resources and saved money.

- ◆ Reducing use of unsustainable materials reduces your carbon footprint.

- ◆ Helping customers reuse and return packing materials helps extend the life of the resources.

- ◆ Using less material and reducing the size and weight of materials cuts costs and reduces emissions.

Chapter 14

Cost Analysis of Getting to Market

In This Chapter

- ◆ Greening your fleet
- ◆ Using less fuel cuts costs
- ◆ Finding fuel-efficient shippers
- ◆ Supporting local businesses and reducing shipping costs

The American Physical Society (APS), an organization of 46,000 physicists, released a report titled *Energy Future: Think Efficiency* in October 2008. It stated that the United States could reduce dependence on foreign oil and greenhouse gas emissions dramatically and immediately by increasing efficiency in transportation and building fuel usage. The report points out that efficiency is easy and inexpensive to implement.

"The bottom line is that the quickest way to do something about America's use of energy is through energy efficiency," Burton Richter, the chairman of the study panel and a 1976 Nobel Prize winner in physics, told McClatchy News. "Energy that you don't use is free. It's not imported, and it doesn't emit any greenhouse gases. Most of the things we recommend don't cost anything to the economy. The economy will save money."

The report states that the transportation sector uses 70 percent of our petroleum fuel and emits 30 percent of greenhouse gases in the United States. The APS recommends that the federal government invest more money in the development of cheaper, more reliable batteries for electric cars.

"If you look at magically converting the whole fleet to plug-in hybrids that get 40 miles per charge, greenhouse gases would be reduced by 33 percent and gasoline use by 60 percent," Richter told McClatchy News, adding that the result would cut oil imports by 6 million barrels per day—the amount the United States currently imports from OPEC nations and a little less than half of all oil imported to the United States daily.

Let's examine how we can put this information to work by increasing fuel efficiency and reducing emissions for your sustainable business.

Choosing a Green Vehicle

Although many alternative fuels are being experimentally presented to the market, their viability varies greatly. Some options, such as corn ethanol and biodiesel, show limited promise but are unlikely to solve fuel efficiency needs for most consumers.

Hybrid cars, which have been developing a strong market from Japanese carmakers, are demonstrating a good alternative to traditional vehicles, and American auto-makers are quickly following suit with an array of hybrid vehicles on the horizon. However, the best solution to low-emission, low-fuel vehicles appears to be the electric vehicle, which is regaining popularity after being shelved for several years.

The big issue in using electric, in addition to longevity of power supply and availability of recharging facilities, is the source of electricity. If renewable energies take the lead in electricity generation, these cars will be a boon for emission reduction. If we're powering our cars by burning more coal or oil, we won't be making much progress toward alleviating global warming. So let's take a closer look at the options available today and on the horizon.

Hybrid SUVs

Trucks and SUVs are popular and sometimes necessary when transporting products and supplies, but some of these vehicles can be the most expensive to operate because of poor fuel economy consumption. Although some SUVs are being developed today with better fuel efficiency than in the past decades, called "hybrid SUVs," they still are among the most consumptive vehicles on the road, and emission reports are not impressive. If you have an old, low miles-per-gallon (mpg) truck or SUV, you could improve your costs for fuel and emission output by trading in for a newer model with higher mpg and reduced emissions. But there may be better options for you.

Is Ethanol a Green Fuel Choice?

Ethanol enjoyed a wild ride of publicity at the outset of the current "oil crisis" thanks to generous subsidies from the U.S. government to farmers who could grow corn to be used as fuel. Although the farming community celebrated this new market for their product and sucked up the subsidies as fast as they became available, corn ethanol quickly hit the skids, primarily because its use as a fuel additive was never a suitable option. Why? Because corn is an important food source for both people and livestock, and diverting its use from food to fuel created food shortages which drove up prices in many communities and countries.

Furthermore, ethanol production requires a high energy input, rendering the benefit of using ethanol as an additive to displace petroleum a relatively ineffective means of cutting emissions.

Finally, there just isn't enough corn in production to meet our need for alternative fuel. If we used all the available corn—leaving none for food—we could make only 1.5 million barrels of ethanol per day, yet we use 21 million barrels of oil each day in the United States.

Brazil has created a more successful ethanol market using sugar cane, which produces more energy and is more efficient, but again, sugar cane is not a crop easily grown in the United States, so it doesn't show much promise as our solution to alternative fuel needs.

Enviro-Fact

Scientists at the Union for Concerned Scientists do project that ethanol made from waste cellulosic material, such as corn stalks or weed grasses that have no competing value, could show promise for large-scale ethanol production in the future, and research and development on this option are underway.

A plus for ethanol is that it can be used in any conventional vehicle in blends of up to 10 percent, and you'll notice that many fuel pumps today provide a mix of ethanol and petroleum.

Adapt Delivery Vehicles to Biodiesel Fuel

Biodiesel fuel has gained some popularity, especially for trucks that require diesel fuel and have low mpg efficiencies. Biodiesel is an oil made from plants (such as soybeans) and can also be made from used fryer oil. Because diesel-burning vehicles can be adapted fairly easily and at low cost by the mechanically inclined, it has become popular among environmentalists to adapt vehicles and fuel them with waste oil collected from restaurants. Of course, as soon as this became semi-popular, the restaurants that once happily unloaded their waste oil to travelers for free began charging for the oil when they recognized a new source of revenue.

Biodiesel can be blended with petroleum or made from 100 percent vegetable oils, but it still produces carbon emissions when it's burned as fuel, so it's still contributing to greenhouse gases. Diesel fuel emits 10 to 20 percent more toxic particulate emissions than gasoline, so it also contributes to air pollution, which can be hazardous to our respiratory systems. Also biodiesel is often produced from crops that are grown using unsustainable practices. Check to see if your biodiesel provider is producing his fuel from local waste vegetable oil or commercially grown crops to determine how sustainable it is. Because fryer oil and oil derived from vegetables is in limited supply, biodiesel is a short-term solution to our fuel needs.

> **Hazard**
>
> Biodiesel and waste vegetable oil are not the same thing. Biodiesel is vegetable oil that has been converted to fuel. It is best to convert your diesel vehicle's engine before you run it on pure waste vegetable oil. To purchase conversion kits, visit www.goldenfuelsystems.com.

I visited a sustainable small business in Burlington, Vermont, that produces biodiesel from vegetable oils collected from area restaurants. Its owner, chemist Scott Gordon, doesn't anticipate biodiesel becoming the mainstream fuel for vehicles in the future because of vegetable oil availability, the cost of processing, and the fact that it's not a truly clean solution to our emission issues. However, Gordon does project that biodiesel could be a viable alternative for home and building heating oil.

In 2007, Clif Bar, a company that produces energy bars, switched its delivery vehicles to B99, or 99 percent biodiesel made from used vegetable oil. As a result, it cut its carbon emissions from 255 tons to 15 tons in a single year.

Low-Carbon and Fuel Standard

California has led the way (as often seems to be the case with innovative technology and environmentally friendly initiatives) by setting a low-carbon fuel standard as a legislative mandate. The standard established a mandate for lower carbon emissions, which is expected to spur technology of various alternative fuels while reducing oil consumption and greenhouse gas emissions. The plan is hailed because it provides an incentive to markets to develop more-efficient and lower-emission fuels in response to consumer demand.

Enviro-Fact

Willie Nelson, the Texas singer-songwriter who tours the country in a big diesel bus, has partnered with a fuel company in his home state to create a biodiesel business that is establishing biodiesel fuel stations across the country as an option for commercial truckers. Although BioWillie won't cut down much on costs or emissions, it does help to relieve our dependence on petroleum fuel. The National Renewable Energy Laboratory reports that B20, a blend of biodiesel and petroleum, cuts petroleum consumption by 19 percent, reduces carbon dioxide (CO_2) emissions by 16 percent, and reduces hydrocarbon emissions by 20 percent. Converting your existing trucks to use biodiesel is an alternative worth considering if other high-mpg and low-emission options won't work for your fleet.

Massachusetts has announced an interest in establishing a similar standard based on advanced biofuels—those derived from nonpetroleum, nonfood vegetable sources and producing emissions of at least 50 percent less than fossil fuels. A state task force estimates that an advanced biofuel industry could contribute $280 million to $1 billion per year to the state economy by 2025 while reducing petroleum dependence and emissions.

Other states are considering similar options, and according to the Natural Resources Defense Council, the European Union, British Columbia, and Ontario have adopted a low-carbon fuel standard.

As a business owner, you can anticipate that more states and perhaps the federal government will follow these initiatives. You'll want to plan ahead for the low-carbon fuel standard because it may become a law in your area. Even if it doesn't, adopting these low-carbon fuel standards for your own fleet is a great move toward greening your business.

Freight Options

If your business requires freight shipping options for large quantities of product, you want to consider the various options for mass transit of cargo. Let's take a look at the best choices.

Hybrid Truck Fleets

Companies with fleets of delivery vehicles can reduce costs by switching to more fuel-efficient vehicles. You may even take advantage of government incentives to upgrade your fleet to more efficient, lower-emission vehicles. The Environmental Defense Fund provides an updated list of incentives available from the federal government, as well as states, and also offers a listing comparing the efficiencies and costs of various hybrid and efficient delivery vehicles (see Appendix B for contact information).

PHH Arval, a leading fleet management service in North America, provides out-sourced fleet management solutions for delivery vehicles. With the Environmental Defense Fund, the company has established PHH GreenFleet, the first and most comprehensive greenhouse gas management program for fleet vehicles. More than 60,000 vehicles in their management program have collectively reduced emissions by 14 percent and reduced operating costs by 4 percent (see Appendix B for contact information).

Rail Transit

Although trains traditionally were fueled by diesel fuel and thus left behind high emissions and particulate pollution, recent advances in rail diesel technologies are helping make trains a better choice for moving freight than in the past. In September 2008, the Environmental Protection Agency (EPA) announced a funding program allocating nearly $50 million to programs developing clean diesel fuels for trains and trucks.

Some rail lines are reducing their pollution levels by using smaller diesel, hybrid, or electric engines. If rail cargo is part of your shipping and distribution program, check with your carrier about its fuel and emission policies, and seek out those that are helping reduce their carbon footprint and pollution output.

Going Green

The EPA SmartWay Transport Program provides information, assistance, and incentives to implement more efficient and environmentally friendly transportation options, such as innovative financing and grants to help green the fleets of small businesses. SmartWay certifies vehicles that meet its standards for efficiency and emission reduction. It also provides fuel reduction tips, information on alternative fuels, and a Green Vehicle Guide that compares vehicle choices based on SmartWay standards (see Appendix B).

Choosing Existing Green Shippers

Many commercial shippers have discovered great savings by converting their fleets to hybrid and fuel-efficient vehicles. If you don't have your own fleet, you can still take advantage of their investment by utilizing their services. When you contract with shippers, ask them specifically if your packages will be carried on a hybrid or fuel-efficient vehicle. Letting these businesses know that you appreciate their efforts helps them as well as your business—and the planet.

FedEx, also working with the Environmental Defense Fund, was the first commercial shipper to introduce hybrid vehicles into its fleet, with 172 of its 30,000 vehicles now using hybrid technology. The vehicles represent a 75 percent cost increase, but returns on investment (ROI) in terms of reduced gas cost and emissions are significant. According to an April 2008 report from *Business Wire*, FedEx's hybrid trucks improve fuel economy by 42 percent, reduce greenhouse gas emissions by about 30 percent, and reduced particulate pollution by 96 percent.

By October 2008, the company had not added any further vehicles to its fleet because of the high cost and lack of government incentives. Hopefully its commitment to environmental improvement will soon be rewarded with greater incentives, which will reduce the cost of efficient vehicles and increase competition in the field. Even at 172 vehicles, FedEx maintains the largest fleet of commercial hybrid trucks in North America.

According to a *Christian Science Monitor* report in November 2007, UPS has one of the largest truck fleets in the nation. The company uses 50 hybrid vehicles for local deliveries, saving 44,000 gallons of fuel per year and cutting emissions by 457 metric tons of CO_2. The company has also instituted a software program to help minimize driving time and reduce fuel use, and it is reducing its jet fuel consumption by reducing idle time of its fleet of 600 jets—one of the largest fleets in the world—with better coordination of flights, according to *The Wall Street Journal* (March 11, 2008).

The United States Postal Service (USPS) claims it has the largest civilian fleet of alternative vehicles. The USPS uses some hybrid technology, biodiesel, ethanol, and compressed natural gas for about a third of its fleet of nearly 150,000 delivery vehicles. It worked with General Motors to test a hydrogen fuel cell minivan—the first commercial use of a fuel cell vehicle in the nation—and uses some electric vans, which are zero-emission vehicles. For more information, see Appendix B.

Port Support

If your business is near a major shipping port and you need to send your products far and wide, you might investigate shipping by boat as an option. Cargo ships do present some environmental problems, though. According to Grist.org, the Bluewater Network says that a single container ship emits more pollution than 2,000 diesel trucks. On top of that, ships carry ballast water, which is typically exchanged in a different port from where it was collected, and release sea creatures in the water, fostering exotic populations that can be damaging to local environments.

Going Green _____

The Clean Cargo Working Group, convened by the Business for Social Responsibility, is a network of cargo shippers working to clean up the environmental impact of ocean-going cargo. If you need to ship via the seas, you might consult this group and make arrangements to utilize shippers dedicated to reducing their environmental impact.

Local Sales Focus

One of the best ways to reduce your shipping costs is to focus more sales on the local market rather than far away. Have you been marketing via the Internet and perhaps overlooked your potential local customers? Take another look at your local community; you might have potential customers at your doorstep who may be unaware of your products because of your more global marketing efforts. Reach out to potential local customers to help support your local business community, raise visibility of your own company, and reduce your shipping expenses and emission output.

Increase Local Market to Increase Profits

Selling your product or services to customers in your local market can benefit you in many ways beyond just increasing sales. If you've been focusing on distant markets, reduce your shipping costs and delivery times by selling to local customers. Although sales may be smaller, you should be able to compensate for volume through reduced costs of shipping, and you are likely to establish more repeat business and stronger referrals through your local markets. At the same time, you'll be supporting your local business community by becoming more involved in the regional field.

Reduce Shelf Time

One benefit of maintaining local markets is that you can get your product off the shelves and into the hands of your customers more quickly if they're in a regionally accessible delivery zone. Moving product benefits you in terms of inventory and taxes—you've got less to store, and you won't be paying taxes on assets in inventory.

Reduce Transportation Costs

It costs less to ship within your regional zone. Whether you're providing delivery or shipping through commercial carriers, your cost to get the product to your consumer is reduced if the distance is shorter. In addition, you're reducing fuel usage and fuel emissions, which reduce your carbon footprint.

Support Local Businesses

Providing products to local businesses helps reinforce the local business market. Networking with other businesses is also likely to help expand your reach for additional sales and present opportunities for working within the community on nonprofit and sustainable initiatives. Sharing your expertise with your local business community will help increase sales and support the local economy.

As you can see, you can reduce your shipping costs and fuel emissions in many ways that will result in lessening your carbon footprint and increasing profits. As you increase your local sales market, you can also let your local community and other customers know about your commitment to the environment and your company's efforts to create a healthier planet. It's another win/win for people, the planet, and profits.

The Least You Need to Know

- There are a variety of fuel-efficient vehicle options available to your business.
- Reduce your costs by reducing your shipping fuel expenditure.
- As you reduce fuel usage, you reduce your emissions and carbon footprint.
- Switch to more fuel-efficient vehicles for your own deliveries or use fuel-conscious commercial shippers.
- Focusing more sales in local markets reduces shipping costs and increases sales.

Part 4

Your Business Practices and Cost Benefits

This part deals with sustainable practices at your place of business. In addition to creating a sustainable product and facility, you can green your office practices and employee routines. As you develop sustainable practices, it's important to record your progress so your stakeholders can learn more about your efforts and applaud your investment in going green.

We show you ways to green your team and how best to share your progress with employees, customers, and shareholders. And we help you calculate the value of going green in concrete terms that everyone can understand and use.

Chapter 15

In-House Office Systems

In This Chapter

- ◆ Save electricity and energy
- ◆ Reduce electronic waste
- ◆ Choose recycled paper products
- ◆ Recycle paper supplies
- ◆ Use nontoxic inks

Creating a sustainable building environment and product is important, but you also need to green up your office routines. By making your office more eco-friendly, you'll save money on energy used, which reduces emissions, your carbon footprint, and your supply purchases. You can also reduce the amount of waste your business sends to the landfill and reduce the toxicity of products in your office as well as in your waste stream.

In this chapter, we give you many ways to make your office more sustainable and resources for more information. If you're looking for a quick checklist, go to www.sustainableindustries.com, where you'll find a guide to the green office full of information provided by *Sustainable Industries* magazine.

Electronic Efficiency

Technology is a valuable tool for running a business, as it enhances speed, work quality, and profits. Electronics also play a key role in the green factor. An office that uses its technological gadgets responsibly enjoys substantial environmental—and financial—rewards.

How many packs of paper (and trees) do you save when you send routine office memos by e-mail? Add to that all the training manuals, job applications, and purchasing orders you can route via desktop, and you can see a mountain of paper through the forest.

Obsolete File Storage: Save to Disk

Electronics enable offices to make efficient use of square footage. You can store tons of information in digital formats rather than packed away in bulky filing cabinets. An easy-to-access electronic filing system also boosts workers' efficiency, as they can retrieve a piece of information at their keyboards rather than sorting through papers in filing cabinets.

Electronic "Paperwork"

Plenty of businesses are taking full advantage of electronics for business transactions that traditionally involve paper. By using electronic job applications, billing, and payroll, businesses can cut back on paper with relative ease.

According to the Minnesota Pollution Control Agency, Wilderness Inquiry, a nonprofit Minneapolis-based organization that provides wilderness trips, enjoys various advantages through switching to website and electronic communications for its marketing materials and registration information:

◆ For those inquiring about a trip, the information is immediately available by computer rather than via snail mail. Potential customers appreciate this convenience along with the environmental aspects.

◆ The electronic communications process is more efficient for the staff, as workers don't copy and mail as much trip information and forms.

◆ Money is saved on postal fees.

Power Down: Unplug Unused Equipment

Technology helps keep an office running smoothly, but some equipment may be running unnecessarily.

With so many documents routed by e-mail, printing and fax machines might be idle. When computers and other equipment are not being used, save energy—power them down, turn them off, or even unplug them.

"Use a power strip as a central 'turn off' point when you are done using office equipment to completely disconnect the power supply. Even when turned off, electronic and IT equipment often uses a small amount of electricity when plugged in," states the Environmental Protection Agency (EPA). "Don't forget to unplug battery chargers or power adapters when equipment is fully charged or disconnected from the charger." See Appendix B for more information.

Take advantage of the energy-saving features that automatically put computers, monitors, and other office equipment on a low-power mode when temporarily inactive. It's an effortless way to reduce energy consumption, as computers and monitors easily reactivate by simply touching the mouse or keyboard. Read the product information to set up the equipment to your desired specifications. The more energy a business saves, the more that business is doing to protect the planet.

> **Enviro-Fact**
>
> The Alliance to Save Energy reported that companies could have saved up to $46 million over the three-day July 4th holiday in 2008—if they would have turned off their computers. If the estimated 104 million workers using personal computers at work left the machines on during the holiday weekend, they would have generated enough electricity to emit 474 million pounds of carbon dioxide (CO_2).

Screen savers are not intended to save energy, and they don't. According to the EPA, graphics-intensive screen savers might require twice as much energy as computers not using screen savers. Also the screen saver might prevent a computer from entering the power-saving sleep mode.

"Power management has the potential to save up to $50 per computer annually," states the EPA. "If all office computers and monitors in the United States were set to sleep when not being used, the country could save more than 44 billion kWh or $4 billion worth of electricity and avoid the greenhouse gas emissions equivalent to those of about 5 million cars each year."

Various types of power management features are available. The EPA provides the following tips for making Microsoft Windows programs more efficient (note that these apply to personal computers using Windows):

♦ System standby—Drops monitor and computer power use to 1 to 3 watts each, wakes in seconds, and saves $25 to $75 per computer a year.

♦ System hibernates—Drops monitor and computer power use to 1 to 3 watts each, wakes in 20 or more seconds, saves work in the event of power outage, and saves $25 to $75 per computer a year.

♦ Turn off monitor—Drops monitor power use to 1 to 3 watts, wakes speedily, and saves about $10 to $40 a year.

EPA's advice is to set computers to enter system standby or hibernate after 30 to 60 minutes of inactivity. Save more by setting monitors to sleep after 5 to 20 minutes of inactivity. "The lower the setting, the more energy you save," the EPA states.

For more information, see www.energystar.gov/index.cfm?c=power_mgt.pr_power_mgt_faq.

Greener Electronics

Not all electronic products are equal—at least from an environmental standpoint. Think green when evaluating the array of items on the market.

Purchasing and Manufacturing Processes

Purchase products equipped with energy-saving features. If practical, consider buying electronic equipment that's made with recycled materials.

> **Enviro-Fact**
>
> According to the EPA, businesses that use office equipment with Energy Star qualifications may benefit from additional savings on air conditioning and maintenance. The efficient designs often run cooler and enhance durability.

A useful tool for selecting greener electronics is the Energy Star program, a part of the EPA. Products earn the Energy Star designation by using 30 to 75 percent less energy than standard counterparts.

Green America, which provides a green office resource page on their site (see Appendix B), reports the EPA calculates that a home office outfitted exclusively with Energy Star equipment (computer, monitor, printer, and fax) can save enough electricity to light the entire home for more than four years. You can achieve similar results at your place of business.

Another resource for businesses interested in greening their office functions is Earth 911, an organization that promotes recycling and other facets of sustainability. Some points they offer on their website regarding electronic equipment are:

◆ Laptops use less energy than desktop computers.

◆ Ink jet printers use less energy than laser printers.

Update Equipment

Update your computer equipment, but do so wisely. Before going off to order something technologically fresh and new, consider accessories and maintenance programs that would refurbish and tune up existing equipment. Weigh the advantages of acquiring updated, more efficient equipment against the expense and the environmental facets of discarding old equipment.

When replacing machinery, order only necessary items. Some existing older accessories, such as cables, the mouse, and keyboards, might be perfectly fine to use with new equipment, suggests Earth 911.

Before you ditch the old computer because it's just moving too slowly, try a software cleaning program to bring back the speed and perfection. Large Software is a company that provides a software program called PC Tune-Up that helps clean up your existing system and restore it to sleek functionality (see Appendix B).

Managing E-Waste

With so many tempting gadgets on the market, electronic equipment tends to be something we regard as outdated and obsolete. However, it's not something to toss casually into the trash. Every piece of electronic equipment represents a wealth of natural resources, most of which continue to be useful even after the machine becomes functionally obsolete.

A United Nations University publication, *Computers and the Environment* (2004), says it takes 530 pounds of fossil fuels, 50 pounds of chemicals, and 3,300 pounds of water—a total of 1.8 tons—to make a desktop computer and monitor. In 2005, Americans sent an estimated 1.5 million tons of electronics to our landfills. That is a complete waste of useful resources! And chemical contamination concerns also exist because electronic gadgets may contain potentially hazardous materials. The Basel Action Network (BAN), a Seattle-based nonprofit that works to reduce the spread of toxic trash, says there are 500 million computers in the world containing 6.32 billion pounds of plastic, 1.58 billion pounds of lead, and 632,000 pounds of mercury. BAN reports that 70 percent of heavy metals in U.S. landfills come from electronics.

Going Green

Apple has just introduced a notebook computer that it hails as the greenest notebook ever made. The new MacBook uses recyclable materials without many of the toxic substances typically used in computers. The machine is designed to maximize energy efficiency by coordinating software and hardware, and packaging for the notebook has been reduced. For more information, see www.apple.com/mac/green-notebooks/.

The ecologically preferable approach to disposing of unwanted equipment is to put it to good use elsewhere—perhaps a local school, business, or organization. Use online classified services and web-based trading organizations such as www.freecycle.com to determine if there's a potential taker.

If you can't easily put the machinery to another use, recycle it responsibly through a qualified recycling service. Sort out and reuse some parts, such as copper and plastic components, in other equipment. Earth 911 states, "E-waste should not be considered waste. It is a resource. Useful materials such as glass, copper, aluminum, plastic, and other components can often be extracted and reused. Some manufacturers have even referred to e-waste as a valuable source of materials."

Various manufacturers and some retail merchants offer take-back programs. When you buy new electronics, find out how the manufacturer and retailer can help you recycle the equipment when you're done with it.

Many local government agencies provide programs especially geared to collect unwanted electronics along with other potentially hazardous disposables. To determine what programs and services are available in your area, log on to Earth911.org, which provides information on recycling and reuse services based on geographic location. The EPA also provides a listing of places that will recycle your electronics (see Appendix B).

Reduce Paper

Reducing paper use is an obvious way to cut down on waste, and part of accomplishing this task is pleasantly simple. Think. Think before you reach for a fresh sheet of paper to jot down a phone number. Instead, flip over paper you'd throw into the recycling bin.

When reading a document, think before you press the "print" button. Maybe you only need a section of that 10-page report, or perhaps you don't need any of it.

When workers start thinking about paper, the "use less" approach becomes automatic. Why bother with a separate cover sheet for a fax when the "to" and "from" information fits nicely on the first page?

> **Enviro-Fact**
>
> The Minnesota Pollution Control Agency reports that Americans throw away enough office paper each year to build a 12-foot-high wall stretching from New York to San Francisco—that's 10,000 or so sheets per person.

The Minnesota Pollution Control Agency agrees that attitude is key to reducing paper. "Promote a 'think before you copy' approach. Are you really going to re-read that report? Consider sharing some documents with co-workers. Print only the number of copies needed for the meeting; don't make extras."

California acknowledges paper-reduction achievements as part of its Waste Reduction Awards Program (WRAP), sponsored by the state's Integrated Waste Management Board. One WRAP winner is F&F Multiprint, a print and graphic design business in Yolo County.

According to the awards information, F&F Multiprint invites consumers to bring in their single-sided paper waste to be made into scratch pads at no charge. F&F Multiprint also saves on paper with a proofing system that enables clients to approve designs online.

Use Recycled Paper

The "recycled content" symbol is hot among green-minded folks and is featured on many paper products, including general white office paper, colored paper, envelopes, file folders, business cards, and gift certificates.

The amount of recycled content ranges from 30 to 100 percent. Another factor is type of recycled content—either pre-consumer or post-consumer waste. Environmental advocates generally prefer post-consumer waste because it's reusing products consumers previously used and recycled.

> **Enviro-Fact**
>
> If your company indulges customers with holiday greetings or thank-you notes, consider using recycled card stock for them, or better yet, send electronic greeting cards.

The Green Office (www.thegreenoffice.com) in San Francisco says that prices for 100 percent post-consumer recycled paper may be about 10 to 20 percent more than the cost for a comparable product made without any recycled material, but that's easily compensated for by using techniques to reduce the amount of paper used.

In addition to papers made from 100 percent post-consumer waste, the assortment available at The Green Office includes some tree-free papers featuring fibers made from byproducts of harvesting coffee and produce, including mango and lemons.

CD sleeves and other office supplies can be made with recycled materials.

(Courtesy Sustainable Group)

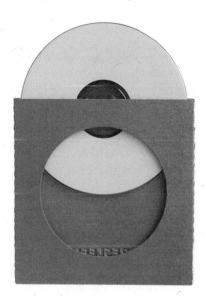

Print on Both Sides

Paper generally offers two sides, but plenty of workers habitually grab a blank sheet for each task. Tossing away paper that's only been partially used is tossing away valuable resources. Using paper to its fullest potential saves money, preserves forests, and reduces pollution associated with paper production and distribution.

Make a point of using both sides of all paper in the office. When purchasing copiers and printers, choose a product that offers double-sided features and set up the machines to print on both sides.

Keep a collection bin near printers and fax machines to gather discards with one clean side. Then put that clean side to use. For example, grab a stack of sheets, cut them into squares, assemble squares into a pile with the clean side facing up, and staple. Now you have a handy scratch pad for jotting down phone numbers or notes.

Recycle Waste Paper

Set up a recycling program and make it easy and convenient for the staff to comply. Designate a recycling coordinator or a team to guide the project. Earth 911 suggests someone who volunteers and is enthusiastic would be a good leader.

Work with local recycling providers to determine which types of papers and cardboards they accept and whether they need to be sorted. When speaking with the recycling service, based on guidelines from the Paper Industry Association Council, ask these questions:

- ◆ What are the potential costs and benefits of recycling?

- ◆ Will a decrease in the amount of material going to disposal help cover the costs of recycling?

- ◆ Which materials can be recycled most cost effectively?

- ◆ What grades of paper do you handle, and what is the minimum amount required for pickup?

- ◆ How will material be collected? What are the common contaminants for each material? Will we be notified if material is not accepted because of contamination?

- ◆ Will we receive updates on the quality and quantity of materials collected?

- ◆ Will additional containers or other equipment be required for the collection of recyclables?

> **Enviro-Fact**
>
> According to the American Forest and Paper Association, the amount of paper and paperboard products recovered for recycling in the United States in 2007 amounts to almost 360 pounds for each man, woman, and child in the nation.

With a recycling program in place, set up receptacles at appropriate locations. Some businesses, including Sustainable Group, provide a recycling bin at each work station.

Bins don't need to be fancy. Old cardboard cartons recycled from office packages work just fine. Label each appropriately, and specify what types of paper are allowed and what types are not.

Promoting the program also is important. Discuss the guidelines with the staff and encourage everyone to participate.

Going Green _____

Make a personalized recycling poster using this online template: www.paperrecycles. org/workplace_recycling/ dynamicposter/index.html.

Monitor the effort and applaud the staff; keep track of how much you recycle, and calculate the money saved from reduced purchases, energy saved, and emissions reduced. Showcase the achievements. Your green-minded customers and business associates are going to appreciate your effort. And you may inspire others to take on similar projects.

Various environmental organizations and government agencies offer recognition for noteworthy recycling endeavors, among them The American Forest and Paper Association. This organization holds an annual competition for businesses, individuals, and schools to showcase their outstanding programs for recycling high-quality paper. For information on that event, log on to www.paperrecycles.org.

Enviro-Fact

According to the Paper Industry Association Council, the following are ways that different paper products can be recycled:

- Newspapers can be recycled into newsprint, egg cartons, and paperboard.
- Used corrugated boxes can be recycled into new boxes or paperboard.
- High-grade white office paper can be recycled into almost any new paper product, including tissue.

Reduce Toxics

Greening your office includes reducing the exposure of your staff and the environment to toxic chemicals. Paper bleached white is often made with chlorine, a process that pollutes our waterways, and inks are often made with toxic chemicals.

Chlorine-Free Paper

The emphasis on green approaches to manufacturing includes reducing chlorine in the paper-making process. By selecting and purchasing papers designated as chlorine-free, businesses are boosting demand.

The Green Office reports that its most popular green office paper is a version that's 100 percent post-consumer waste that's recycled and chlorine-free. According to Alex Szabo, CEO and Founder of the business, the quality and durability of recycled paper matches that of paper made entirely from virgin wood and processed with chlorine.

The paper processed with chlorine may be slightly brighter, but this is the only notable difference. As we understand the importance of reducing chlorine pollution of our environment, getting used to unbleached paper products should be easier.

Soy-Based, Vegetable-Based, and Water-Based Inks

When ordering professionally printed documents or packaging, ask about the types of inks available. The global emphasis on eco-friendly business practices is prompting professional printers to work with products that are healthier for the planet, according to representatives of the National Association of Printing Ink Manufacturers (NAPIM).

Depending on the type of project and printing process, you might substitute a water-based ink or vegetable-based ink for a less eco-friendly petroleum-based ink. The water-based inks and inks made with vegetable oils (such as soy, linseed, and sunflower) use sustainable resources and emit fewer volatile organic compounds (VOCs), according to the NAPIM.

The Least You Need to Know

- Skip paper when it's practical. Instead, create electronic documents and send memos by e-mail.

- Office electronics and paper products create huge amounts of waste. Reduce your waste by reducing your paper usage.

- Electronic equipment contributes toxic chemicals to landfills. Make your electronics last longer and dispose of them properly to avoid contaminating landfills.

- Choosing environmentally friendly paper supplies can help reduce the pollution in our waterways from bleached paper.

- Recycle office supplies to reduce expense and reduce your business's contribution to toxic pollution.

Chapter 16

Greening the Commute and the Workweek

In This Chapter

- ◆ Mass transit
- ◆ Commuting
- ◆ Reducing travel needs
- ◆ Trading expenses and emissions for profit

At your place of business, you can make daily life more sustainable in several ways. By cutting back office or manufacturing facility hours, reducing transportation costs, and developing creative ways to conserve and save, you'll save money as well as help the planet.

Support Mass Transit

Some companies encourage employees to move closer to work by providing incentives, including down payment assistance, location-efficient mortgages, and rent subsidies. Locating your business in an urban center with easy access to mass transit options such as subways, buses, or rapid light transit systems is also good since mass transit is much more efficient in energy use.

Many businesses encourage employees to utilize these systems with incentives such as free tickets, cash rebates, and scheduling that complements transit opportunities.

Enviro-Fact

The American Public Transportation Association (APTA) estimates that by reducing vehicle travel miles, public transportation can reduce harmful carbon dioxide (CO_2) emissions by 37 million metric tons a year. The APTA states that a single person commuting a 20-mile roundtrip alone by car can reduce his personal CO_2 emission by 4,800 pounds per year by switching to public transportation. This results in a 10 percent reduction for an average two-adult, two-car household. Swapping one car for public transport can save up to 30 percent of CO_2 emissions.

Provide Public Transport Stipends

The APTA reports that the Transportation Equity Act for the 21st Century (TEA-21), a federal law amended in 1998, provides tax-free benefits for employers and employees who take advantage of public transportation or van pooling options. Employers can provide up to $115 (as of January 2008) in monthly stipends or cash back to employees who choose this mode of transport. Employers can deduct the cost from their taxes and don't have to pay payroll taxes on the stipend. In addition, employees don't have to pay income tax on this benefit. The APTA cites several additional benefits: no parking or gas expense; reduced emissions and pollution in the community; reduced traffic congestion; and a relaxing commute where riders can rest, read, or do paper-work instead of facing a stressful drive during rush hour.

All federal government employees in the Washington, D.C., metro area are eligible for this benefit, and employees of many federal agencies around the country are, too. The stipend tax benefit is available to private businesses and nonprofits as well as government agencies; however, self-employed individuals, sole proprietors, and independent contractors are not eligible.

Help Employees Green Their Commute

Commuter Choice is an organization that provides information for businesses interested in setting up a commuter program or incentive system for employees, including information on options available around the country. In its list of benefits, Commuter Choice estimates that providing such tax-deductible benefits in the form of transit credits or incentives can even be less expensive for employers than giving a cash raise because of the tax incentives to both employer and employee. For contacts and more information on benefits, see Appendix B.

This example comes from www.commuterchoice.com:

A company gives an annual raise of $780:

- ◆ Cost to business: $840 (salary plus FICA)
- ◆ Actual salary increase: $455 (salary minus income and FICA taxes)

The company gives a $780 Commuter Choice benefit instead:

- ◆ Cost to business: $470 (benefit minus corporate tax deductions)
- ◆ Actual salary increase: $780 (tax-free benefit)

Carpooling

Clif Bar, a privately-owned company with about 200 employees based in Berkeley, California, implemented a program called Cool Commute to encourage employees to make eco-friendly transit choices. Employees earn points if they carpool, walk, bike, or take public transportation to work. They can then trade these points for public transit vouchers or gift cards to eco-friendly stores such as Whole Foods. Employees can also choose to apply their points to support environmental causes or to buy carbon offsets.

Several existing electronic carpool matching programs are available to businesses and individuals. Most are free, and some provide additional services to business participants. Here are a few; you can easily find more with an Internet search for carpooling:

- ◆ RideSearch.com is a free service that helps match up people interested in carpooling nationwide. The site offers tips on finding suitable carpool partners and incentives for businesses implementing the program.

- ◆ Avego.com is a new carpooling connection service that's based on emerging technologies. Riders and drivers can connect on a nearly immediate basis using their computers and mobile phones. Riders help pay for the expense of the trip, 15 percent of which goes to Avego, and drivers enjoy the reduced cost for their commute. The company, which has offices in the United States and Europe, wants to reduce cars on the road by increasing shared rides.

- Carpoolconnect.com provides an instant, free Internet resource for finding rides going your way. Just enter your location and your destination to find out if anyone has signed on with similar travel plans.

- Carpoolworld.com matches drivers and riders worldwide for free, also using the Internet. The company, started in 2000, claims the fastest, most precise trip matching possible.

- Dividetheride.com matches carpoolers for business and kid pick-ups, helping families cut costs and reduce emissions.

- eRideShare.com has served more than 1 million carpoolers since its advent in 1999. They offer special features for employers who set up the free service for employees.

- Zimride.com is another carpool service that utilizes Internet technology to connect drivers with riders. They can even be found on Facebook.com.

Another popular way to cut down on driving expense and emissions is to use cars on a temporary basis instead of owning one. This way, drivers have the convenience of a car when they really need it.

Zipcar is a member-based organization with cars in selected cities. It is similar to car rental agencies, except they have conveniently located cars around the country that you can access with their pre-programmed plastic membership card. If you need a car for a trip, you check their website to locate the nearest car, reserve it, pick it up, and go. The card unlocks the car and starts the ignition. Zipcar says each car in their international fleet has the potential to take 15 cars off the road and that users save an average of $5,000 per year. The agency also has a special program for businesses, Z2B, which offers reduced rates to business customers (see Appendix B).

For a quick ride, you might choose a hybrid taxi service. Yellow cabs in New York City are converting to hybrid vehicles, and OzoCar in New York City and the northeast region provides an all-hybrid fleet of Toyota Prius and Lexus cars plus free wireless; they even include a laptop in the backseat for your use. PlanetTran provides similar hybrid car services in the greater Boston area and San Francisco. It also provides corporate discounts, specialized accounting services, and environmental impact analysis assistance. For contact information, see Appendix B.

Cash Incentives for Employee Bicycles and Hybrid Cars

Many companies are providing incentives to employees to switch to hybrid vehicles, according to www.hybridcars.com. Clif Bar rewards its employees with a $5,000 bonus if they buy hybrid cars or use 100 percent biodiesel (B100) fuel for their cars. Software firm Hyperion also offers $5,000 to employees who make the switch, part of a $1 million company-wide incentive program. Bank of America offers a similar $3,000 incentive to employees. Google also awards $5,000 to employees who buy qualified high-efficiency vehicles and a $2,500 contribution toward leased vehicles. Timberland offers a $3,000 bonus to long-term employees who purchase hybrid cars, and Patagonia offers $2,000 or helps employees retrofit their diesel vehicles to use biodiesel.

Parking Incentives for Hybrid Cars

Many companies, organizations, cities, and states offer incentives such as free parking, use of high-occupancy vehicle (HOV) lanes, and rebates to those who buy and use hybrid and alternative fuel vehicles. A few examples:

- The University of Miami rewards its faculty and students by issuing half-price parking passes to those who use hybrid vehicles on campus.

- The state of Maryland offers discounted parking at city garages for hybrid owners.

- Salt Lake City offers free metered parking to alternative fuel vehicles.

For an updated list of regional incentives, visit www.hybridcars.com.

Remote Employees

Do you really need to have all your staff under your nose every day using lights and computers, taking up space, and requiring heating/cooling expenses? It might be worthwhile to consider allowing staff to work from home or remote locations some of the time.

Telecommuting Full Time or Part Time

Employees who work on a computer are in an excellent position to work from home a day or so a week or even all the time. Some employees thrive on the group atmosphere of being at work, and others work best under supervision. However, some people are self-directed or self-disciplined enough to get the work done on their own and can realize many personal benefits from the telecommuting arrangement. Employees save time by losing the daily commute, which of course means saving money on fuel and eliminating emissions. They save money on work clothes and meals away from home during the workday, too. Your company might want to experiment with telecommuting as an option for the right people and the right jobs.

Reduced Costs = Increased Profits

Consider that having employees work from home could reduce your costs of running an office, which means saving money on electricity and reducing emissions. Reduced costs mean added savings and increased profits.

Sales and Meeting Travel Offsets

If you can reduce your company's travel needs, you can reduce your travel costs. Try mixing the following techniques for reducing business travel to find a combination that serves your business well. If making a trip is unavoidable, you can still find ways to reduce the energy and emission costs by choosing greener travel options.

Promote Efficient Business Travel

In addition to the daily commute to work, businesses can also make an impact on their environmental footprint by taking a look at business-related travel. Business trips for meetings, conferences, and presentations can represent a significant expenditure of time, money, energy, and emissions. Finding ways to green up business travel is beneficial to the planet as well as to your bottom line.

Reduce Business Travel

Begin by taking a closer look at individual trips, and consider whether sending staff to distant locales is really necessary. Measure the cost benefit of potential sales and networking using actual sales results from similar previous trips against the cost of making the trip; don't forget to factor in the environmental costs of energy and emissions expended. You might be able to reduce your carbon footprint—and your travel expense—simply by being more judicious about the value of the trip. Perhaps you can connect with your colleagues and customers in other ways besides actual face-to-face contact—at least sometimes.

Teleconferencing Instead of Fly-In Meetings

Teleconferencing has become increasingly popular and effective with the advent of the Internet. I'm a member of a nonprofit organization, the American Society of Journalists and Authors, which has members throughout the country. Our 12-member board meets monthly via phone. Our executive director sends us dialing instructions and a code, which enables us all to join a party line for our two-hour meeting. We meet in person just twice each year at an expense of about $10,000 for the organization, which covers our flights and lodging for the trips.

Some such services are free and provide a toll-free number for user access, others charge a fee for enhanced services (such as recording), and some require a long-distance charge to individual callers. We use our voice over Internet protocol (VOIP) phones (such as Vonage or Skype) or cell phones to reduce the cost—because most of us have unlimited minute plans with these providers, we don't have to pay anything extra for a two-hour call. There are even free and low-cost video conferencing services available that are easy to use. Teleconferencing is much more cost-effective for our small nonprofit than meeting in person and serves our needs perfectly well. It could be just as much a cost-saver for your business as well. Of course, when you're not traveling, you're also saving energy and reducing emissions, so chalk up another one for your sustainability plans.

The following are some teleconference providers:

◆ FreeConference.com offers basic services for free plus a selection of premium services, such as toll-free dial-in.

◆ Go To Meeting is a web conferencing service that makes meeting online easy.

◆ Ready Talk is a web-based conference service that delivers audio and web meeting services.

◆ Office Depot offers conference calling for a monthly or per-minute fee, including toll-free access and web-based services so conferees can review web-based material during the call.

◆ Live Office Teleconferencing offers several services, including recording and website access for a per-minute fee.

Purchasing Travel Offsets

For those events that do require your presence or the presence of your staff at an out-of-town event, improve your sustainability by purchasing travel offsets to help counterbalance the emissions produced by the trip. Companies like NativeEnergy provide calculators to help you determine the energy and emission cost of your trip. You then pay them an amount of money determined by their calculator, which they invest in alternative energy research and providers to produce the same amount of energy without emissions. In this way, the energy you're using today can help build the alternative energy infrastructure that will provide a better solution in the future.

NativeEnergy helps support wind farms and methane digesters, which provide clean electricity with no carbon emissions. It works with businesses large and small to develop customized offset programs for their businesses and travel needs that help companies reduce their carbon footprint and become more sustainable. Find the NativeEnergy travel calculator and contact information in Appendix B.

Sustainable Travel Choices

As with your other business partnerships, if you can work with companies who have made a commitment to improve their sustainability, you can help improve your own sustainability as well. Virgin Airlines has proven to be a leader in finding ways to reduce the heavy carbon footprint of not just its own planes but for air travel across the board as well. Working as a sustainable business, the company applies many familiar principles to its operations, such as becoming paperless and serving Fair Trade teas and coffees. The airline posts its 29-step plan for sustainability online.

Virgin is working with Boeing to develop more sustainable airplanes. Company owner Richard Branson has pledged to invest in the development of biofuels or alternative fuels that will work in planes, and his company has proven that planes can run on such fuels with a demonstration flight in February 2008. Branson also ponied up a $25 million incentive prize to the person or firm who can develop technology to remove greenhouse gases from the atmosphere. Announced in February 2007, the contest closes in February 2010. See Appendix B for contact information for Virgin Airlines and the Virgin Earth Project.

Continental Airlines was the first North American airline to use biofuel in March 2008. Continental, like many other airlines, works to conserve fuel with slower flights and helps customers offset their travel emissions online. Continental reports that it has reduced its CO_2 emissions by 35 percent in the past decade and other greenhouse gases by as much as 75 percent. Also like many airlines, the company practices recycling with its in-flight service.

When planning your next business trip, check to see whether the carrier you're considering is making strides toward sustainability by going to its website and asking questions about emissions, offsets, fuel, and other sustainability issues.

Although train travel is not as accessible or as attractive in the United States as it has been in Europe for more than a century, it is gaining a bit in popularity as gas prices rise. At the same time, railway operators are greening up their lines by improving pollutant emissions with the use of new, cleaner diesel fuel and biodiesel. If you can afford the extra time to travel by train, you might consider it as a way to reduce the emissions and energy costs of your travel.

If you're planning to rent a car for travel, ask if a hybrid vehicle is available. Many companies do provide at least a few for their fleet, and you'll save money on gas while reducing the emissions.

Also if you or your company has joined Zipcar, you might find that using the Zipcar option at your destination is preferable to renting a car.

After you've reached your destination, consider staying in a green hotel to help support other businesses making a difference to the planet and to reduce your own travel footprint. Many hotel chains are adopting greener policies, such as increasing recycling, using energy-efficient heating and cooling systems, dispensing soaps in bulk instead of single-use disposable bottles, and implementing the linen reuse program, which is saving thousands of gallons of water and reducing the energy needed to dry loads of towels daily by an estimated 5 percent. See Appendix B for help finding green hotels.

Tinkering with Time Clocks

Another way to reduce the carbon footprint of your business through workday routines is to adjust the schedule to reduce energy usage. If you can't put the whole force to work at home, maybe you can juggle workdays.

Flextime

Flextime allows employees to adjust their time at the office to accommodate their schedules, their families, and their commute. Being flexible with the time clock gives employees the chance to bypass rush hour by arriving and leaving work earlier or later in the day. By staying off the road during the most congested hours, they can reduce their commute time and be available to their children before and after school.

Four-Day Workweek

In 2008, many cities and companies began switching to a four-day workweek and closing the office one day a week. Utah became the first state to move to a mandatory four-day workweek for its 17,000 state employees in August 2008. The result saves energy used by the offices with attendant reduced emissions, a reduction of fuel and emissions spent getting employees to work, and a reduction of traffic congestion and pollution. Utah projects a savings of $3 million in utility costs in its first year.

Many four-day programs involve 10-hour workdays which some employees and businesses appreciate but others find difficult because they can be tiring and disruptive to family life. Some professions can suffer from tired technicians whose skills can be compromised by the extension of the workday, so the move may not be appropriate for certain jobs where safety for workers or customers is a risk.

Other companies, such as Green America, are moving instead to a four-day, 32-hour workweek, thus avoiding the exhaustion factor and day-care difficulties for employees. Proponents of this plan point to several benefits. It reduces absenteeism, increases productivity, and increases employee satisfaction, thus reducing staff turnover.

Aaron Newton, author of *A Nation of Farmers: Defeating the Food Crisis on American Soil* (New Society Publishers, 2009) and a sustainable land use planner, makes a strong case for moving toward a shorter workweek: "The idea of a 40 hour workweek (5 days × 8 hours) is based on nothing more than an idea put forth by the federal government almost 70 years ago. This was certainly an improvement in the lives of many Americans who were at the time forced to work 10-plus hours a day, sometimes 6 days of the week, but today it's time for another change to a shorter workweek."

Increase Family Time

Those who are unable to get their work done during the shortened week have the option of using their three-day weekend to catch up. But one of the greatest benefits is the added time employees have for themselves and their families. More time to relax bolsters creativity and helps parents provide personal care for their children.

The Least You Need to Know

◆ You and your employees can save money by adopting more efficient means of traveling to and from work and on business trips.

◆ There are resources to help your company develop the best plans for commuting.

◆ Helping employees implement your sustainability goals as part of their work life produces great benefits for you and your staff.

◆ Some green innovations in the workweek can save substantial amounts of money and energy and also give employees more free time for their families.

Chapter 17

Employee Issues

In This Chapter

- ◆ Improve employee relations
- ◆ Promote healthy food choices
- ◆ Provide incentives for preventive health
- ◆ Enhance employees' lifestyles

In creating a sustainable business, you must involve employees in the process. Employee satisfaction, productivity, and engagement are important values you must incorporate into the overall plan. Creating a sustainable corporate culture means enriching employees' lives through better health and wellness as well as providing a meaningful work experience that engages their intelligence, creativity, and critical thinking skills. Creating a more fulfilling workplace benefits your company as well as your employees. Engaging employees to help achieve your plans for a sustainable business gives them a sense of ownership of the idea, the process, and your company's success.

Employee Relations

Building relationships with your employees beyond the traditional employer-employee status keeps employees happy, productive, and committed to your organization. It takes an entire team to make a business successful! Engage employees in issues that speak to them and relate to their values, and tie this back to your organization so your employees feel a sense of belonging.

All Business (www.allbusiness.com), a resource for business owners and managers, provides 10 tips for building relationship capital with your employees:

1. Preach trust, and be worthy of employees' trust.

2. Treat your employees with respect.

3. Periodically admit your weaknesses.

4. Keep your promises.

5. Support your team.

6. Lead with your heart.

7. Create growth opportunities for your employees.

8. Don't just act interested, be interested.

9. Say thank you.

10. Be an open communicator.

Clif Bar is a company that takes great pride in its employees and takes advantage of its independence to customize work life for owners and employees. When owners invited employees to tell them the kinds of benefits they'd like to have, they created a friendly workplace.

Employees can participate in a 401(k), join a tuition reimbursement program, get help buying a first home, and receive incentives to choose eco-friendly transportation. They can create flexible schedules, enjoy a vacation for the winter holidays when the company closes from December 25 to January 1 each year, and earn a paid sabbatical leave of six weeks every seven years.

Providing benefits like these that go beyond traditional work perks supports a company's sustainability goals and engages employees in sustainable lifestyles. It also supports the employees' access to more rewarding lifestyles, which helps attract valuable candidates for employment and keep them on the job.

Build Green Values into Corporate Culture

Building your green vision and values into your corporate culture is vital to the success of any green or sustainability program (see Chapter 3). So think of creative ways to engage all your employees by educating them on the vision, values, and goals you have developed. Get employees excited about your new green initiatives through trainings and workshops or activities and contests. Inviting everyone to feel a personal connection with the overall organization's green vision, values, and goals is the only way employees will care enough to make your sustainability program a success.

Heather once worked with an organization whose goal was to increase its waste diversion rates. To get people to change their everyday habits of throwing their soda cans, paper, and food scraps into the same bin, she needed to think of a creative way to engage all employees. She encouraged the use of new recycling and compost bins scattered around the office by developing a contest between departments. After conducting a general training session educating everyone on the new waste system, she tracked the diversion rates of each department. At the end of the week, the winning department received an incentive for their hard work. As a result, employees kept up their newly formed recycling and composting habits, and the organization met their increased waste diversion goal. Without engaging employees and building the green value of eco-friendly disposal, the program would not have been a success.

Helping employees incorporate their values of sustainability into their own lives is an important part of creating a sustainable business, and it's attractive to potential employees who want their work to be a meaningful contribution to society and to their lives. For the company, it's a great way to build a strong staff that's committed to shared goals of creating a more sustainable business and product.

Going Green

Clif Bar supports employee involvement in community service by working with several nonprofit organizations and encouraging employees to volunteer on company time. Staff members maintain a community garden; deliver meals to homebound elderly; collect food, clothing, and goods for local food banks, shelters, and families in need; and raise funds for disadvantaged youth. A contingent of Clif Bar staff made the trip to New Orleans to help rebuild homes with Habitat for Humanity. In 2007, 92 percent of Clif Bar employees participated in these community service programs, donating an average of 22 hours each year.

Support Employee Creativity

Inviting staff to help make your business greener connects them to your cause and multiplies your supply of brainpower. Helping employees think greener can spark their creativity and unleash a wealth of good ideas, which is the foundation on which we're all building as we forge new and better ways to conduct business and our lives in better harmony with the earth.

Supporting employee creativity fuels innovation, which can make or break an organization. These days, "business as usual" is becoming a fading mantra replaced by words such as "innovation," "efficiency," and "cutting edge." Your employees will deliver cutting-edge ideas and technologies only if you create an environment that spawns creativity and thought exchange among them.

In his article in *Innovative Edge*, "Six Steps for Encouraging Employee Creativity," company president Jeffery Govendo points out the following ways to actively support creative thinking and innovation.

1. Create a safe haven for new thinking. Encourage employees to share new ideas.

2. Employ a process for developing new ideas that have been offered. Make it possible for new ideas to evolve into innovations.

3. Cross-pollinate ideation groups. Generate discussion of new ideas among experts and employees.

4. Have a neutral facilitator conduct ideation sessions. A facilitator will help keep new ideas alive during the process of evaluating them and putting them into action if warranted.

5. Support employees for engaging in the process. Encourage creative brainstorming by allowing time for discussion of new ideas and development of implementation plans.

6. Assure follow-through. If new ideas are deemed worthy of pursuit, help employees make a plan to explore possibilities.

Clif Bar challenged staff in conservation efforts by conducting a company contest to see how employees could find ways to conserve energy and water and reduce waste. Creating a dialogue and forum for creative thought—in this case for the issue of energy, water, and waste reduction—allowed employees to develop innovative strategies for tackling the problems set forth. Engaging employees brings out their best ideas and gets them involved in company-wide initiatives, which they carry into their home lives and share with friends.

Rewarding Employees

Making employees feel valued through rewards helps keep them loyal to your organization and encourages them to give 110 percent when coming to work each day. And you don't have to break the bank in rewarding employees. There are plenty of cost-effective ways to make your employees feel valued, wanted, and inspired to keep up the good work.

Simple gestures, such as sending a handwritten note (on eco-friendly paper, of course) or offering to buy a cup of coffee, go a long way. Providing priority parking that rotates between hardworking employees is another great way to boost morale.

Another great way to reward employees is to encourage the use of flextime (see Chapter 16). Offering employees flexible work hours allows them to maintain balance between their personal and professional lives. The less an employee worries if she will be reprimanded for taking time off to visit the eye doctor or pick up her sick child from day care, the more productive she will be. This perk also builds a relationship between employees and supervisors as they communicate about schedules and trust each other to accomplish the week's work.

Working from home can be a welcome reward for any employee, especially those who are accustomed to braving the rush-hour commutes. It's also a great way to incorporate sustainability into your organization by reducing your employee's commute carbon footprint.

Reward effort as well as success. Not every idea is going to produce award-winning results, but you still want to encourage employees to generate those ideas. Without a few failed ideas, you might never reach the one that positions your organization for continued success.

Clif Bar, who provides incentives to employees who choose alternative vehicles or use mass transit, also provides on-site services to make life easier for staff, including laundry facilities, a hair salon, and a car-washing service. Taking care of these mundane domestic chores while at work means more time to relax at home. In most cases, there is no additional expense to the company—it's just a matter of contracting with local businesses to provide these services.

Encouraging Healthy Food Choices

Healthier employees are more productive employees, and encouraging healthier food choices will reflect your sustainability values. Look into local fruit delivery services that will stock your employee kitchen with fresh, healthy, local snack options. Also consider encouraging employees to buy into a *Community Supported Agriculture* (*CSA*) program. CSA programs connect local farms directly with local consumers by offering produce subscriptions. Buyers receive a weekly or monthly basket of produce, fruit, eggs, meats, milk, flowers, or any variety of agriculture products. If you have a kitchen where employees can cook meals, consider purchasing a CSA program for your office.

def•i•ni•tion

A **Community Supported Agriculture (CSA)** program consists of a community of individuals who pledge support to a farm operation so that the farmland becomes the community's farm, with the growers and consumers providing mutual support and sharing the risks and benefits of food production. A CSA's focus is usually on a system of weekly delivery or pick-up of vegetables and fruit, but can also include dairy products and meat. The term *CSA* is mostly used in the United States, but a variety of similar production and economic subsystems are in use worldwide.

Provide Incentives to Choose Healthy Lunches and Build Community

Consider offering gift certificates to area organic restaurants and groceries as incentives for employee performance. If your company has (or volunteers with) community gardens or CSA programs, develop a contest to create exciting new meals utilizing the fresh produce and herbs from the gardens. Encourage employees to pack healthy lunches and snacks to satisfy their hunger throughout the day by providing healthy recipes in your company newsletter and on your company bulletin boards.

Organize Meals Featuring Local Organic Produce

Most offices hold employee parties or meals throughout the year to celebrate birthdays, engagements, and other milestones. Holiday parties that include food and drinks are also popular.

When holding company breakfasts, lunches, or other gatherings, include local ingredients in your meals. Using greener raw ingredients is a sure-fire way to reduce your environmental impact (see Chapter 10). In both instances, you have the added bonus of improving the health of your employees.

Clif Bar hosts a breakfast meeting each week, a low-cost organic salad bar twice a week, and fresh organic fruit and Clif products daily. Employees can purchase healthy take-out dinners at the office a few days each week to cut down on cooking time at home and to encourage healthier family meals.

Think Green for Business Meeting Meals

If you're planning a business lunch or dinner for employees or customers, consult with the caterer, restaurant, or chef to incorporate healthy food choices into the menu. Select locally grown organic produce for a memorable meal that reflects your company value of sustainability. From the type of coffee you serve (choose Fair Trade certified organic!) to the cup you serve it in, think about how your purchasing decisions reflect your values. Your clients need to see you walk your talk, and what better way to show them than to offer a delicious, holistic meal served up with local, seasonal ingredients?

Green Up the Snack Room

In your snack room, skip the traditional candy bar and soda machines filled with mass-produced, fatty, sugary snacks and drinks. Instead, provide a basket of fresh fruit and fruit juices and healthy munchies such as nuts, natural energy bars, and yogurt. Keeping employees energized and healthy on the job is good for them as well as for your company and helps maintain their productivity levels with nourishing brain foods.

Plath and Company, a builder located in San Raphael, California, encourages healthy food choices by stocking its kitchen with healthy foods, snacks, and drinks. After embarking on a sustainability program, it rid its kitchen of sugary sodas and fatty snacks and replaced bottled water with filtered water. More often than not, employees grabbed lunch from the employee kitchen and ate in the building, either at their desks or in the community room. Replacing unhealthy food brought an increase in employee energy and productivity and a feeling that their employer was looking out for them.

One organization located in Pittsburgh, Pennsylvania, chose to follow a similar path as Plath and Company. Because they didn't have as many options for delivery of local organic fruits and vegetables to their office, they designated an employee each week to pick up office food during a trip to the grocery store. The only requirement was that the employee had to purchase healthy snack food. Within two months, most employees not only showed an increase in energy but also a decrease in their waistlines!

Eliminate Disposables

Replace paper plates and plastic cups in your kitchen with real dishes, cups, and silverware. Assign a rotating schedule for kitchen clean-up if you don't have janitorial service, or simply require individual users to wash their own dishes or put them in the dishwasher. When washing dishes, use an eco-friendly dishwashing soap or a dishwasher detergent that is biodegradable.

If you must use disposables, choose compostable fiber board and bioplastics made from corn, starch, and other natural materials that you can compost. If you do use compostables, be sure to actually compost your disposables. Throwing compostable containers into a garbage can destined for the landfill will not promote biodegradability.

Going Green _____

If your municipality does not offer a composting option, consider building or purchasing a worm bin for your office kitchen. You can compost food scraps (excluding meat and dairy), tea bags without staples, and coffee grinds right in your kitchen. For more information on how to make a worm bin, visit http://your.kingcounty.gov/solidwaste/composting/wormbins.asp.

Provide Recycling Receptacles

Providing visible recycling stations throughout the office encourages and reinforces the need for increased waste diversion and overall awareness of sustainability practices. Locate recycling bins for paper, plastic, and compostables in your dining area as well as throughout your facility, and do some investigative research to make sure your materials are being properly disposed of. Too often employees make the effort to sort their waste to dispose of it in an environmentally preferable manner just to have the night janitorial staff toss everything into the trash. Properly train everyone involved in your organization's waste stream on how to dispose of all waste.

Double-check with your waste management company to make sure they can compost the compostable cups, plates, and cutlery you're using. If these aren't properly disposed of, their sustainable value is invalidated, and they just add to the lost resource collection at the city dump.

Employee Health Options

In addition to a traditional health-care plan, many sustainable companies are including credits or coverage for alternative and preventive health care. Taking good care of our bodies before we get sick is much more cost-effective than treating disease when our defenses have been worn down. Gym memberships, massage, and acupuncture all maintain health and prevent illness.

You might also consider this idea for an employee perk or reward. Dow's on Ninth, a jazz club and restaurant located in Pittsburgh, Pennsylvania, provides its employees, wait staff, and kitchen staff the opportunity to receive a 15-minute chair massage at the end of a busy Friday or Saturday night. This helps keep the employees feeling fresh and allows them to work faster and harder, providing better service for Dow's guests.

Group Activities: Exercise, Yoga, Tai Chi, and Biking

Group activities increase the health of your employees, keep them mentally sharp, and build the skills necessary to engage in teamwork and collaboration, all of which are key to making a business function successfully.

KACO Solar is a carbon-neutral company that creates inverters for photovoltaic power systems. The small company, founded in 1914 and with offices in Germany and the United States today, holds morning workouts for staff, provides subsidies for gym memberships, and provides time off for employees to participate in marathons.

Clif Bar provides an onsite gym and allows daily workouts (with personal trainers) on company time. The company also offers nutrition counseling, free yoga classes, and bargain-priced massages.

Credit for Alternative Health Choices

You can incorporate all these benefits into your employee benefit plan to help improve the lifestyle of your employees. Providing credits or subsidies for alternative health care (such as massage and acupuncture) as well as incentives for preventive measures (such as increased exercise and healthier eating habits) can reduce overall health-care costs. At the same time, you'll be supporting your employees' involvement in healthier, more sustainable life practices. These kinds of innovations help draw employees to your place of business and reinforce your overall impact of sustainability.

The Least You Need to Know

◆ You increase your business sustainability when you extend it to employees and their activities.

◆ Encouraging exercise and healthy diets is a valuable benefit for employees.

◆ Healthy employees are happy employees.

◆ A strong, healthy workforce reduces turnover and increases productivity, which is good for your bottom line.

Chapter 18

Green Your Company Events

In This Chapter

- Applying environmentally sound business practices to meetings and events
- Making your meetings green
- Saving business money when making events green
- Improving your business reputation by going green

Now that you've greened up your business facility, systems, and products, it's time to carry the healthy theme through to your company events. Green meetings are increasingly popular, and for good reason: the meeting and event industry produces a lot of unnecessary waste and greenhouse gases. Meetings involve expenses for transportation and fuel to attend cross-country events, heating and cooling large spaces for hundreds or thousands of attendees, feeding participants, and dealing with waste—the biggest culprit of all. From name tags to hand-outs to disposable dinnerware and water bottles, crowds of people produce tons of trash. And it all adds up to a lot of energy.

In this chapter, we share some good ideas on how you can green your meetings—and why this is such a good idea. You may be surprised to learn that while you're saving the planet, you're saving money, too. By minimizing resources and reducing waste, you're cutting costs.

Green Meeting Possibilities

According to MeetGreen, a typical five-day event for 2,500 people will use 90,000 bottles, 75,000 paper cups, and 87,500 napkins. That translates into many tons of embodied energy used to create the products, producing tons of greenhouse gases and ending up as tons of waste in the landfills. We can do so much better, and that's what going green is all about. Although most small businesses won't be working on events of such large scale, the same practices applied here can be used for smaller events as well.

Co-Op America (now Green America) has been putting on Green Business Conferences for several years. Its 2008 event in Seattle hosted 30,000 attendees yet proved remarkably green. Only 3 percent of the waste from the two-day event went to landfills—that means 97 percent was recycled and composted. You can do this, too! Even if your event is much smaller, you can reduce waste by instituting a recycling program.

The Environmental Protection Agency (EPA) announced in May 2008 that it would give preference to facilities that minimize waste and conserve resources when selecting sites for its meetings and events. The EPA has partnered with many meeting associations and hotels to make it easier for meeting planners and meeting venues to meet green standards for efficiency.

Many cities and states are initiating similar programs in support of green businesses. For example, in Florida, Governor Charlie Crist has launched a green initiative by declaring that all government meetings must be held in green-certified facilities and meet green standards of efficiency. This kind of policy is moving us in the right direction, and it's a great example of a nonpartisan cooperative effort to lead the way and show the world how we can make the new green economy and a healthy green environment work.

Choose a Green Venue

First on your checklist in creating a green event is to choose a green venue. Choose a site that has been LEED-certified by the U.S. Green Building Council (USGBC) or that meets local green building requirements with various standards of efficiency and low impact. If you have out-of-town guests, choose green-rated hotels or those that at least offer a linen reuse program and bulk dispensers for shampoos and soaps in guest suites. The Green Meeting Industry Council reports that the linen reuse program saves tons of water, energy, oil, and cleaning products while preventing toxic bleach from getting into the environment.

Going Green _____

LEED certification is provided by the USGBC to help facilities develop more environmentally friendly buildings. While many hotels and other buildings are striving to achieve LEED certification for their facilities, many others are making strides in green innovations without meeting the stringent LEED requirements. Talk with facility managers about their green innovations to find one that applies at least some energy and efficiency measures, even if they are not LEED-certified.

These hotels have made an effort to reduce the environmental impact of meetings and events:

◆ The Green Meeting Industry Council reports that the Fairmont Sonoma Mission Inn and Spa in Sonoma, California, switched to compact fluorescent light bulbs and saved $61,000 in one year while preventing 300,000 pounds of greenhouse gases from polluting the atmosphere.

◆ The new InterContinental Hotel in San Francisco is working toward achieving LEED certification for its new facility. The newly constructed building is a testament to the possibility of being green while meeting the luxury standard expected by guests willing to pay for five-star accommodations.

◆ InterContinental Hotels are making green an initiative worldwide. In the United States, they've replaced incandescent bulbs with more than $1 million worth of compact fluorescents, saving more than $2.28 million worth of electricity annually and preventing more than 90,000 tons of carbon dioxide (CO_2) emissions, the equivalent of taking 17,416 cars off the road.

◆ The Willard InterContinental Hotel in Washington, D.C.—where Abraham Lincoln and both Presidents Roosevelt have stayed—has evolved into an environmentally friendly venue over the years. The International Hotel & Restaurant Association recognized the Willard with its Environmental Award for Hospitality Sustainability. The hotel offers sustainable food, beverages, and supplies and is 100 percent powered by wind energy. They compost organic waste, use nontoxic cleaning products, and save more than 100,000 gallons of water annually through conservation programs.

♦ The newest hotel on the InterContinental block is the Innovation Hotel in Windsor, England, which is a demonstration project of a luxury hotel employing all the green principles possible. The hotel employs solar panels to heat water and wind turbines for electricity, harvests rainwater for irrigation and to flush toilets, has a green roof garden to help insulate, uses recycled materials for windows and furnishings, and donates nonperishable leftovers to charities and food banks.

♦ Kimpton Hotels, a leader in greening its properties, has launched its "Great Meetings, Great Causes," program to help meeting planners organize green events at its facilities worldwide.

♦ Devil's Thumb Ranch in Colorado provides an environmentally friendly resort and spa designed with sustainability in mind.

For a more comprehensive listing of green hotels and meeting venues, see Appendix B.

Seek Building Efficiency

Try to find a meeting venue that recognizes green principles and has made the transition to a more energy-efficient environment. When first contacting a venue, ask if it has green policies. You might use the EPA list provided later in this chapter to develop the questions to ask and the types of innovations you're looking for. Many new buildings are studying the standards set forth by the USGBC and striving for LEED certification in new construction. Some cities are requiring that new construction meet LEED requirements. Instead of costing millions, as once feared, it's paying off.

What should you look for in building efficiency? The opportunity to unplug from the power source. Coordinate with the meeting venue to ensure that energy, lights, and air conditioning will be turned off when rooms are not in use. For example, the Seaport Hotel Boston reports saving $100,000 in one year by installing occupancy sensors in its hotel rooms. If no occupancy is detected after 14 minutes, the room air conditioning/heating system goes into sleep mode to ensure comfort and avoids wasting energy when it's not needed. Some venues are installing room key sensor systems that turn lights and air conditioning on when occupants are in the room and off when they exit.

> **Enviro-Fact**
>
> *Meetings and Conventions* reports that the Washington State Convention and Trade Center saved nearly $200,000 in 2004 by switching to energy-efficient lighting.

Request rooms with windows to maximize daylight use. Again, look for places that use automatic sensors to save energy. Use rooms that maximize daylight—natural light saves energy and creates an atmosphere more conducive to sales. The Green Meeting Industry Council says you can even increase sales by up to 40 percent with natural lighting.

Green Interiors

Look for a building that off-gases as little volatile organic compounds (VOCs), formaldehyde, and other toxic airborne particles as possible. Exposure to synthetic petrochemicals can have a numbing effect on our senses as well as cause a slight decline in our intelligence quotient over time. Some chemical components of paints, fabrics, adhesives, air fresheners, and cleaners can also trigger asthma attacks or allergic reactions. Choose places furnished with natural materials. Solid-surface floors such as tile or bamboo are preferable to carpet, although some carpet manufacturers create less-toxic flooring materials that are recyclable. Ask if they used no- or low-VOC paints, wall coverings, and furnishings in the interiors.

Clean Cleaning Agents

Nontoxic cleaning products are far less damaging to indoor air quality than traditional cleaning agents, and green laundry products are gentler on fabrics. Cindy DeRocher, manager of The Gardens Hotel in Key West, has worked to make her facility the first green lodging in Key West. She said that asking staff to avoid the use of bleach products in cleaning and laundry was challenging because of the powerful cleaning properties of bleach. Still, her facility uses nontoxic products and energy-efficient laundry machines. They have replaced complimentary soap products with bulk in-room dispensers to reduce waste and cut costs. Ask the facility you're considering whether they use green cleaning products and practices.

Convenient Location Reduces Transportation

Choose a convenient venue that's close to attendees to cut down on travel and transportation costs and energy. Make it easy for attendees to walk or carpool to events—you and your guests could save an estimated $10,000 a day in transportation costs and energy, according to Meeting Strategies Worldwide. And eliminating shuttle bus transportation and selecting hotels and meeting facilities within walking distance eliminated $30,000 to $40,000 for one three-day meeting, according to the organization.

The EPA has developed a list of items to consider when searching for a green venue:

◆ Do you have a recycling program? If so, please describe.

◆ Do you have a linen/towel reuse option that is communicated to guests?

◆ Do guests have easy access to public transportation or shuttle services at your facility?

◆ Are lights and air conditioning turned off when rooms are not in use? If so, how do you ensure this?

◆ Do you provide bulk dispensers or reusable containers for beverages, food, and condiments?

◆ Do you provide reusable serving utensils, napkins, and tablecloths when serving food and beverages?

◆ Do you have an energy efficiency program? Please describe.

◆ Do you have a water conservation program? Please describe.

◆ Does your facility provide guests with paperless check-in and check-out?

◆ Does your facility use recycled or recyclable products? Please describe.

◆ Do you source food from local growers or take into account the growing practices of farmers who provide the food? Please describe.

◆ Do you use biobased or biodegradable products, including biobased cafeteriaware? Please describe.

◆ Do you provide training to your employees on these green initiatives? Please describe.

◆ What other environmental initiatives have you undertaken, including any environment-related certifications you possess, EPA voluntary partnerships in which you participate, support of a green suppliers network, or other initiatives?

For more info, go to www.epa.gov/oppt/greenmeetings/pubs/current_init.htm.

Hazard

Be aware that since "green" is the new gold in hotel properties, some facility marketing materials may make claims that don't add up. Be sure you're well informed of the sustainability issues that concern you so you can ask the right questions to make sure the property isn't just claiming to be green.

Help in Finding Green Space

The EPA is currently developing standards for green meetings, but in the meantime, several organizations and individual meeting planners are available to help you make your events as green as they can be. The Green Meeting Industry Council and Meeting Strategies Worldwide provide ample resources to meeting planners and organizations who wish to learn more about greening their events (see Appendix B).

Firms Specialize in Connecting Venue to Client

If finding a green venue seems too difficult for your staff to tackle, several firms specialize in helping businesses and organizations find the perfect venue for events and meetings. Green consultants have recognized an increasing desire among clients for green venues and can offer a great deal of assistance in matching the perfect venue to client needs. If your staff doesn't have the time or expertise to vet green venues, find a firm that specializes in this area to help make sure you're locating your event in a genuinely green facility. See Appendix B for a list of firms specializing in placing green festivals and events.

Consultants Go Green

Spitfire Agency is dedicated to supporting businesses in moving toward a healthier global future. Founder Sarah Haynes has told listeners of the "People Speak" radio show that her mission is to have minimum impact on the planet and maximum impact on people. She has made a name for herself as the Queen of Green Meetings, applying Spitfire staff and skills to make music festivals and events as green as possible. She worked with Richard Branson and Daryl Hannah to green the Virgin Festival in 2007, a music festival held in Baltimore, Toronto, Calgary, and Vancouver each year. Biodiesel fuel and solar power–generated electricity and even stationery bikes were hooked up to run compact fluorescent light bulbs. All materials, such as plates and cups, were made from biodegradable materials, which a local service composted with a goal of producing "near zero" waste. Haynes has worked with many events worldwide to help switch to greener systems.

Haynes offers an interesting way to help consumers break their buying habits and reduce their waste: carry around your own trash for a week. Her friend, Julia Butterfly Hill, famous for living in a tree for more than a year in protest of timbering operations, challenged her to do this. Haynes says that carrying her garbage in a backpack really helped her pay attention to selecting items with less packaging and to simply resist acquiring things she didn't really need.

"The solutions exist—it's really not that hard," Haynes said in an interview on "People Speak" in August 2007. "If someone's committed to [go green], they can. It's a lot of work and a lot of time, but this is definitely something we can all handle." Seven Star, Inc. organized the Chicago Green Festival in 2006. Ten tons of waste were recycled, with just 4 percent of the festival garbage going to landfills. One secret to the success of composting and recycling was stationing volunteers and staff at recycling and compost bins to help ensure that garbage was properly disposed of.

> **Enviro-Fact**
>
> *Meetings and Conventions* reports that San Francisco's Moscone Center began a recycling and donating program that saves $500,000 a year on the cost of hauling trash.

These are just a couple examples of large organizations and consultants that have successfully found ways to reduce waste and conserve resources for meetings and events. Regardless of your company's size, if you learn from their experiences, you can apply the same techniques to your business events.

Reducing Waste Is Key

Learning to make do with less and cutting back on consumption is an important part of going green. All the stuff we move to our landfills is poisoning our air, water, and soil. Choose recycled and recyclable items for your event, such as pens, paper, and awards. Request that recycling and compost bins be placed in visible locations to avoid sending reusable resources to the trash dumpster.

Select Eco-Friendly Gifts

Every meeting planner wants to offer a gift to attendees, but often these gifts are kitschy things that fall by the wayside and into the trash soon after the event. Cut back on the cute gifts and focus more on useful, reusable, eco-friendly items that will have a more positive impact on the planet. Make sure items really are green, not just greenwashed.

Many promotional product companies specialize in eco-friendly gifts, but always make certain the gift meets green standards. Ask about the areas your firm has considered to make your business green: Will gift recipients use the item over the long term? Where does the item come from? How much does transportation cost in bringing it to you? Is it made with recycled materials? Are they nontoxic and biodegradable, recyclable, or reusable? How much waste is in the production process and packing? If the item is imprinted with a company logo and the medium permits, do they use soy- or vegetable-based inks? These are just a few questions to consider when selecting the best eco-friendly gift for your meeting guests.

Here are a few ideas for appropriate gifts whose useful life extends far beyond your event. Send your green message via www.gogreengift.com, the original eco-starter kit. Instead of offering bottles of water or plastic refillable bottles, give your guests stainless steel bottles—they won't leach anything into the water. Reusable bags will come in handy at the grocery store and help cut down on the plastic we use. Jump drives (loaded with conference handouts and resource materials) will be useful and reusable in the office. Items made with recycled materials trump cheap plastic logo items.

Request Green Dining

Our eating needs represent a huge contribution to greenhouse gas production and environmental contaminants. Scientists say that raising meat produces more greenhouse gases than our transportation industry. The impact of the chemical industry on agricultural practices results in contaminating our fruits, vegetables, meat, and milk with pesticides, antibiotics, and other synthetic chemicals we wouldn't otherwise have introduced into our bodies. These chemicals take petroleum and energy to produce and are polluting our air, soil, and water supplies. Choosing to eat without them is a decision that's gaining a lot of support—organic food is the fastest-growing segment of our food industry today.

You'll have to weigh the cost-benefit advantages of greening up your meals. Although organic foods typically cost more than conventional, the trade-off of getting clean fruits, vegetables, and meats not contaminated with synthetic petrochemicals and pharmaceuticals and produced with less greenhouse gases represents a value measured by our health rather than our checkbooks. Consider the health and environmental impact of your meals when deciding whether you can afford to choose organic options. You can reduce the cost of organic meats and produce by selecting local growers. Also if you reduce the amount of meat on the menu and replace it with vegetables, you'll cut down on the cost because meat costs more than produce.

Locally Grown Menu Items

Work with the chef to develop a delicious organic vegetarian meal using fresh local produce. Although vegetarian meal options can sometimes seem boring, such as spaghetti or sauce-less steamed vegetables, there are more creative alternatives. Find a chef who's willing to create a truly memorable meal with vegetables, grains, and beans. An added bonus: going vegetarian is good for the wallet *and* the waistline.

Does the hotel or conference facility have an arrangement to send leftover food to a local shelter? Does it compost scraps to help nourish the garden or landscape? Both of these practices can ensure that food is used as sustainably as possible—eat what is edible and feed the rest to the plants that will create the next meal.

Reusable Dining Ware

You've heard reduce, reuse, recycle. It matters. Use reusable plates and silverware instead of disposable.

The Environmental Defense Fund says that using disposable plasticware uses 10 times more energy (in resources and manufacturing) than you'd use with reusable ware, even calculating in the water and energy used to wash it.

A popular new product is compostable plates and flatware made from corn or other starch. These are good because they are made from a renewable resource and are biodegradable. But throw them into the compost bin, not the garbage can, and make sure they make it to a municipal composting site for proper disposal. These types of bioplastics will not break down in a natural environment and need to be sent to an industrial composting facility, not the plastic recycling center. Ask for visible and accessible recycling and composting bins.

Request Bulk Condiments

Buy in bulk. Ask the hotel to use bulk dispensers for sugar, salt, pepper, cream, and other condiments. The Green Meeting Industry Council says that bulk cream is 62 percent cheaper and sugar costs half as much when dispensed in cream pitchers and sugar bowls instead of individually wrapped packets. Ask for salt and pepper shakers and condiment bottles instead of individual packets, too.

Three Stream Waste Stations

If you do use some plastics and paper, request that recycling bins be located in visible, easy-to-access spots so attendees can properly dispose of them. If you're using compostable materials, offer a compost bin as well. Most often, recycling bins are blue, composting bins are green, and garbage bins are black. Clearly label each bin, and ensure all attendees understand where to throw their waste. Ask a trained volunteer or employee of the venue to man the waste stations and help educate guests on where to place their waste. This will ensure a successful, zero-waste event.

Pitchers of Tap: Skip Bottled Water

Please don't distribute water bottles—give your attendees stainless-steel, refillable bottles or locate water dispensers and fountains conveniently and serve water only by request at meals. Avoid plastics (water bottles, bags, and packaging)—they're made with nonrenewable resources and create pollution and waste problems. A pile of plastic the size of Texas lays in the Pacific Ocean today, and it's killing hundreds of thousands of birds, fish, and marine life each year. If we stop using it, they'll stop making the stuff.

At Greenbuild 2004, the USGBC Conference provided water in bulk containers with compostable cups, saving $25,000 and preventing 48,000 plastic water bottles from hitting the landfills or oceans, where they often end up.

Enviro-Fact

Meeting Strategies Worldwide has created a White Paper outlining the savings meeting planners can achieve by going green. Reducing shuttle travel was shown to save $60,000 for a five-day meeting of 40,000 attendees, using efficient lighting saved $51,000 per year for a hotel, and providing water in pitchers saved an estimated $48,000 over furnishing bottled water to 1,200 attendees at a five-day event. These are just a few examples of cost-saving environmental initiatives that meeting planners can achieve. See the full report at: www.meetingstrategiesworldwide.com/files/docs/Meeting_Strategies_Worldwide_Economy_and_Environment.pdf.

Cindy DeRocher at the Gardens Hotel in Key West says she stopped buying 15 cases of bottled water each week, which in turn had to be trekked 150 miles out of the island chain to a landfill. Instead, she provides guests with complimentary refillable water bottles and locates water dispensers throughout the hotel grounds for guests' convenience. She's confident that the move will save her hotel money.

Reduce Paper

Reducing our paper waste output makes a big dent in cutting back on our carbon footprint. We save trees which help process the CO_2 in the air, and we save energy and reduce emissions from the paper production process. Bleaching paper is damaging to waterways that serve as receptacles for pulp mill waste. They become contaminated with dioxin through the process, which is a known carcinogen. So think of ways you can cut back on using paper.

Communicate Electronically

Reach out to your potential conference attendees through e-mail and organizational websites they might visit. Sending an ad online instead of in print is faster and far less expensive, plus it saves paper and the transportation cost of mailing.

Electronic Registration

Trade paper for electronics. Create a conference website and let potential participants register online without costly and lengthy paper transactions. Keep in touch with registrants using e-mail.

Handouts on Jump Drive

Instead of printing handouts, provide electronic links to useful information. With your jump drive, you have no paper, no bleach, no chlorine, no trees, and much less trash.

Promotional companies sell jump drives, also called flash drives, in bulk lots of 25 to 1,000 or more. The cost can be as low as $4 or $5 each if you're buying a lot of them, or up to $40 or more if you need a large-capacity drive or you only need a few. You can generally find a flash drive, which will hold plenty of data to replace the paper you won't be buying or disposing of, for around $7 if you can buy 50 or so. When you compare the costs of electronic versus paper, remember, too, that your attendees will reuse their flash drives for years to come, so consider the item one of your gifts.

Name Tags

Use recyclable name tags. Although they're made of plastic, you can insert a paper name tag and any other material into the plastic sleeve. When the event is over, attendees can drop the necklaces into recycling bins as they leave, and you can reuse them for your next event. You can also use name tags made of biodegradable plastic. The Sustainable Group (www.sustainablegroup.net) offers compostable badges.

Provide Recycling Receptacles

For things that you must print, use recycled paper and vegetable-based inks and print on both sides of the page. Also provide adequate recycling opportunities for guests so that paper stays in the chain instead of being thrown away.

Cost-Benefit Analysis

Some green innovations won't be financially feasible for your company, whereas others will actually reduce the cost of your event. You'll need to conduct a cost-benefit analysis of various options and then decide which work best for your business and your event.

Weighing Cost Savings Against Additional Expense to Go Green

You may find that venues that have gone the full mile and invested in creating a top-level green building are too costly for your event. Certification is an expensive process and sometimes requires expensive heating and cooling systems or renovations. However, don't let a venue's green status keep you from requesting a bid proposal—you might be surprised that even though a facility has made the investment in environmentally friendly heating, air conditioning, and water and waste systems, it is still competitive with conventional arenas. The consumer price may reflect lowered energy expense.

Creating the Best Combination for You

You'll have to compare prices of conventional meeting spaces and green venues and then decide which meets your priorities and goals. You may not be able to create a completely green event, but if you make some strides in some areas, such as meeting space and waste reduction, you'll be making steps in the right direction. Next time, you can add in greener dining options or electronic jump drives.

Let your guests and the press know what you're doing for the planet, and maybe they'll join in. It feels good to go green.

The Least You Need to Know

- ◆ Finding a green venue for your event will help save energy and emissions.

- ◆ With proper planning, you can reduce waste from your event by as much as 95 percent or more.

- ◆ Choosing organic and locally grown food at your event provides a great opportunity to make strides in protecting the planet.

- ◆ Replacing paper with electronic communication saves paper and waste—a win/win!

Chapter 19

Sustainability Reporting

In This Chapter

- Defining a sustainability report
- The history of sustainability reporting
- Areas of a sustainability report
- The business values of a sustainability report
- Understanding the meaning and need for a report
- Applying it to my business

Sustainability has certainly become a buzzword within the going green movement, but in its short life span within environmental language it has become watered down and misused. Often sustainability—which is representative of environmental, social, and financial bottom lines—only touches on its first pillar of environmental initiatives. For example, a consulting organization that states, "… we provide sustainability services, through calculating and substantially reducing the GHG (greenhouse gas) emissions of your business …" is seeing only a part of the puzzle. An environmental assessment or carbon footprint can definitely have a place in a sustainability program but does not encompass the full realm of a credible program or report. Before we can define a *sustainability report*, we need to have a solid understanding of sustainability to avoid this common pitfall of partial reporting.

What Is a Sustainability Report?

Sustainability has many definitions. The concept formally originated during the Brundtland Commission in 1987, when they defined sustainable development as follows: "Sustainable development is development that meets the needs of the present without compromising the ability of future generations to meet their own needs."

In basic terms, we should live our lives and do business in a way that meets our needs and enables success but doesn't inhibit the ability of people in the future to do the same. It is a simple yet humanistic concept.

In the business community, sustainability is referred to as the "triple bottom line" or the "integrated bottom line" and can be accompanied by the motto "People, Planet, and Profit" (see Chapter 1). These phrases refer to a business focus on three things: the environment, social well being, and the financial bottom line. Most consultants or professionals in the sustainability industry use these definitions only as starting points. You might consider how these definitions work and don't work for you and then come up with your own definition of sustainability, keeping in mind the underlying principles.

The following table shows a sustainability report that outlines areas of sustainability.

def•i•ni•tion

A **sustainability report** is a company-specific document which can follow various protocols—i.e., Global Reporting Initiative (GRI), measuring an organization's performance through key performance indicators (KPI) in the focus areas of financial, environmental, and social. The collected data is tied in to anecdotes, stories, and quantitative representations which relate to the organizational goals and values.

The Integrated Bottom Line: Areas of a Sustainability Report

Environmental (Impacts on living and nonliving natural systems)	Social (Impacts on the social systems in which an organization operates)	Economic (Impacts on the economic interests of stakeholders)
Air quality	Labor practices	Sales, ROI, and profits
Water quality (and usage)	Human rights	Employee wages

Environmental (Impacts on living and nonliving natural systems)	Social (Impacts on the social systems in which an organization operates)	Economic (Impacts on the economic interests of stakeholders)
Energy usage	Workplace diversity	Jobs created
Waste produced	Community impacts	Community development
Greenhouse gas emissions	Product responsibility	Customer collaborations
Land use	Operating ethics	Customer satisfaction

Sustainability reporting helps companies communicate their sustainability vision and values and demonstrate what they have committed to and what actions they are taking to achieve this vision.

Survey after survey reinforces the fact that sustainability reporting has significant benefits. We've summarized some of our favorites and what we believe are the most meaningful to a wide range of organizations so you can choose the best approach for your business.

The History of Sustainability Reporting

The initial sustainability reporting initiatives have roots in history earlier than you might think. The first sustainability reporting was done when pioneering corporations attempted to go beyond financial reporting more than 35 years ago in Germany.

Here in North America, we have been a little slower to respond to the sustainability reporting movement. The initial reports started showing up after the 1987 Brundtland Commission, when sustainable development was defined.

In the 1990s, sustainability reporting closer to its current format began when several companies launched the practice of disclosing their environmental performance. Their reasons were partly self-serving and partly good business practice. High-profile global firms such as BP, Shell, Toyota, Hewlett-Packard, and General Motors responded to investors' questions around the financial performance, record on human rights, labor practices, and resource conservation (or lack of) by sustainability reporting. As more companies realized they could not build trust or model transparency with their stakeholders after a huge public relations crisis, such as a catastrophic oil spill in an environmentally sensitive marine area, the sustainability report was a proactive solution.

The Business Value of a Sustainability Report

When we look at a sustainability report, we are looking at the value of disclosing the information to external stakeholders. A sustainability report is a valuable tool to understand, measure, and analyze a company's performance from the inside.

In the past, many organizations decided to create a sustainability report in response to a crisis. You may be aware of the stories of sweatshop exposés in the mid-1990s. In 1996, an article in *Life* magazine titled "Six Cents an Hour" featured the Nike organization. In this article was a picture of a 12-year-old boy named Tariq surrounded by the pieces of a Nike soccer ball which he would spend most of a day stitching together. His pay for the work was about 60 cents. At the same time, Nike was paying millions in endorsements to sports celebrities. The public responded relentlessly. Within weeks, activists all across North America, armed with pictures of Tariq, were protesting Nike stores, urging customers to not purchase Nike products.

Since this public relations nightmare, Nike has become a leader in the sustainability movement but continues to be suspect in the minds of the general public.

This example shows that it's always better to be proactive rather than reactive. For small- to medium-size enterprises, the trend in sustainability reporting has been a proactive approach out of a desire to be more transparent with stakeholders. We can see examples of this with Seventh Generation, Ben and Jerry's, Green Mountain Roasters, and Guayaki Sustainable Rainforest Products. It's important to understand how we operate, interact with, and impact the markets we work with. A sustainability report helps map out that story and enables you to measure and manage the process. We'll show you how to create such a report for your business.

As we enter into a more interconnected age of social networks and a huge variety of media sources, increasing pressure is placed on companies large and small to operate in a more accountable and transparent manner. This pressure comes from a variety of stakeholders, including customers, communities, employees, shareholders, and regulators. Credible reporting on all aspects of a company's performance—economic, environmental, and social—is a way to enhance corporate accountability and transparency.

Enhancing Reputation

Sustainability reporting opens up many doors for an organization. The public opinion of your company changes, and you are seen as a leader in your industry, which will satisfy investor trends in the desire to invest in progressive companies. It also showcases your initiatives industry wide and has the potential to open up new markets.

Again, more and more individuals are aligning their values to the money they spend. Nearly $1 out of every $10 under professional management in the United States today—9.4 percent of the $24.4 trillion in total assets under management tracked in Nelson Information's Directory of Investment Managers—is involved in socially responsible investing.

Improving Internal Operations

Sustainability reporting is like taking inventory of your whole organization. We might compare it to a home renovation; you look at the vision of what your dream house would be and you build it. The areas of the home that weren't functioning 100 percent are now new and improved. It tends to highlight inefficiencies in areas such as resource consumption and waste generation. Wearing your new sustainability vision and goals on your coat sleeves shows your commitment and excites and empowers your staff. It also sends a message to stakeholders and individuals looking at your organization that you put your words into action. This will help attract and retain high-quality employees, people who want to associate themselves with such leading organizations.

Building Relationships

Cost savings are ultimately a part of any sustainability program, and these savings typically are seen through supply-chain innovations. In leading supply-chain initiatives and collaborations, you'll strengthen relationships with key stakeholders. Being proactive is always better than reactive, and all this work will improve the management of sustainable development issues.

Who Will Use the Sustainability Report?

A sustainability report isn't only for external use but can also be beneficial internally for measuring and managing specific areas of organizational development and growth. It has value in determining key criteria for green and ethical supply chain purchasing, outlining areas of inefficiency and waste, and empowering staff toward creative solutions.

The following chart outlines some of the areas and stakeholder groups who will use the report and how it applies to them.

Stakeholder Group	Areas of Interest
Communities	Health and safety Economic opportunities Environmental concerns
Customers	Product safety Customer satisfaction Ethical performance
Investors	Risk and opportunity factors Major capital inputs as a factor of production Ethical performance
NGOs	Environmental performance Ethical performance What you don't report
Employees	Health and safety Employee compensation Workforce demographics
Regulators	Ethical performance Environmental performance Environmental compliance

Does This Apply to My Business?

This is a question most small and medium enterprises (SME) face. Do we need a sustainability report?

You'll need to consider several factors when making your decision, but more often than not, the ultimate determining question will be the bottom line: do you expect sustainability reporting will benefit your company?

We've already covered the extensive benefits companies have realized through sustainability reporting. However, the two most important questions tend to focus on time and cost. Does your organization have the time required and the budget available?

This list of initial considerations will help outline the resources and time required to produce a thorough sustainability report:

- What is the scope of the report? Are you covering all of the company's operations? One office or all offices? One division or all divisions?

- Do you have current systems to help measure the required information, or do you need to develop these systems?

- Do you have useable information available?

- What is the degree of stakeholder consultation?

- Do you have the internal capacity to develop the report, or do you have to use external parties?

- What level of verification and assurance will you use?

- What is the medium of the report (for instance, print-based versus web-based)?

If you are unsure of your capacity to report on or assess any of these areas, you might think about consulting a third party to help assess your needs. Look to your local chamber of commerce or industries association to see if there is an organization performing sustainability consulting. You can also check to see if there is a Business Alliance for Local Living Economies (BALLE) in your area. See Appendix B for contact information.

How to Begin Your Sustainability Report

This standard 10-step approach to a sustainability report is a great starting place for all SME beginning the path to a more sustainable organization. Large organizations typically use the GRI, which isn't practical for smaller businesses. There is a GRI program called "High-5" designed for SME, but before you purchase that, go through the following list. It's great for organizations wanting to move forward through in-house initiatives. You can transfer your work here over to the GRI if needed.

Use headings in the following list to help map out the sustainability reporting process and start putting a timeframe and team members around the activities associated with these tasks.

- Build the business case

- Re-plan decisions

- Map out the reporting process

- Identify key issues and map data points

- Engage stakeholders

- Develop performance indicators

- Collect information and data

- Prepare and design the report

- Verify and assurance

- Publish, distribute, and evaluate the report

Build the Business Case

Building the business case is a way for you to share your ideas, and some high-level details, to help engage buy-in for your sustainability reporting project. In building the business case, you're going to need all your cheerleading skills to rally your troops. First, look for buy-in by identifying and obtaining a commitment from a senior management sponsor who will champion the sustainability reporting process. If this is you, you are halfway there!

The next step takes a little more time, but is well worth the effort. Here are some suggestions on what to tie into your business case for sustainability reporting:

Look for links to the strategic direction and priorities that the company's board and senior management have laid out—can other current projects dovetail sustainability? Is it consistent with the company's culture—for instance, values stated and lived by management and employees (charity work, happy workforce)? Does it reflect what drives the corporate performance—for instance, maintaining or enhancing reputation, attracting and retaining talented employees, increasing short-term shareholder value, competitive position?

You get the picture: always look at the vision and goals and keep working it back. To make it easier, you may want to break it out into two parts: internal and external value for the company.

Preplanning Decisions

Now let's look at conceptualizing what the report will look like and scope out the following. Remember nothing here is written in stone; you just want to get an idea of the key considerations you'll need for your report.

Focus of Report

Deciding what kind of report works best for your company will depend on how senior management wishes to position your company's commitment to sustainability. Remember how in the previous step you linked to your company's strategic direction? Now use that information you already have available. Many companies begin by reporting on one focus area, such as environment, and then expanding coverage and level of integration in subsequent reports.

Level of Integration

Will you aim to achieve economic, environmental, and/or social factors? This is pretty straightforward; just know who you are writing your report for—keep the audience at the forefront in making these decisions (look at your stakeholder list).

Boundary of the Report

What facilities, organizations, and time period are you using? Think big, but start small! Decisions on boundaries are important because they will affect the content, cost, and reception of your report. You will want to be sure all members of the reporting team are collecting data and information for the same part of the company and over the same period.

Medium of Reporting—Printed or Electronic?

Some companies start with a hybrid approach to reporting because they need to share with multiple communities and stakeholders. Some companies use this approach to reduce costs and to keep their reports to a manageable size. A hybrid report involves printing a paper report as well as using the company website to supplement it.

Communications Messaging and Design of the Report

Communication is important, so speak to your audience. Avoid jargon or overly technical explanations; save that for the website as a page for those who are interested. The widest range of audience members need to understand the report, so make it easy to read. If you are not a graphic designer, this is *not* a good place to practice. Bring someone in who can get the message across with an effective and attractive layout, using photographs or illustrations that will enhance the overall presentation of the information in the report. This applies to both the printed version as well as the web version.

> **Going Green**
>
> Publishing your first sustainability report online will allow you to not only be more environmentally responsible, but will also enable you to make changes to content and add information as it becomes available.

As Paul Scott, director of Next Step Consulting, points out, "The graphic clichés—smiling kids in baseball caps, happy chairmen planting trees, cupped hands cradling the globe—will be seen for the unnecessary padding they are." Look for images that are real and relevant, that speak to the tone and culture of your organization—images that invoke the senses of your readers that show the words of the report in action. For example, tell about staff that helped out at a volunteer day event.

Level of Verification or Assurance to Use

Verification and other forms of assurance can lend credibility to a corporate sustainability report. Verification is not a stamp of approval on good sustainability performance, but a tool to enhance the credibility of your performance reporting. So even in the preplanning step, decide to include verification and assurance within your reporting process. The AA1000 created by AccountAbility is one of the most accepted assurance standards; building your report based on this methodology will pave the way for a smooth third-party verification of your data in the future.

Stakeholders can also play an important role in the assurance process. Involving stakeholder review in the reporting process, for example, can be an effective means of verifying report quality and ensuring credibility. Stakeholders are more likely to question whether a company is reporting on all the relevant issues to its operations and doing so in a balanced way.

Information Gathering

Now it's time to start some discussions, take some surveys, or organize focus groups to determine your needs and develop your goals for sustainability.

Map Out Sustainability Process

Organize a working group that includes representatives from a variety of different business units. Discuss sustainability and what it means to your company so the working group understands; have them explain it back to you as well—there is a lot of info here, and everyone needs to be on the same page.

Develop a process for managing sustainability reporting (for instance, some companies establish internal reporting procedures). Google docs is a great tool if your company doesn't have a shared point server.

Set responsibilities and reasonable timelines. Share workload and responsibility. Incorporate collaboration by ensuring that all working group members learn, share, and grow through the process. This is what sustainability is all about.

Assign appropriate employee hours resources (external assistance may be required in some areas), and let people do what they do best.

Identify Key Issues and Map Data Points

The person responsible for identifying key issues needs to …

◆ Identify the key issues the report will address.

◆ Identify company-specific key data points already available. For instance, does staff satisfaction survey data exist? Does your company already have stakeholder feedback on their website?

◆ Look at reports from other companies around the world to generate ideas and collect examples. Have everyone on your team look at another company's sustainability report and tell you what he likes and dislikes about it.

This is one place where you might hire external help for advice and direction. Have you ever heard the saying "you can't see the forest for the trees"? You may be too involved in the details of a problem to look at the situation as a whole. Objectivity and another set of eyes will also lend credibility to your report.

Stakeholder Engagement

Stakeholder engagement helps ensure that your sustainability report meets the needs of your key stakeholders. As Mieko Nishimizu of the World Bank said in a 2002 keynote address on the 50th Anniversary of Japan's Bretton Woods Membership Symposium in Tokyo, "We are tied, indeed, in a single fabric of destiny on planet earth."

Map out the stakeholder engagement process and include it in your report. Describe how your company has identified its key stakeholders, how it solicits their input, and how their input is considered in the company's decision-making processes and in determining the content of the report.

Remember how we stressed clarity in preplanning and writing for your audience? If you are not clear on who your audience is, including their interest areas, you won't have a clear report.

Going Green

Here are common stakeholder groups:

- Communities
- Consumers
- Customers
- Employees
- Financial institutions
- Government authorities
- Nongovernmental organizations (NGOs)
- Shareholders
- Suppliers

Make sure you do the following:

- Identify the key stakeholders the sustainability report will target

- Determine the extent of stakeholder engagement in the reporting process and in what stages:

  a) Identification of issues to be included in the report

  b) Development of key indicators of performance

  c) Perceptions of company performance

  d) Formal verification of company performance

- Undertake stakeholder engagement at the appropriate stages

Develop Performance Indicators

A performance indicator is a point of data that enables you to monitor and measure an aspect of your business. It describes organizational performance in a clear, balanced, and unbiased way—one of the major challenges of effective sustainability reporting.

Things to remember:

- Select appropriate and meaningful indicators. Are they manageable and modifiable?

◆ Ensure that selected indicators make sense to your business and your stakeholders; always check in with your vision and the feedback from your stakeholders. Many companies ask stakeholders to review their indicators before using them internally. This is also a requirement under the AA1000 assurance framework.

Enviro-Fact

The AA1000 framework helps organizations build their accountability and social responsibility through quality social and ethical accounting, auditing, and reporting. It addresses the need for organizations to integrate their stakeholder engagement process into their daily activities. The framework provides guidance on how to establish a systematic stakeholder engagement process that generates the indicators, targets, and reporting systems needed to ensure greater transparency, effective responsiveness to stakeholders, and improved overall organizational performance (see Appendix B).

◆ Know where to store indicator data and how to collect it. If you have an indicator that requires five steps in the collection process, collect it regularly (and on time) and measure it accurately.

◆ Understand what you are currently measuring and how it can dovetail into the sustainability indicators.

Creating indicators may seem like a daunting task and a fairly dull part of the whole sustainability program, but it is well worth the upfront investment for any successful organization.

Collect Information and Data

The secret to this step is to ask for help. Most of the data you are looking for is stored somewhere in the organization. By engaging team members and colleagues, you will save valuable time and energy and get another pair of eyes on the information to reaffirm the meaningfulness of the indicators you developed. Follow these steps:

◆ Collect, collate, and analyze relevant data and information. Put that Excel spreadsheet to work.

◆ Assess the reliability of data.

◆ Collect data regularly and systematically, and ensure that collection procedures guarantee data reliability. Document the data collection process so you can duplicate it in the future if the contact person shifts departments.

Don't be overwhelmed to the point of inaction over these ideas. Collect what you can and report what is relevant. If you can't find the data for an indicator you've developed, state that in your report. The whole idea behind the report is transparency and "warts and all" reporting. Stating that an indicator needs further development is nothing to hide; your stakeholders will respect you more for being upfront and open.

Going Green _____

Follow these tips to find sources of information for your sustainability report:

- ◆ Regulatory reports
- ◆ Inventory and production records
- ◆ Financial and accounting records
- ◆ Purchasing records
- ◆ Environmental review, audit, or assessment reports
- ◆ Environmental training records and so on

Prepare and Design the Report

Remember the preplanning section of this chapter? Align your notes from there with the following steps:

- ◆ Identify key messages
- ◆ Formulate the text of the sustainability report
- ◆ Determine the appropriate report design, layout, and use of graphics
- ◆ Receive management sign-off prior to printing

Verification and Assurance

Again, revisit the preplanning exercise and look at what you found on verification and how it aligns with your sustainability goals.

Check the quality of the information and data you have collected and are reporting. Many experts recommend having an external party do this, as it lends to the credibility of the report. However, if cost is a consideration, have a couple senior-level staff members look at the process and check the data.

Publish, Distribute, and Evaluate

Congratulations, you've done it! This is the last step in a very rewarding project. Now how are you going to share what you have found?

Here are a couple tips:

- ◆ Publish the report either electronically or in printed format.

- ◆ Determine the launching strategy, and share the report with key stakeholders.

- ◆ Find out how you did through some form of feedback mechanism(s), such as online comments or surveys, and incorporate the feedback into future reporting processes and the ongoing management of sustainability issues.

You are now a sustainability reporting master!

The Least You Need to Know

- ◆ A sustainability report is a roadmap which can be as detailed or simple as your want; use it to understand where you are and where you want to go.

- ◆ Stakeholders are key to any reporting process; use them to help as much as you can.

- ◆ Everyone needs to start somewhere; think big and start small. Brainstorm the highest goals you can achieve and then begin.

Part 5

Marketing Your Green Message

Letting customers, colleagues, and competitors know you've gone green—and why—is an important step in helping create a healthier planet, and it is a great way to increase sales and profits for your business. In this part, we give you tips for developing a marketing campaign to capitalize on your green status and provide the important points you want to make as you tell the world about your progress. We also include ideas about groups you can work and network with to help leverage your position in the new green marketplace and green economy.

Chapter 20

Spreading the Word

In This Chapter

- ◆ Clarifying your green story
- ◆ Creating a credible green message
- ◆ Understanding environmental marketing guidelines
- ◆ Press releases and publicity

Having put so much effort into making your business environmentally and socially responsible, now you can really capitalize on your achievement by letting the world know what you've been doing. This chapter covers how to create a credible green story by clarifying your marketing messages and adhering to environmental marketing guidelines. As you shape your publicity and marketing campaigns, you'll want to carefully craft your message to represent the issues accurately and to avoid falling into the increasingly common trap of overstating claims of greenness. Although some companies are jumping on the green bandwagon with the single intent of turning a profit, you are joining a revolution that promises to change the way our world does business and protects our future. Be proud of your accomplishment and make sure your customers and competitors understand the distinction.

Develop Your Green Story

The first step in creating a successful green marketing campaign is to actually reduce the environmental impact of your organization and products and improve your social footprint. Now that you have transformed your organization and implemented our suggestions, it's time to tell your story. A successful marketing and branding campaign detailing your green story is the finishing touch to any sustainability program. And remember to keep credibility and truth behind your messages; it's the only way you can truly gain customer loyalty and improve brand value. If you simply green-wash, customers will lose trust in your product line and ultimately your organization.

Gaining a comprehensive understanding of how and why your organization and products are green is essential to the success of any green marketing campaign. It is often referred to as creating your green story. Think of it as a two-part process: part one looks at your organization, and part two assesses your products.

Why Is Your Company Green?

List all the sustainability initiatives you've implemented and anything your organization is doing to go green. Write down both the social and environmental initiatives your organization is working on. This could be anything from improving employee education programs surrounding green issues to improving energy efficiency and waste reduction at your corporate headquarters. Refer to the green vision you developed (see Chapter 3) and the sustainability action plan (see Chapter 4) and outline your organization's sustainability initiatives.

Only include initiatives you have acted upon and implemented in your organization when you outline your green story. Marketing green ideas, programs, or products you've not yet implemented could be grounds for greenwashing. It is extremely important to maintain authenticity and transparency when creating your green story!

How You Made the Transition

An authentic green story tells of both your organization's successes and its challenges. Talk to your audience about how you embarked on your journey toward sustainability and what inspired you to do so. Refer to the sustainability vision you created and tell your customers what inspired you to begin incorporating green and sustainable practices into your organization.

Earlier we talked about New Belgium Brewery in Fort Collins, Colorado, and its environmental footprint reduction efforts. New Belgium built its green story not only around what it is doing to move toward sustainability but also how it was inspired in the first place. The company started its journey with a simple red bicycle. When first forming the brewery, the owners decided to give each employee a red cruiser bike to encourage them to use their bicycles for work commuting and trips within town, promoting exercise and environmental awareness. This simple action ingrained sustainability into the DNA of New Belgium's organization and serves as the foundation of not only New Belgium's logo but also for its current "Follow Your Folly" marketing campaign. If you have a similar inspiring story, be sure to tell it!

How Are Your Products Green?

When assessing your products, look at a product's entire life cycle from cradle to grave (see Chapter 10). First, think about how and where the raw materials were extracted, harvested, or recovered. Were they extracted or harvested in an environmentally and socially responsible manner? If the materials are recovered or recycled, how were they collected and reprocessed? Next, think about the manufacturing process. Was the product manufactured with green or lean manufacturing techniques?

> **Enviro-Fact**
>
> Odelle's Brewing in Fort Collins, Colorado, manufactures all their kegs and bottles of beer using renewable energy. They also retrofitted their building with skylights to reduce the amount of energy needed to light the facility on sunny days. In addition to reducing energy use and purchasing energy from renewable sources, Odelle's recycles all recyclable waste generated at its facility, purchases local bottles whenever possible, and is involved in numerous community initiatives and donation programs.

After assessing the impact of the manufacturing process, look at how far both the raw materials and finished product traveled to reach the end user. The farther the travel distance, the greater the environmental footprint. Different transportation modes have varying degrees of environmental impact. Generally, rail has the least, followed by ship, truck, and air transportation.

Also look at how the product is used and what environmental impact it has or health impacts it might have on the consumer. Is the *environmentally preferable product* replacing a nonenvironmentally preferable one? Does the product improve the health of the consumer? For example, many green cleaners are environmentally preferable because

def•i•ni•tion

An **environmentally preferable product** is a product proven to have a reduced environmental impact when compared to a similar product in the same category.

they are biodegradable and less toxic. Many also have the added benefit of emitting zero volatile organic compounds (VOCs). Eliminating VOCs from cleaning agents adds an additional health angle to the product's green marketability.

Another example of a product which reduces the consumer's direct environmental impact is a reusable water bottle. By using these bottles, consumers reduce the amount of plastic they purchase, use, and dispose of—most likely in a landfill. When we use a reusable bottle, we also protect our health from toxic chemicals that leach from the plastic into our water. A more complete green marketing story is created if the bottle itself is composed of recycled material, is recyclable, and the organization producing the bottle operates in a sustainable manner.

Speaking with suppliers about environmental and social practices often takes some investigation. Be sure to verify all claims made by any supplier; untrue or unclear supplier claims will ultimately affect the validity of your green story.

The last thing to consider when assessing your product's green attributes is to look at the end of the product's life. Ask yourself, how is the product disposed of? Can it be disposed of via environmentally responsible means—such as composting, recycling, reusing, or repurposing—or will it be sent to a landfill? Also determine the environmental impact of the product as it breaks down or decomposes. Some products release toxic substances when decomposing. This contaminates air, water, and soil, reducing the quality of our ecosystems and jeopardizing the health of all species, including humans.

Guide to Greenwashing

Above all, avoid greenwashing! If your customers do not trust your story or believe your green claims, they will be less likely to buy your products and support your organization. With so much noise in the market about green and no clear definition, deciphering fact from fiction is often difficult. But one thing is certain: you do not want your organization accused of making false claims.

Make Sure Your Story Is Valid

Before printing any environmental marketing messages, make your story solid and valid. Providing back-up documentation to both concrete and vague claims will add credibility to your organization's message. If you are stating claims you can document with scientific evidence, always complete the proper testing and documentation procedures and create a cut sheet or white paper for all staff to have on hand. This will allow them to quickly send any necessary back-up documentation to interested parties if they question the validity of your claims. For example, if your organization claims that it reduced its carbon footprint by 20 percent over the course of two years, be prepared to support this claim with verification data. You will need to have your carbon footprint calculations from two years ago readily available, as well as your current carbon footprint calculations.

Most green product claims—claims that an organization is "going green" and claims of implementing a comprehensive sustainability platform or individual programs into an organization—can be documented and verified. The key is to determine your baselines and benchmark your current sustainability performance for both your organization and products to demonstrate how each have improved over time. See Chapter 5 for more information on how to assess your organization's current environmental and social footprint in creating benchmarking metrics.

> **Going Green**
>
> Often environmental claim documentation can be prepared in-house following certain guidelines and standards, such as the International Organization of Standards Type II Self Declared Environmental Claims (ISO 14021, 1999) guidelines. Or hire an outside agency to prepare claim verification documentation for you. See Chapter 22 for detailed information about environmental marketing guidelines.

When possible, have back-up documentation on file for all green/sustainability marketing claims. The following are examples of claims that generally have available back-up documentation upon request:

- Recycled-content product composition
- Rapidly renewable product
- Recyclability
- End-of-life take-back programs
- Biodegradability
- Compostability
- Energy, water, and waste reduction—company/organization
- Energy, water, and waste reduction—product

- Carbon footprint reduction and carbon neutrality
- Low/zero VOC

Greenwashing Sins

In the spring of 2007, Terra Choice Environmental Marketing, the Canadian marketing agency responsible for administering the Environmental Choice EcoLogo, conducted a study assessing the green product claims of 1,018 products. Research teams visited six big-box retail stores and recorded every product-based environmental claim they found along with the nature of the claim, supporting information, and references offered for further information.

After recording 1,753 environmental claims on the 1,018 products, they tested the claims against current best practices for environmental marketing, including the International Organization for Standards (ISO), the U.S. Federal Trade Commission (FTC), the U.S. Environmental Protection Agency (EPA), Consumers Union, and the Canadian Consumer Affairs Branch. The result of this study was the development of the "Six Sins of Greenwashing." Terra Choice discovered that all but *one product* committed at least one greenwashing sin.

According to Terra Choice, the Six Sins of Greenwashing are as follows:

- **Sin of Hidden Trade-Off:** This sin is committed by suggesting a product is "green" based on a single environmental attribute (the recycled content of paper, for example) or an unreasonably narrow set of attributes (recycled content and chlorine-free bleaching) without attention to other important issues such as energy, global warming, water, and forestry impacts of paper. Such claims are not usually false but are used to create a "greener" picture of the product than a more complete environmental analysis would support.

- **Sin of No Proof:** Any claim that cannot be substantiated by easily accessible supporting information or by a reliable third-party certification commits this sin.

- **Sin of Vagueness:** This committed by every claim that is so poorly defined or broad that its real meaning is likely to be misunderstood by the intended consumer.

- **Sin of Irrelevance:** This sin is committed by making an environmental claim that might be truthful but is unimportant or unhelpful for consumers seeking environmentally preferable products. It is irrelevant and therefore, distracts consumers from finding a truly greener option.

♦ **Sin of Lesser of Two Evils:** These are green claims that might be true within the product category but that risk distracting the consumer from the greater environmental impacts of the category as a whole. The Sin of Lesser of Two Evils is committed when environmental qualifiers such as "organic" or "green" are placed on products in which the entire product category is of questionable environmental value.

♦ **Sin of Fibbing:** This sin is committed by making environmental claims that are simply false.

Environmental Marketing Guidelines

Contrary to popular belief, environmental marketing guidelines and standards do exist. Most people are unaware that there are rules and regulations to follow when crafting green marketing messages. Following these guidelines will ensure that your marketing messages are credible and verifiable.

The EPA and the FTC teamed up in 1999 to create the FTC Environmental Marketing Guidelines, which provide a framework for the use of environmental marketing claims. According to the EPA, "National guidelines issued by the Federal Trade Commission (FTC), with the cooperation of the U.S. Environmental Protection Agency (EPA), are available to help companies make sure their green claims don't run afoul of the law. The FTC Act prohibits deceptive acts or practices, including deceptive representations in advertising, labeling, product inserts, catalogs, and sales presentations."

Truth in Advertising

Can we really enforce truth in advertising? Consumer agencies are beginning to crack down on corporations making erroneous green marketing campaigns. Companies adhering to environmental marketing guidelines are also beginning to make their voices heard by suing companies in the same market segment for stating untrue green claims.

Referencing the FTC environmental marketing guides when creating your green marketing messages could ultimately mean the difference between feeling the wrath of the greenwashing accusers and building trust with your consumer base.

The FTC's "Guide for the Use of Environmental Marketing Claims" applies to environmental claims included in labeling, advertising, promotional materials, and all other forms of marketing. This includes words, symbols, emblems, logos, depictions, product brand names, or any other means.

Environmental Marketing Claims

Basically, anytime you want to make a green claim, refer to the marketing guidelines to make sure you are creating a credible, valid, nondeceptive message. Following is an overview of the FTC environmental marketing guidelines, but see Appendix B for a link to view the complete guides.

The general principles laid out in the guides are:

◆ Qualification and disclosure: This refers to the way the actual environmental claim is printed and the clarity of the language being used to talk about the claim.

◆ Distinction between benefits of product, package, and service: You must state clearly whether your green marketing claim is highlighting a service, a product, or a product's package.

◆ Overstatement of environmental attribute: Don't overstate any green attribute of your product, services, or packaging. Also avoid talking about green claims that are not relevant.

◆ Comparative claims: Any green claim making a comparison to another product or service must make the basis of comparison clear and understandable to steer clear of deceiving the consumer.

In addition to explaining general principles and rules to follow when creating green marketing claims, the guide also provides guidance about the use of eight specific environmental marketing claims. The following show claims with examples that are acceptable and deceptive to consumers.

General environmental benefit claims: Unless you can substantiate and qualify broad based green claims, do not make them!

Example: A product with a spray pump is labeled "environmentally safe," yet this product contains VOCs which react with sunlight to create ground-level ozone or smog. This is a deceptive claim because while the packaging could potentially be environmentally preferable, the product itself is not remotely environmentally safe because it contributes to air pollution.

Degradable/biodegradable/*photodegradable*: To make a claim of degradability, biodegradability, or photodegradability, it is necessary to substantiate the claim with scientific evidence. Products or packages that carry claims of degradability, biodegradability, or photodegradability must include information about where the product must be disposed of to properly break down and the rate of degradation.

def•i•ni•tion

Photodegradability is the process that occurs when materials break down to smaller particles when exposed to sunlight.

Example: A garbage bag package states that the product is degradable but does not accompany the claim with any qualifier statements, and the garbage bags are normally disposed of by incineration or land filling. Because both means of disposal do not create environments where the product can easily break down, this claim is deceptive to the consumer.

Compostable: Like claims of degradability, biodegradability, and photodegradability, any claim that a product or package is compostable must be backed up by scientific testing and documentation. Products and packaging that claim to be compostable must break down into healthy, usable compost in either a backyard composting pile, inside a composting bin, or in an industrial composting facility. When making claims of compostability, note if the product needs to be composted at an industrial composting facility and if those facilities exist in the area where the product is sold or if it can be composted at home.

Example: A manufacturer of unbleached paper cups claims on the product's packaging that the cups are compostable. If the manufacturer can substantiate this claim with supporting evidence, the claim is not deceptive. The supporting evidence does not have to be printed on the packaging, but the manufacturer must be prepared to share supporting evidence when questioned.

Recyclable: If a product or package can be collected, separated, and reprocessed into a raw material for a new product, it can bear the recyclable symbol. If you are labeling a product as recyclable, make sure it is logistically feasible to actually recycle the product.

Example: A product composed of multiple types of plastic is labeled recyclable. Because it is a mixed-plastic product, it must be sent to a facility that has the technology to recycle products composed of multiple plastic types or back to the original manufacturer for reprocessing. These facilities are not common. Unless the product manufacturer has designed a take-back program for the product or the product is sold in an area where it can be easily recycled, the claim is deceptive.

Recycled content: If a product or package is composed of recovered materials that would have otherwise been sent to a landfill, the manufacturer can claim the product is composed of recycled content. Remember from Chapter 10 that there are two types of recycled content: pre-consumer and post-consumer. When making a recycled content claim, it is extremely important to quantify the amount of pre-consumer and post-consumer recycled content in the product or package for which you are creating marketing messages.

Example: A product contains 30 percent recycled content purchased scrap from another manufacturer's operations and 30 percent recycled content recovered after consumers utilized it. The product's claim that it is composed of 60 percent recycled content—30 percent post-consumer and 30 percent pre-consumer—is a valid claim.

Source reduction: Any claims of reduction in weight, toxicity, or volume for products or packaging must be qualified.

Example: A product advertisement claims that the product packaging now uses 15 percent less plastic than it previously used. If the manufacturer can substantiate this claim with qualifying data, then the claim is not deceptive.

Refillable: To make the claim that a package or container is refillable, two criteria must be met—a system must be in place for the collection and return of the package or container so it can be refilled, or the consumer must be able to buy the product used to refill the package in bulk in order to refill the package or container themselves.

Example: Soap is sold in an 8-ounce container that is marked refillable. The same soap is also sold in bulk at the location where the consumer purchased the 8-ounce container, allowing the consumer to refill the smaller container with contents of the bulk container. This refillable claim is not deceptive.

Ozone safe and ozone friendly: For products making claims of reduced detrimental impact on the ozone layer, the product must not contain ozone-depleting substances.

Example: An aerosol hairspray can is labeled "Zero CFCs," but it contains HCFCs, an ozone-depleting substance. Because consumers might associate a "Zero CFC" claim with ozone protection, this claim is deceptive.

Publicity

Now that you have the tools you need to make sure your green claims are valid, it's time to hit the PR circuit. To grab the attention of editors and publishers, make your headlines unique. Headlines such as "Corporation X is going green" and

"Corporation X makes a 15 percent energy reduction" are overplayed and nondescriptive. Also steer clear from using "eco" and "environmental" without any substance. Catch the eye of the people who have the power to publish your stories by specifically defining your story. Sure, you are going green, but what exactly are you doing? Talk about the innovative programs your organization has implemented to integrate triple bottom line values into your organization.

When sending out press releases, use agencies that focus on spreading the word about environmental and sustainability stories, such as CSR Wire and E-Wire.

Going Green _____

CSR Wire (www.csrwire.com) and E-Wire (www.ewire.com) are news wire services that focus on environmental and social issues. Each focus on the following subjects.

CSR Wire: academia, activism, business ethics, clean technology, community development, corporate governance, diversity, employment and appointments, environment, events and entertainment, fair trade, finance, green building, heath and wellness, human rights, natural/organic products, philanthropy/corporate contributions, ratings and rewards, renewable/alternative energy, research reports and publications, socially responsible investing, sustainability, volunteerism, and workplace issues

E-Wire: environment, health, science, and technology

Electronic Resources

An effective, eco-friendly way to spread the word about your green products and organization is to send *e-blasts* and e-newsletters to the people you want to reach with your message. With the advent of new technology, the days of snail mail direct-mail campaigns are slowly ending. E-marketing campaigns enable you to track the number of recipients who receive, open, and read your e-mails, providing you with concrete data that will help you make more informed decisions about the effectiveness of your marketing efforts and give valuable feedback to what you should adjust for future marketing campaigns.

def•i•ni•tion _____

E-blasts are mass e-mails sent simultaneously that you can customize with individual information.

Collect e-mail contact information from customers when they visit your website, when they place orders, and whenever you're in contact with them by asking if they'd like to be added to your e-mail lists. If they value your products or services, they'll be pleased to have you stay in touch with them and keep them informed of new developments with your company and products. Electronic messaging is less invasive than phone calling and doesn't involve the paper waste, postage, or energy expense of direct mail. A word of caution, though: if you over-inundate your valuable customers with too much information, you run the risk of driving them away. Respect your customers' time and attention by reaching out to them with news they can use, not relentless sales pitches.

A few electronic marketing resources that can help you shape your e-mail message, collect and manage addresses, track results, and ensure a successful e-mail campaign are: Constant Contact, eBlast.com, Emma E-mail Marketing, and Campaign Monitor. See Appendix B for contact information.

Reflecting on the path your company has taken in its quest to become a more sustainable business will help you develop the most accurate message to share with the world about your success and products. Your customers, colleagues, and competition will recognize your integrity and gravitate to your business over others who don't meet their personal goals and standards.

The Least You Need to Know

- ◆ Carefully craft your message to convey your green values.

- ◆ Customers and colleagues will be pleased to learn of your environmental and social commitment. Learn the importance of environmental marketing guidelines.

- ◆ Do not overstate your case or greenwash your product—you'll lose your audience.

- ◆ Take advantage of electronic publicity opportunities, but don't overwhelm customers with more information than they want.

Chapter 21

Promote, Support, Expand

In This Chapter

- ◆ Determine your target market
- ◆ Green consumers value green products
- ◆ Green buyers expect product integrity
- ◆ Educate consumers

So far, you've learned how to incorporate sustainability into your everyday organizational activities, green your products, and craft a credible green story. It is now time to focus on promoting and expanding your business.

Who's Buying?

The Birkenstock-wearing tree hugger is not the only consumer purchasing green products these days. From SUV-driving soccer moms who want to save the planet for their kids to the thrifty consumer who purchased his hybrid because of fuel cost savings, the profile of purchasers of all things green is rapidly changing. According to BBMG, a branding and marketing firm that focuses on branding for sustainability, more than one third of Americans say the term *conscious consumer* describes them very well, and nearly 9 in 10 Americans say the term describes them well.

Defining Conscious Consumers

The conscious consumer is one who takes multiple values into consideration when he purchases products or services. Many people think that conscious consumers are those that purchase on environmental or green values alone, but according to studies conducted by both BBMG and Mind Click, eco-purchasing is not the sole driver of the conscious consumer.

To sell your products to this growing, diverse consumer sector, you must define your specific green consumer to develop the best branding and marketing strategy for your product or service. Remember, without an authentic sustainability story, you will not create an authentic sustainability brand or marketing message. Can you tell that we are trying to drive this point home? Building your sustainability program inside your organization from the top executive level down and the hourly employee up is the key to success. And remember to benchmark and track your progress!

def•i•ni•tion

A **conscious consumer** is one who makes purchasing decisions based on values such as environmental responsibility, honesty, integrity, and social responsibility.

As a general rule, "green" is not the first, second, or even third reason for purchasing a product. More often than not, the age-old mantra of convenience and price trump green for even the most dedicated conscious consumers. You can't expect people to purchase your products or services just because they have a green or sustainability angle. You still have to produce quality products and deliver impeccable service at a price that the consumer is willing to pay. Think of green as a value-added selling point, the third or fourth trigger that makes a consumer purchase your product instead of your competitors'—who might be doing nothing to incorporate sustainability into their operations or green their products in any way.

Enviro-Fact

"Many companies are honestly looking to engage in sustainable business practices and become more socially responsible," says Raphael Bemporad, founding partner of BBMG. "But in a world of green clutter, conscious consumers expect companies to do more than make eco-friendly claims. They demand transparency and accountability across every level of business practice."

An important thing to realize about the conscious consumer is that once they begin to understand the ramifications of their purchases, they are more likely to purchase with their values. After we understand the importance of changing our patterns of behavior to better protect our health and the environment, it's really not hard to recycle more or carry a cloth bag for groceries. Cutting back on energy and water saves us money, which provides an instant incentive to develop new habits. Educating consumers will help them join your business in making changes that can change the world.

In 2008, Mind Click conducted a study that assessed the green purchasing habits of consumers and gauged the concern for global warming among a varied sample of our population. Research showed that 47 percent of consumers in the United States are highly concerned about global warming and are fully engaged in green activities and purchases. That is almost half of our country's population! Mind Click further breaks down that 47 percent into the five following categories:

Alarmist—11 percent

♦ Consumers who are extremely concerned about global warming

♦ Consumers who feel that businesses and the government are responsible for combating global warming

♦ Consumers who are fully engaged in green activities and purchases to combat global warming

Enthusiast—15 percent

♦ Consumers who are concerned about global warming

♦ Consumers who feel that climate change is being addressed

♦ Consumers who are engaged in green activities and purchases to combat global warming

Active Awares—21 percent

♦ Consumers who are highly concerned about global warming

♦ Consumers who believe climate change is not being addressed

♦ Consumers who make lower levels of green activities and purchases

Passive Awares—16 percent

♦ Consumers who are highly concerned about global warming

♦ Consumers who believe climate change is not being addressed

♦ Consumers who make levels of green activities and purchases

Indifferents—24 percent

- Consumers who are undecided/moderately concerned about global warming
- Consumers that expect business/government to provide solutions
- Consumers who make lower levels of green activities and purchases

Nonbelievers—13 percent

- Consumers that deny global warming exists
- Consumers that do not expect solutions
- Consumers who make nominal green activities and purchases

According to Mind Click, the most prominent green behavioral changes include recycling, installing energy-efficient light bulbs, and washing clothes in cold water instead of hot. Conscious consumers changed their purchasing habits by selecting higher concentrate laundry detergent, buying in bulk, and visiting the farmers' market. Perhaps the most encouraging piece of data to emerge from this study is that up to 55 percent said they would participate in simple changes to further engage in green activities.

Defining Your Green Consumer

To define your green consumer, first look at what your product or service has to offer (see Chapter 20). Does your product cater to those who are motivated by environmental conservation, improved health, or cost savings? Identifying the key green attributes of your products and services will help you define which segment of the conscious consumer you should target.

According to the Natural Marketing Institute, there are five types of conscious consumers:

- Life Styles of Health and Sustainability (LOHAS)—This consumer has a progressive attitude on the environment and society, is looking for ways to do more, and isn't too concerned about price.

- Naturalized—This consumer is primarily concerned about personal health and wellness, uses many natural products, and would like to do more to protect the environment.

- Conventionals—These consumers are practical, like to see the results of what they do, and are interested in green products that make sense in the long run.

- Drifters—These buyers are not too concerned about the environment, figuring people have time to fix environmental problems, and so don't necessarily buy a lot of green products.

- Unconcerned—These folks have other priorities, are not really sure what green products are available, and probably wouldn't be interested anyway; they buy products strictly on price, value, quality, and convenience.

Think about who purchases your product, create a customer profile for them, and identify which segment of the green market is most likely to buy your products or services. Remember that marketing to the conscious consumer is not just about green or the environment; it's about sustainability. Don't forget to highlight benefits such as increased health and positive social impact as well as environmental attributes.

Value-Driven Purchasing

Consumers are increasingly purchasing with values in mind in addition to price, performance, and quality. People want to feel good about what they buy. As consumers become more educated, this struggle for value-driven purchasing will increase. Are you ready?

In their inaugural *Conscious Consumer Report*, BBMG, the marketing and branding firm, describes five values that drive the conscious consumer. The BBMG team researched the values behind 24 consumers' purchasing decisions in Kansas, New York, and California, choosing different areas of the country to make sure the results represented a varied demographic. Let's briefly examine these values from BBMG's report. To download the full report, visit www.bbmg.com.

Health and Safety

Conscious consumers seek natural, organic, and unmodified products that meet their essential health and nutritional needs. They avoid chemicals or pesticides that can harm their health or the planet, and are looking for standards and safeguards to ensure the quality of the products they consume.

Honesty

Conscious consumers insist that companies reliably and accurately detail product features and benefits. They will reward companies that are honest about processes and practices, authentic about products, and accountable for their impact on the environment and larger society. Making unsubstantiated green claims or over promising benefits risks breeding cynicism and distrust.

Convenience

Faced with increasing constraints on their time and household budgets, conscious consumers are practical about purchasing decisions, balancing price with needs and desires and demanding quality. These consumers want to do what's easy and essential for getting by and make decisions that fit their lifestyles and budget.

Relationships

These consumers want more meaningful relationships with the brands in their lives. They ask questions similar to the following:

- Who made it?

- Where does it come from?

- Am I getting back what I put into it?

Conscious consumers seek out opportunities to support the local economy when given the chance, want to know the source of the products they buy, and desire more personal interactions when doing business.

Doing Good Feels Good

Conscious consumers are concerned about the world and want to do their part to make it a better place. After all, contributing to the greater good just plain feels good. People are feeling a new sense of purpose by aligning their purchasing decisions with products and companies that are improving our homes, our lives, and our planet. From seeking out environmentally friendly products to rewarding companies' fair trade and labor practices, they are making purchasing choices that can help others. These consumers want to make a difference, and they want the brands they support to do the same.

Conveying Your Green Status to Customers

You must be transparent when talking to consumers about the green or sustainability attributes of your products and services. Most likely, you don't have it all figured out when it comes to green. But don't worry, not many organizations do. We're all making our way on this exciting and challenging journey into the new frontier. Discussions, issues, and concepts surrounding the field of sustainable business change every day. In this young, promising arena, you need to recognize the strengths of your organization and product, but also let the consumer know what areas you are unsure of and are trying to figure out. When creating marketing materials that convey your green status, use the information you learned in this chapter to better focus your messages on the conscious consumer. Align your green or sustainability goals with their values consistently in all of your marketing messages.

You want your customers to understand what is green about your products or services and how to properly use these to get the most benefit for themselves and the planet. Educate your consumers on the most efficient way to use your products. For example, if you are selling a product that increases energy efficiency in the home through a programmable thermostat, the consumer must know how to properly use the device to ensure a reduction in energy use actually occurs.

Educate Customers About Recycling Products

You must also educate consumers on how to properly dispose of products after using them. Often people try to do the right thing by purchasing and using compostable cups, plates, and cutlery made from bioplastics only to throw these items in the trash. When compostables are thrown into the trash, they don't break down as intended, so the product is misused and its intended purpose of environmental footprint reduction is jeopardized.

We also see this same problem with plastic products. Many municipalities can only recycle certain types of plastics, mainly #1 and #2. While certain recycling programs accept plastics labeled #1 to #7, these are few and far between.

When marketing a product as recyclable, inform the customer if the product can be recycled in his area and how to dispose of it properly if it's not eligible for municipal recycling. If your product must be sent to a special facility, make it clear on your packaging.

Following is a list of common plastics and their corresponding recycling numbers. Check the type of plastic your product is made of by looking for a recycling symbol containing a number in the center. Use the following list to determine what type of plastic the product is made of.

- ◆ #1—PETE/PET
- ◆ #2—HDPE
- ◆ #3—PVC
- ◆ #4—LDPE
- ◆ #5—PP
- ◆ #6—PS
- ◆ #7—Other

> **Hazard**
>
> Not all municipalities have recycling systems in place to handle plastic and glass. If they do, it is not likely that they can recycle all types of plastic. Be sure to check with your local municipality to determine what types of plastics they accept for recycling. If you are selling products, make sure consumers know how to properly dispose of them.

Don't Overstate Benefits

To build an authentic, credible, and sustainable message, you must remain true to your customers. Remember, honesty and relationships are two main purchasing values of those buying green products and supporting sustainable companies.

Overstating a product's benefits, green or otherwise, will line you up for disaster. If word spreads that you are being dishonest, consumers will lose faith in your brand and scrutinize your products. This point is especially important because of the rapid ability to share information over the Internet. Blogs and websites pick up information just as it is posted and spread it like wildfire. You don't want to be on the losing end of a PR nightmare. Remember to back up your marketing messages, especially those that can be qualified with scientific evidence. Use this data when creating your message to ensure you do not overstate your benefits (see Chapter 20).

Customizing Your Marketing Message

Now that you understand a bit more about green consumers and what drives their purchasing decisions, it is time to customize your marketing message.

Focus on how to spread the word about your organization and products, and target meaningful marketing outlets. Developing a highly detailed, well-planned marketing strategy will aid in the successful execution of your marketing campaign.

Staff

Spreading your green message internally is just as important as marketing your message to the external audience. Your employees are your most effective brand angels—people who love and support your brand—and if they don't understand your marketing messages and the actions you are implementing to back them up, you can't expect your external message to be powerful. Customize your marketing messages to speak to your employees as well as your customers and external audience.

Customers

Use the customer profile you created when defining your green consumer to pinpoint exactly who you are marketing to. This will help you focus your marketing message and customize it to your audience. Look at the values your target customers embrace. Are they reflected in your marketing messages and woven into the products and services you are selling?

Media

Research various media outlets and channels that will be an effective means of spreading your message. This includes online resources such as blogs, e-newsletters, and news websites as well as print media. When researching, remember to ask yourself, "Will this marketing channel be beneficial to spreading the word about my product? Will we see increased interest from consumers that will translate into increased awareness or sales?"

Look to magazines that specialize in your industry for both advertising and editorial opportunities, but be aware that just because you advertise in a magazine, it does not guarantee you will be featured in an editorial. Many publications draw a thick line between their editorial and advertising departments. Check with your advertising rep on the policies of the particular publication you are advertising with. Often, if there is a separation between departments, your advertising rep will connect you with the appropriate member of the editorial team who has the authority to vet and publish stories.

Measuring Your Success

Knowing where your marketing efforts are a success and where they are falling short will help you create better marketing campaigns. More than ever before, marketing professionals are facing an increased demand for marketing accountability. In order to best measure the effect of your marketing campaign, create a system based on best practices. It may be useful to involve other departments in your organization—such as sales, accounting, and customer service—to develop your marketing metrics. Be sure that upper management is clear on what metrics they want to review before implementing any marketing metric measurement system or dashboard. Once established, you can use this measurement tool for your current and future marketing campaigns. Track your metrics, analyze them, review them, and learn from them.

The Least You Need to Know

- A substantial segment of the market seeks sustainable products.
- Define your customers.
- Develop your product to meet sustainability standards.
- Establish marketing materials that acknowledge the green consumer's concerns.

Chapter 22

Stamp of Approval

In This Chapter

- ◆ Finding eco-labels for your business
- ◆ The value of eco-labels
- ◆ Confirming legitimacy
- ◆ Understanding the wide selection of labels

One good way to let your customers and colleagues know you're working to make your business sustainable is to seek the stamp of approval from bona-fide green certification programs. When you can demonstrate that you've passed through the highest standards, whether by obtaining LEED certification for your building from the U.S. Green Building Council (USGBC) or as a green business member of Green America, your customers will know you're vetted as a genuinely green and sustainable business.

Because many green credentials are popping into the market, you should know the validity of available programs so you can choose the best allies for your business. In this chapter, we provide a review of several eco-label programs we hope will help you make the best, well-informed decisions for your company. This chapter reviews only a fraction of the eco-labels available today. To access a comprehensive guide to eco-labeling, visit www.greenitgroup.com.

Navigating the Sea of Endorsements

The increase in green marketing initiatives has spawned a rampant increase in the number of certifications available in the green marketplace. Many different types of organizations—including nonprofits, for-profits, and government agencies—have developed *eco-labels*. The validity, breadth, and issues each address vary. From energy efficiency to organic food, it's often tricky to differentiate the good, better, and best. Sorting through the sea of certifications can often be a grueling task.

Understanding the Endorsement

Understand that just because a product has an eco-label doesn't mean every aspect of that product or company is green. For example, GreenGuard provides an eco-label for indoor air quality, and products bearing the GreenGuard seal of approval meet certain tests for improved indoor air quality and volatile organic compound (VOC) emissions.

def•i•ni•tion

An **eco-label** identifies a product that meets specified environmental performance criteria or standards. Awarded by a third-party organization to products or services, this document provides an overview of eco-labels, including a summary of programs for electronic products in the United States and abroad.

But just because one aspect of the product is green does not necessarily mean the entire product is a green product. For example, GreenGuard certification does not cover other green product aspects, such as raw materials, end-of-life disposal, or production and company sustainability practices. Another example would be an Energy Star–certified product. This eco-label, which you can find on many kitchen appliances, washing machines, and computers, focuses on energy use during equipment operation. Again, meeting this standard does not necessarily mean the entire product has been scrutinized through a lens of sustainability.

The International Organization for Standards (ISO) is the world's largest developer and publisher of international standards. Comprised of a network of 157 countries, this nongovernmental organization forms a bridge between public and private sectors. According to the ISO, three broad types of environmental labels exist:

- ◆ Type I environmental labeling (ISO #14024:1999)—This voluntary, multiple criteria–based, third-party program awards the license to use an eco-label developed by the third party. These types of labels assess multiple product criteria, are based on the life cycle of the product, and are awarded to the best environmental performers.

An example of this type of eco-label is the Green Seal. It assesses a product using a multiple-criteria, life cycle–based method. Products that pass the testing criteria are awarded the Green Seal.

◆ Type II self-declared environmental claims (ISO #14021:1999)—These claims are made by the company (hence, self-declared) and are often difficult to verify. Text, symbols, and eco-friendly terminology are used to emphasize a particular environmental aspect of the product or service. Type II labels cover only one eco aspect of a product.

If a manufacturer creates a recycled content label for their product, claiming that the product contains x amount of recycled content, they are following the Type II guidelines.

◆ Type III environmental declaration (ISO/TR #14025:2000)—These voluntary programs provide quantitative environmental data of a product under pre-set categories of parameters set by a third party and verified by that third party. Think of this type of label as a report card that shows how much water, energy, and materials the product uses.

An environmental product declaration (EPD) that is verified by a third party is an example of a Type III claim.

Accuracy in Verification

Consensus shows that eco-labels influence consumer-purchasing behavior. Consumer demand for green everything has led many organizations to create a green story, backing it up with a homemade eco-label. In 2008 alone, countless new eco-labels have hit the shopping isles, promising everything from a reduced carbon footprint to being just plain green without qualifying why or how. Often, these labels are based on a lack of knowledge about environmental issues and green product criteria as marketing departments just seek out an angle, design a label, and slap it on a product.

Recently a major clothing retailer debuted an eco-label highlighting the green products in a number of stores. The label, which adorned a wicker basket, made the claims of biodegradability and eco-friendly. However, the overall product was composed of certain components that were not *biodegradable*. This self-made eco-label is a liability both for the store and the customer purchasing the product. Not only is the retail outlet misleading the customer by making false environmental claims, but the customer could also cause further environmental damage by disposing of the

def•i•ni•tion

A material is called **biodegradable** when microorganisms such as bacteria, enzymes, and fungi can degrade it. This degradation produces water, carbon dioxide (CO_2) and/or methane, and in some cases nontoxic residues.

product in an improper manner, which could lead to increased disposal costs. This is a good example of greenwashing.

Verifying the accuracy and validity of eco-labels is extremely important. Ask yourself the following questions:

◆ Is this eco-label made by the same company that is producing the product?

◆ Is the eco-label self-certified?

◆ Is a credible third party providing the eco-label?

◆ What standards does the product or organization have to meet to obtain the eco-label?

◆ Are the standards that the product or organization has to meet publicly available?

◆ Is the label consistent in its meaning?

◆ Does the organization have verifiable data to back up the claims made on the eco-label?

◆ Was the label developed with pubic and industry input?

Signs of Genuine Value

When a credible outside source gives an eco-label to a product or organization, there is a greater chance the label will be genuine. Third parties who provide transparent labeling criteria provide measurable, replicable standards for products and add a tremendous amount of credibility to any eco-label. Transparency is the key to success, so look for eco-labels that list their green product criteria for all to review. And beware of third parties who sell eco-labels without allowing the public to view their certification criteria.

An example of a genuine eco-label is Forest Stewardship Council's (FSC) certification for sustainable forestry initiatives. Formed in 1993, FSC is an international, independent, third-party group of certification bodies that assess forest management for sustainable forest management activities and chain-of-custody tracking of sustainable wood products that originate from FSC-certified forests. Third-party certifiers work with landowners to bring their forests up to transparent standards, which were developed by a large group of external stakeholders.

Other eco-labels are not so transparent. An organization in Florida that certifies businesses for being green charges a fee for certification. After it collects the fee, the organization sends out guidelines. The participating business has to fill out the guidelines, sign them, and fax them back. Then the business receives a plaque, a green plastic wristband, lapel pins, and a window decal. There is no verification of the participating business's answers to the questionnaire, nor any guarantee that the participating business is implementing environmental reduction strategies into their business model. Also the guidelines are proprietary, not transparent, and are not available for public review or comment. Although this certification is not transparent or third-party verifiable and auditable, it is a positive step in an overall shift in awareness and adoption of green business practices. But do be aware that the green movement, like any new market trend, provides business opportunities that can be exploited by less-than-scrupulous people looking to make a buck without any real interest in the underlying goals of the movement. Watch out for unnecessary middlemen selling snake oil.

Hazard

When searching for the appropriate eco-label for your product or organization, make sure the standards required to meet the labeling criteria are publicly available. For the most genuine eco-label, seek independent third-party verification for your certification.

If you are looking to certify your organization for its efforts in implementing green or sustainable business practices, research B Corporation and Green America's green business membership. These are two credible organizations that offer sustainable and green business certifications. Also check to see if your city or town has a reliable, transparent green business program and certification.

Pseudo Sanctions

Eco-labels are not always what they seem; many are irrelevant, and even more boast ambiguous claims that may be unfounded or irrelevant. Labels such as natural, free range, and *CFC-free* all sound wonderful, but what are these environmental labels really saying?

According to Ecolabels.org, a food labeled "natural" can contain artificial sugars and oils or partially hydrogenated oils. Meat labeled "natural" pertains only to how the cut of meat was processed and not how the animal was raised. Depending on the type of meat, natural meat may contain added synthetic antibiotics and hormones. According to the USDA, producers of free-range meat must demonstrate that the poultry was allowed access to the outside, not that they necessarily spent time outdoors.

CFC-free means a product does not contain any chlorofluorocarbons, chemical substances that can deplete Earth's protective ozone layer. The ozone layer absorbs 93 to 99 percent of the sun's ultraviolet light, and this protection is vital to the existence of life on Earth. According to the Federal Trade Commission (FTC), CFCs were banned in 1978 for use in propellants in nearly all consumer aerosol products. A CFC-free eco-label is therefore irrelevant and misleads consumers by portraying the product as eco-friendly when it is simply complying with the law.

def•i•ni•tion

CFC-free means free of chloro-fluorocarbons (CFCs), synthetic chemicals that can damage the layer of atmospheric ozone protecting Earth. CFCs were banned from products in 1978.

When assessing eco-labels for products you produce and the products you purchase, look beyond the logo and analyze the label in depth. Labels are not always what they seem.

Third-Party Certifications

Third-party certification and verification is one of the most trusted ways to obtain an eco-label. Products that bear a third-party logo are often the most authentic in terms of environmental claims, as long as the third party provides transparent certification criteria. Utilizing a well-recognized third-party provider of eco-labels is an effective way of creating a credible green story.

Third-party agencies work with product manufacturers and suppliers to obtain the necessary data needed to analyze the product to meet the certain criteria for each specific certification.

Following are a few examples of third-party-certified eco-labels.

Green Seal

Green Seal provides science-based environmental certification standards that are credible, transparent, and essential in an increasingly educated and competitive marketplace. Founded in 1989, Green Seal is well respected in the environmental community, utilizes internationally recognized standards, and is nonprofit. To earn a Green Seal stamp of approval, products must meet the outlined environmental standards developed for the specific product category, undergo scientific testing, and provide a tour of the product's manufacturing facility. Green Seal reviews the manufacturing process and the use and ultimate disposal of the product. A product performance review ensures that all certified products work as well or better than other products in their individual product category. All Green Seal standards are set through an open, collaborative process that includes stakeholders from all industry sectors, including consumer groups, government, universities, trade associations, manufacturers, and the public. Each year, products that received Green Seal certification must participate in a review. For a list of Green Seal–certified products, visit www.greenseal.org.

Green Seal stamp of approval.

(Courtesy Green Seal program)

Scientific Certification Systems

Scientific Certification Systems (SCS) offers a diverse range of eco-labels. Since 1984, SCS has been providing independent verification of environmental claims made by manufacturers regarding products and service qualities such as biodegradability, recycled content, and water efficiency. SCS also is a certifier for the previously mentioned FSC certification and Veriflora, a sustainably grown floral certification.

Veriflora seal.

(Courtesy Veriflora)

Scientific Certification Systems seal.

(Courtesy Scientific Certification Systems)

LEED Certification: Leadership in Energy and Environmental Design

Perhaps the most well-known third-party eco-verification label is the USGBC's Leadership in Energy and Environmental Design (LEED) certification. The USGBC is a nonprofit, nongovernmental organization whose mission is to transform the way buildings and communities are designed, built, and operated, enabling an environmentally and socially responsible, healthy, and prosperous environment that improves quality of life.

The USGBC, formed in 1993, has grown to comprise over 15,000 organizations from across the building industry. According to the USGBC, members include building owners and end-users, real estate developers, facility managers, managers, architects, designers, engineers, general contractors, subcontractors, product and building system manufactures, government agencies, and nonprofits.

The LEED certification system is a tiered system that addresses the built environment. Buildings earn LEED certification through the accumulation of points from four levels: certified, silver, gold, and platinum. With the LEED rating system, the USGBC transformed the building industry by creating a certification for buildings. It also created a certification for people qualified as LEED-accredited professionals. Building product manufacturers, architects, designers, city planners, and consultants all work together to create a more sustainable built environment and achieve the stringent LEED rating standards. LEED is the perfect example of a successful, third-party eco-certification that unified industry to create a market shift toward sustainability.

USGBC seal.

(Courtesy U.S. Green Building Council)

Fair Trade

Eco-labels cover more than just environmental issues. The Fair Trade Certified logo ensures that strict environmental and social criteria were met in the production of trade and agricultural products. Purchasing Fair Trade Certified products ensures that you are contributing to the empowerment of farmers and farm workers. Procurers of Fair Trade Certified products provide high wages to farmers, allowing them to rise out of poverty and reinvest in their communities. This certification encompasses environmental protection as well as social development.

Fair Trade Certified seal.

(Courtesy Fair Trade Certified)

Government Eco-Labels

The U.S. government provides its Energy Star certification program to let consumers know that products bearing its seal have been assessed and approved as the most energy-saving, efficient models on the market. The EPA introduced Energy Star in 1992 as a voluntary eco-labeling program developed to promote energy-efficient products to consumers and reduce greenhouse gas emissions. The widely recognized eco-label is seen on appliances such as refrigerators, stoves, washing machines, office equipment, home electronics, lighting, and much more.

Recently, the EPA Energy Star ratings have come under fire recently. In its October 2008 issue, *Consumer Reports* reported that its tests of Energy Star appliances indicated some were less than half as efficient as the manufacturer claimed and the Energy Star label backed up. The magazine said standards are lax and that several loopholes exist that give the sales-promoting certification to products which don't deserve it.

The EPA responded that it stands by the integrity of the program and its certifications.

Energy Star seal.

(Courtesy EPA Energy Star)

The EPA recently launched the WaterSense program to make it easier to purchase products that save water. Much like the Energy Star program, products which meet EPA standards are labeled with the WaterSense logo. According to the EPA, "When you use products bearing the WaterSense label, you can expect exceptional performance, savings on your water bills, and assurance that you are saving water for future generations." To find products that meet WaterSense criteria, visit www.epa.gov/watersense/pp/index.htm.

WaterSense logo.

(Courtesy EPA Water Sense)

International Eco-Labels

Eco-labels exist around the world. The United States is actually behind the times when it comes to labeling products for environmental and social attributes.

The following is a list of well respected eco-labels from around the globe:

◆ Blue Angel (Germany)—The Blue Angel is Germany's eco-label. Created in 1977, it is one of the oldest eco-labeling programs in the world.

◆ Eco Mark (Japan)—The Japan Environment Association develops environmental standards and permits products to bear the Eco Mark symbol.

◆ Environmental Choice (New Zealand)—The New Zealand Ecolabelling Trust is a voluntary, multiple specifications–based environmental labeling program initiated and endorsed by the New Zealand government.

◆ Environmental Choice Program (Canada)—The Environmental Choice Program (ECP) is Environment Canada's eco-label program which certifies environmentally preferable products based on multi-attribute life-cycle criteria.

◆ Environmental Label Award (Croatia)—The Environmental Label is awarded by Croatia's Ministry of Environmental Protection for products certified as meeting specific environmental performance criteria.

◆ European Commission, Green Public Procurement—Policies, resources, and guidance from the European Commission are designed to increase the level of green public procurement in the European Union member states.

◆ European Union (EU) Eco-Label—The EU Eco-Label is a voluntary program designed to encourage businesses to market products and services that are kinder to the environment. It is used throughout the European Union as well as in Norway, Liechtenstein, and Iceland.

- Global Ecolabelling Network (GEN)—GEN is a nonprofit association of third-party, environmental performance labeling organizations founded in 1994 to improve, promote, and develop the eco-labeling of products and services.

- Good Environmental Choice (Australia)—Good Environmental Choice is Australia's environmental performance eco-label. It is based on product life cycle.

- Hong Kong Green Label Scheme (HKGLS)—HKGLS is an independent, not-for-profit and voluntary scheme for the certification of environmentally preferable products launched in 2000 by the Green Council and the Hong Kong Productivity Council.

- Green Mark (Taiwan)—Green Mark is Taiwan's program to guide consumers in purchasing green products and to encourage manufacturers to design and supply environmental benign products.

- Green Purchasing Network (Japan)—The Green Purchasing Network (GPN) was established in February 1996 to promote green purchasing among consumers, companies, and governmental organizations in Japan.

- Korea Eco-Label—The Korea Eco-Labeling Program certifies qualifying eco-products for excellent quality and performance, as well as general environmental friendliness during the entire production process.

- National Programme for Labelling Environmentally Friendly Products (Czech Republic)—The Czech Eco-Labelling Agency manages the Czech National Eco-Labelling Programme, which labels environmentally friendly products.

- NF Environnement Mark (France)—The NF Environnement mark is the official French ecological certification.

- Organization for Economic Co-Operation and Development (OECD) Environmental Directorate—The OECD Environment Directorate is an international organization that provides governments with the analytical basis to develop environmental policies that are effective and economically efficient.

- GreenLabel (Singapore)—The Singapore Green Labelling Scheme was launched in 1992 by the Ministry of the Environment and awards the GreenLabel to products meeting specific environmental criteria.

- Swan Eco-Label (Nordic Countries)—The Swan is the official Nordic eco-label introduced by the Nordic Council of Ministers.

♦ TCO Development (Sweden)—TCO Development provides certification and environmental labeling of office equipment designed to improve the work environment and the external environment.

♦ Thai Green Label Scheme (Thailand)—The Thai Green Label Scheme, launched in 1994 by the Thailand Environment Institute in association with the Ministry of Industry, awards the Green Label to products meeting specific environmental criteria.

Is It Worth It?

You can choose from many eco-labels, which you'll find on a variety of products whose manufacture and use impact the earth in many ways, from energy, oil, and water usage to waste produced during manufacture and use. These seals can help you ensure that your efforts to make your business sustainable and Earth-friendly will be successful.

The Least You Need to Know

♦ Products on the market use many types of eco-labels.

♦ Most eco-labels are legitimate and use genuine standards to determine the eco-friendliness of a product and/or business.

♦ Invalid label programs are available that cost money but don't provide any useful or legitimate rating.

♦ Taking time to familiarize yourself with labels will help you make the right choices in purchasing as well as in seeking eco-labels for your own business.

Chapter 23

Green Partners

In This Chapter

- ♦ Government partnership programs
- ♦ An avenue for showcasing a business's environmental principles
- ♦ Online resources for rebates, tax credits, and incentives

Local, state, and federal governments are recognizing the benefits of encouraging businesses and homeowners to reduce electricity usage and emission outputs. A diverse array of initiatives and partnership programs are emerging to help you bring your business into the future with renewable energy resources and environmentally sound policies. In this chapter, we've selected a few to get you started.

Government and Organizations as Your Green Partners

Government agencies at all levels work with businesses and other organizations in voluntary partnership programs that revolve around different environmental themes. Your environmental partner can be a business or organization that voluntarily participates in a program that addresses a particular theme or goal. Some environmental partnerships feature a narrow focus and pertain to a specific activity or industry, while others address broader issues and are applicable to a wide range of businesses.

The Environmental Protection Agency (EPA) is a key player in the field of partnerships, offering an assortment of national and regional partnering programs, including Energy Star and the Green Power Purchase program.

If the idea of teaming up with the federal government piques your interest, peruse EPA's list of partnership programs to select something that fits your business's goals and interests (see Appendix B). In addition to EPA partnerships, various other government agencies and organizations offer environmental-themed partnership programs.

The Carbon Trust (a government-funded independent company) is an organization whose mission is to accelerate the move to a low-carbon economy by working with organizations to reduce carbon emission and develop commercial low-carbon technologies. It partners with multiple organizations, both for-profit and nonprofit, and offers resources including information, monetary assistance, and referrals to consulting firms that can help you calculate and reduce your carbon footprint. It has recently expanded from the United Kingdom to the United States and is offering carbon labels for its products (see Appendix B).

Another organization, The Vermont Business Environmental Partnership, asks participants to meet a set of environmental standards before they are designated an Environmental Partner. The standards involve efforts in such areas as recycling, energy efficiency, and promoting the partnership program. From there, participants may work on additional standards to achieve the next level status of Environmental Leader.

Local governments and community organizations are getting involved in supporting environmental initiatives, too. The Silicon Valley Environmental Partnership is a nonprofit organization that works on local environmental issues. The Bay Area Green Business Program in California is a partnership of government agencies and utilities that work with businesses and public agencies on achieving a higher standard of environmental performance.

Regulatory Bane or Benefit?

Participating in an environmental partnership offers distinct business benefits in addition to promoting a healthier Earth. An environmentally friendly business image is among the perks. The affiliation with a partnership program showcases a business's green attitude, which attracts customers who are seeking to support businesses that share their eco-friendly values. Other benefits include the opportunity to use technical support and resources offered through some of the partnership programs.

Regarding potential perks for participating businesses, the EPA website states, "Most EPA Partnership Programs offer technical assistance, professional networking, and public recognition. Many offer financial and environmental analysis tools, training, seminars, guidebooks, toolkits .... Others help businesses identify potential buyers and sellers of environmentally superior products and connect them to environmental financing."

Another potential benefit of the partnership programs is more money. Businesses that employ energy-efficient, water-efficient, and waste-reducing practices often enjoy the savings that go along with them.

The EPA's Waste Wise program is a government partnership program that works with businesses and nonprofit organizations to help them reduce and track their waste. When members join the program, they inventory the total amount of trash they currently generate and submit their findings to an EPA database. They can then find resources on the website about increasing their diversion rates. Stated in 1994, the Waste Wise program has grown to include over 2,000 member organizations from small- and medium-size enterprises to multi-national corporations.

> **Enviro-Fact**
>
> "Businesses and organizations that are leaders in energy efficiency use about 30 percent less energy than their competitors," according to the EPA.

With all these benefits comes some additional work. The business partner often must submit reports outlining accomplishments and areas of compliance as it relates to the program, but the benefits seem to outweigh the extra work.

Tax Rebates in Strategic Areas

Some eco-related projects, such as installing solar panels, may involve a substantial investment. When venturing into such a project, take advantage of available financial incentives that offset the expense. Especially noteworthy is an eight-year extension of the 30 percent federal tax credits for installing solar energy systems, according to the Solar Energy Industries Association (www.seia.org).

Another type of tax credit applies to manufacturers. Those who produce specific types of products, including refrigerators and dishwashers, may be eligible for federal tax credits if the products meet the required specifications.

Purchasing hybrid vehicles for your business is another way to reap tax benefits of greening your organization. To learn more about tax and other monetary incentives available for hybrid vehicles by state, visit www.hybridcenter.org.

> ### Enviro-Fact
>
> The Database of State Incentives for Renewables and Efficiency (DSIRE) offers info on federal and state utility incentives that promote renewable energy and energy efficiency. To browse among some of these programs, visit www.dsireusa.org.

Research tax rebates and incentives specific to your business, industry, and regional location to learn more about how you can financially benefit from going green.

The EPA offers a wide array of partnerships, such as the Energy Star and Green Power Partnerships described in the following section, to businesses of all sizes. These examples apply to a broad range of participants, but you may find it well worth your while to study the DSIRE information to find programs best suited to your needs.

EPA Green Power Partnership

Partners in the EPA Green Power Partnership program agree to buy green power. Green power is electricity from renewable sources such as sun, wind, and water. Also, green power is produced in ways that are less air polluting than standard energy.

To maintain the green power partnership status, a participant is required to buy green power in an amount based on a percentage of its annual energy consumption. The percentage guidelines are outlined in the program.

The participating business may install green power directly at the facility, such as setting up solar panels on the roof, or it may buy green power from a utility provider. Another way to participate is by purchasing renewable energy certificates (RECs). The REC does not provide the purchaser with electricity, but is a certificate verifying the money went to support a green power producer elsewhere. For more about RECs, see Chapter 6.

See Appendix B for contact information for the Green Power Partnership program.

Going Green _____

The EPA offers an online tool that's useful in showcasing the environmental value of green power purchased. The Green Power Equivalency Calculator translates the purchase into an equivalent amount of avoided carbon emissions. To quantify the amount of emissions avoided, the calculator puts the amount in terms of familiar references, such as greenhouse gas emissions from passenger vehicles. The tool is available via www.epa.gov/greenpower/pubs/calculator.htm.

Recognition for Reducing

Various partnerships offer awards or other types of acknowledgment for jobs well done. Those official pats on the back can be parlayed into marketing and PR efforts when dealing with business partners and customers and perhaps even the media. Some partnership programs send out press releases when a business wins an award or earns another level of recognition.

A listing on the sponsoring organization's website is another form of recognition. The Energy Star Awards, for example, showcase winning businesses' pursuits in energy efficiency. Information about the winners is featured online.

Timberland, a retailer that sells outdoor products, earned recognition from the 2007 Green Power Leadership Awards. At the distribution plant in California, an on-site solar energy system provides about 60 percent of the energy. The company also buys wind-based renewable energy credits, and the retail stores promote the wind power concept through brochures and a web link.

Another winner that year was Staples, which sells office supply products. The company purchased green power equivalent to more than 20 percent of purchased electricity in the United States, an amount that qualified it for the EPA Top 25 list.

Enviro-Fact
The EPA recognizes businesses of all sizes in its award program, as well as nonprofits and government agencies. To review the complete list of EPA Waste Wise 2008 award winners, visit www.epa.gov/epawaste/partnerships/wastewise/pubs/WasteWise_08_Award_Winners.pdf.

Strength in Numbers

The EPA's various partnership programs attract thousands of businesses, schools, and organizations. The more companies that work toward saving energy, the better it will be for the planet. The Green Power Partnership states that its top 10 retailers buy green power that's the equivalent of enough electricity to power more than 161,000 average American homes in a year. Among the top 10 retailers for 2008 were: Whole Foods, Kohl's Department Stores, Starbucks, Lowes, Office Depot, and REI. Smaller companies can study the sustainability plans of these larger examples to learn more ways to save energy.

Energy use in commercial buildings and manufacturing plants accounts for nearly half of our country's greenhouse gas emissions and nearly 50 percent of energy consumption nationwide.

Another partnership program, Energy Star, stated that the accomplishments of its industrial partners in 2006 avoided greenhouse gas emissions equivalent to those from more than 4 million vehicles.

Energy Star Partners

Energy Star has partnership programs applicable to a broad assortment of partners.

The objective, according to EPA information, includes energy management that protects the environment and saves money. Various types of partnership programs are offered based on the type of business applying.

For manufacturers, it allows the use of the Energy Star certification logo. For retailers and e-tailers (companies that conduct business over the Internet), the program offers participants networking opportunities with other partners and access to resources, such as staff training materials. Partnership commitments include specific guidelines about how the Energy Star logo is used and how the products are promoted.

Among the noteworthy practices of the Energy Star program is that occasionally businesses promote energy-saving products by offering credits, rebates, or sales tax exemptions on qualified products. Interested customers can type their zip code into the Energy Star website to determine if such offers are available in their community (see Appendix B).

Going Green _____

To become an Energy Star Partner and qualify for the Energy Star award, visit www.energystar.gov and click on the "Go to Partner Resources" tab on the right-hand side of the page. This will redirect you to a page where you can download an application form. Fill out and e-mail the form, and you are on your way to becoming an Energy Star Partner.

Energy-Saving Resources

Energy Star is among the organizations and government programs that offer information and tips for businesses working to reap the environmental, professional, and monetary benefits of going green. In addition to the website, the program offers various free printed materials, including posters, booklets, and brochures, which you can order online or by phone (see Appendix B).

Choose Energy-Efficient Equipment

Remember your energy partner, Energy Star, provides certification of energy-efficient business equipment and appliances. When outfitting your office, take advantage of the expertise Energy Star provides to make sure your equipment is as eco-friendly as it can be. In light of recent skepticism of some Energy Star products cited in *Consumer Reports* magazine, you'll want to be sure you do your homework on the specific equipment you're buying to confirm it provides the best efficiency for your business. But Energy Star can be an important guide and one source of information to help you save money on electricity with energy-efficient equipment and cut down your emissions.

Look around your community and check in with state and federal programs to find incentive and rebate programs to partner with that will help your business achieve sustainability.

The Least You Need to Know

◆ Businesses receive various benefits from working with government through voluntary partnership programs.

◆ In some partnership programs, the participating businesses must submit paperwork outlining the areas of compliance.

♦ Partnership programs are available in an array of environmental themes and activities.

♦ Two popular programs from the EPA—Energy Star and the Green Power Purchase Program—are applicable to a wide assortment of business partners.

Chapter 24

Networking With Other Green Businesses

In This Chapter

- ◆ Reach beyond your business
- ◆ Increase sales through professional networks
- ◆ Benefit from group resources
- ◆ Market through supporting local initiatives

A big part of the green and sustainable movement requires a rethinking of business as usual. Although companies of the past have risen to the top with a spirit of competitiveness considered healthy for business, the new paradigm suggests that cooperating and collaborating may be a more successful way to gain ground in business. Developing a community philosophy of working together and helping one another with shared goals of creating prosperity and a healthier planet for all is the prevailing attitude of the new green economy. Although it might seem contrary to traditional ideas, working with our peers to get ahead can prove to be a successful approach to business. And guess what? It works.

Cooperation Trumps Competition

Most business people have discovered that networking with other professionals can enhance their business through increased contact and visibility in their field. But oftentimes, professional interests are at odds when talking or working with others in the same field. Competition can create a barrier that keeps those with like minds from working together because they're afraid the competition may steal their ideas or their clients. Although the current business mantra deems competition to be good, that's only because it spurs workers to move more quickly than their peers to capture a potential market. Sustainable businesses find that cooperating with peers to achieve goals—instead of competitively hiding information from them—can be a win/win situation for all involved.

The green business approach posits that working together can help achieve even greater goals than a few sales, and the result can be more progress toward shared objectives. Sustainable businesses focus on goals that impact the planet and the health of citizens worldwide while increasing their profits. This approach can lead to greater success for all involved.

Collaborating for Common Good

In the emerging economic climate, which will address green energy and efficiency and create multiple opportunities, saving the planet and turning around hazardous practices becomes a greater good that companies can work together to achieve. Strength in numbers and the power of group energy focused on problems, such as cleaning up polluted water and air, is the only way we will meet these important goals, and these factors are essential to continued life on Earth. Sustainable businesses understand this and factor this knowledge into their design plans. Working together, businesses will be able to achieve these goals more effectively.

Networking with other businesses that share your goals of sustainability will help you find and support suppliers and customers working toward the same planet, people, and profit values that your company supports. You can connect with these companies and avoid supporting businesses that don't share these values. Teaming up to support the same suppliers can result in a discounted cost for purchasing products. Often referred to as a purchasing co-op, many small- and medium-size businesses use this as a cost reduction strategy.

Amy Belanger, Deputy Director of the Green Business Network at Green America, reports a recent example of networking among members resulted in a partnership with Green America; World of Good, an online e-commerce group reserved for products that meet Green America standards for social and environmental responsibility; and eBay, the online auction site that has created revenue streams for many thousands of entrepreneurs. "This was a networking coup in Green America," said Belanger. "It's a concrete outcome of a really good networking relationship."

Benefits Beyond the Bottom Line

Networking with like-minded owners can help businesses gather power on a large-enough scale to affect basic changes in the way they do business and to prevent the worst effects of global warming and a greed-based economy. Part of your sustainable business plan should include benefits such as cleaner air, water, and soil; and employees should have more time to spend with their families or to pursue other creative and intellectual aspects instead of just working to survive. Once considered intangible benefits that had little or no place in the workplace, today the value of these is recognized as important for our health and well-being. They are part of the triple bottom line or integrated bottom line, which provides business benefits for people and the planet as well as profit. Working together can enable businesses to make large-scale changes to help prevent global warming. Remember, sustainable businesses focus on a triple bottom line that includes people, the planet, and profit instead of the traditional single bottom line of just profit.

While large and small sustainable businesses are focusing on more objectives than just profit, by developing sustainable practices, they also benefit from cost savings and increased profits.

Networking Resources

As many business people are learning in the twenty-first century, the electronic age and all its wonderful ability to connect us in myriad ways 24/7 can be a boondoggle to our productivity and a time sapper in our offices. We need to be judicious in our use of electronic resources to make the most of the advantages offered through the Internet. Some companies designate certain times of day, limited hours, or specific employees to maintain electronic networking and research benefiting the company. Also note that the Internet has few filters to help protect us from false claims and wasted money and time. But as tedious as the electronic age may be, there is no doubt that learning to navigate the information highway can lead to better connections with the larger world and opportunities to work with other companies to enhance your sustainability and expansion goals. Working through agencies and organizations that vet members and participants can help focus your efforts on reliable businesses and potential partners, similar to the way certification agencies provide assurance of viability through certification labels.

Green America and the National Green Pages

Formerly known as Co-Op America, the nonprofit organization Green America is dedicated to helping socially and environmentally responsible businesses succeed because it wants to bring about a socially just and environmentally responsible society. Born from a conversation among friends, the group began as a cooperative effort to sell artisan jewelry and tie-dyed t-shirts, but as the need for a network connecting similar businesses became clear, they shifted focus and became a networking facilitator.

"This is a need in the world," says Belanger of the Green Business Network. "If we really want to see dramatic change, we need to get consumers on board, voting with their dollars. Rather than just protesting and trying to change things at the government level, why not change it through the economy?"

Green America created the National Green Pages, a catalog that lists businesses that meet Green America's standards as socially and environmentally responsible businesses. Businesses of all sizes are benefiting from Green America membership because of the resources and networking opportunities it offers.

Going Green

Take advantage of the broad resources available through Green America and find out if your company is eligible for membership at www. greenamericatoday.org.

Operating since 1982, the group has seen a tremendous surge in memberships in the past few years as more business owners seek to apply social and eco-friendly values to their work. Green America provides many services and educational resources for members, and networking with other members can lead to benefits such as discounts and business opportunities, as well as the assurance that colleagues have similar values.

Through the Green Business Network, Green America offers business members connectivity via an e-list, where participants can post inquiries for new products, raw materials, or references and other resources. The group also hosts an electronic lounge for members, where chats and educational resources can be accessed.

Look for the Green America logo on business promotional material and websites and you'll know that the business displaying the seal is genuinely working to help solve the world's problems while conducting a successful enterprise.

Green America logo.

(Courtesy Green America)

Other Sustainability Professional Organizations

The advent of the Internet has made networking much more possible than ever before. Many groups meet virtually online without frequent in-person meetings, and many networking opportunities online help like-minded businesses find ways to work together. The Internet can increase our reach and multiply our marketing efforts when used effectively. LinkedIn, a popular business networking site, enables users to create a profile and connect to one another. Used strictly for business purposes, LinkedIn is a great way to build a professional network. You can also join other groups such as The Green Group, Green and Sustainability Innovators, and The Sustainability Working Group just to name a few.

Green Chamber of Commerce organizations, which are beginning to pop up across the country, are a great place to meet other like-minded green business leaders and potential collaborators. If your city or town doesn't currently have a Green Chamber of Commerce, why not create one? You will increase the presence of your business in the community, serve as a leader, and encourage sustainable business practices throughout your town.

Green Festivals, Conferences, and Networking Groups

Green America hosts annual green business conferences and green festivals in several locations around the country to bring green and sustainable businesses together and to foster education and information exchange. The group anticipates a turnout of as many as 100,000 at its events, which begin with educational programs for business leaders and include a public festival for green products and networking. Many other groups also provide opportunities to connect with legitimate businesses working in the green realm.

Small businesses participating in these events can benefit from exposure through the conferences and from networking with other like-minded firms.

Earth Day Network

Earth Day Network evolved from the original Earth Day in 1970. Today, the international network includes 17,000 organizations in 174 countries, promoting educational and climate-related campaigns around the world. Earth Day Network sponsors Earth Day events to help bring interested parties together to learn more about sustainability.

Green Music Festivals

Earth Day Network partners with Green Apple Festival to produce green music around the United States to celebrate Earth Day. Started in New York City in 2006, the green music festivals were held in eight U.S. cities in 2008, attracting more than 200,000 to the event featuring music and green business vendors and displays. It's billed as the largest Earth Day event in the world. See Appendix B for contact information.

Business for Social Responsibility

Business for Social Responsibility is an organization that helps businesses develop socially responsible sourcing networks and practices. With 250 international business members, the nonprofit group provides advisory services and educational programs. It also networks with civic leaders to help connect members with issues and solutions at the local level and beyond. Its mission statement lists its values as leadership, integrity, and respect and describes its mission as to help businesses develop accountable, sustainable, and competitive success. See Appendix B for contact information.

Green Drinks

Green Drinks International is a group that was founded at a local pub in London in 1989 when like-minded environmentalists pulled their tables together to talk. Thanks to the entrepreneurship of Edwin Datschefski, one of the original group members, there are now 402 cities participating worldwide. You can establish a Green Drinks group in your own area to provide a meeting place for those interested in or involved with environmental issues to learn about one another's programs and how they might

work together. Datschefski advises finding a
local restaurant or other venue that's happy
to host an event one night a month and
then letting attendees buy their own food
and drinks. Arranging for a speaker from
a local government, group, or other green
initiative will help get ideas flowing.

Going Green _____

To find or start a Green Drinks
International group in another
city around the world, visit
www.greendrinks.org.

Net Impact

Net Impact is an organization of students and professionals "using business to
improve the world." It has more than 200 chapters worldwide and 10,000 members
working to support their mutual interests in social responsibility and environmental
sustainability. The nonprofit organization facilitates these initiatives with educational
programming, an annual conference, and online networking for members. "Net
Impact works to enable our dynamic, intelligent, and committed members to transform their ideals into measurable results," according to the group's mission statement.

Net Impact began in 1993 when a group of 16 MBA interns began networking to
"put their business skills to use to both make money and achieve positive social
good." Within a year, 500 students had joined the network. Today the mix is about
half students and half professionals. The group reports that 1,800 attended their
2007 conference, and in 2008 it held two conferences, one in Switzerland and one
at the University of Pennsylvania. Attendees "gain a fresh perspective on the role of
business in society and a new appreciation for their work as business leaders and their
connection to a network of like-minded colleagues." It might be worthwhile to ask
one of your employees to connect with this organization so your small business can
benefit from this network of academics and professionals.

Social Venture Network

Social Venture Network (SVN), founded in 1987, is a group of 500 socially responsible business leaders whose mission is "to inspire a community of business and social
leaders to build a just economy and sustainable planet."

SVN lists several prominent businesses and organizations among those headed
by its members. Gary Hirschfield, founder of Stonyfield Farm, started his yogurt
company in 1983, and a report on the SVN site says the company applied values of
environmental sustainability even then. "We were children of the '60s," he reports in

an SVN article, "and had no choice but to question the conventional models and try to integrate these values." SVN describes the approach as values first and marketing second, but the result was successful—the company grew into the largest organic yogurt company in the world. Hirschfield worked with SVN to found the Social Venture Institute to share his business model and practices with like-minded business owners and entrepreneurs. The twice-annual Institute provides business mentors, problem-solving sessions, and workshops on financing a socially responsible business, sales and marketing, management, and strategic growth.

Working With Community Initiatives

As we move into a new green economy, businesses are taking a leading role in rebuilding a world infrastructure and society that will be a friendlier and healthier place in the future. One of the best ways sustainable businesses can positively affect their communities is to partner with social and government programs to help community members gain footing in the new paradigm. Becoming a player in the new green movement is a more effective way to take advantage of this than sitting on the sidelines bemoaning the changes that are inevitable as we face global warming and a changing economy.

Cause Marketing

Amy Belanger from the Green Business Network has a background in marketing and wrote a chapter for the book *Guerrilla Marketing on the Front Lines* by Mitch Meyerson and Jay Levinson (Morgan James Publishing, 2008). Belanger's chapter, "Guerrilla Cause Marketing: How Marketing with Causes Can Send Your Profits and Your Spirits Soaring," is all about the benefits shared by both the business and the community programs or nonprofits it supports. Belanger says that *cause marketing* is a partnership between a nonprofit and a business where the business provides resources to aid the cause and the cause provides good public relations for the business.

def•i•ni•tion

Cause marketing is a collaboration between a business and a nonprofit organization that provides the chance for the business to help address a social or environmental cause in exchange for publicity.

"Green businesses are often already networking in the community from day one because they started for altruistic reasons. For those who are not, they should be," says Belanger. "They should think of it in marketing terms, not as a donation, because they're not cutting dollars out of their profit. They should consider it super affordable and highly leverage-able mission-based marketing. Every time they contribute to a cause in their community, members of that cause are going to develop a loyalty to their business."

Belanger adds that green business owners often feel uncomfortable marketing their businesses, which often leads to their downfall. Business owners who started out fighting for a social or environmental cause may be wary of becoming too profit-oriented, because that's how our environmental and social problems developed in the first place—through greed. Belanger hopes green business owners will help themselves get past that hurdle: "If you've got a legitimate green business, this is legitimate green marketing that comes together seamlessly—it's not exploitive, it's a good win/win partnership."

Supporting Sustainable Community Programs

Networking opportunities abound in your home community, so look for a cause that the expertise of your business can help. For example, if you're in the green building business or you manufacture or retail green building supplies, check in with the local housing authority to find out if there is a community initiative to develop affordable green housing. If there is, find out how you can help; if no such initiative exists, find out how you can get one started.

If you're in the food business, perhaps you can work with a food bank or a shelter program. Or work with local schools to implement healthier meals using produce from local farms, organic foods, or healthy drinks and snacks.

Are you a sustainable purveyor of green goods? Consider donating your products to local businesses for auctions, fund raisers, or prizes for their incentive programs. Seek out programs that are doing the kinds of work your sustainable values support.

Assisting Nonprofits

Just as you might look for a government program that seeks to fill a need that resonates with your business, you could also look for nongovernment organizations that are serving the community through nonprofit work. You can make donations to support nonprofit organizations, sponsor events to raise funds for such groups, or dispatch volunteer staff to help them in their work.

Clif Bar, maker of all-natural and organic energy bars, has partnered with 1 percent For the Planet to donate 1 percent of their profits to benefit communities. They've also teamed with Focus the Nation to help educate students, businesses, and communities about global warming and environmental issues. The company also provides employee staff time to volunteer for many different community organizations.

Developing an altruistic realm of your business will help your local community, or perhaps a community in a developing nation, and also help your business fulfill your goal of social responsibility. In conclusion, it's clear that developing a business that meets the needs of the planet and people while generating profits is more than a good idea—it's achievable.

Zachary Karabell, president of River Twice Research and adviser to Business of Social Responsibility, wrote in the September 22, 2008, issue of *Newsweek:* "Environmental concerns have suddenly emerged as a dominant driver of global corporations, marrying an old impulse to be good stewards of the planet with an equally ancient desire to make money. That marriage may well eradicate the quaint distinction between profit motive and public good, opening up a brand-new world of business practices and investment opportunities."

This is the new world of possibility and an opportunity to change not just the way we use our Earth's resources but also the way we do business. The new green economy gives us the chance to rewrite the meaning of business and economy in the twenty-first century. As you craft your sustainable business plan, you have the power to affect changes in how we view our economy and how it impacts life on Earth. While developing more environmentally friendly practices, you're reducing your energy usage and waste output and learning how to use resources more efficiently. You're even creating friendlier lifestyles for yourself and your employees. Should the 32-hour workweek take hold on a broad scale, we might have time to pursue hobbies, increase our knowledge through reading or continuing education, and perhaps find time to simply ruminate—the foundation of creative thought, which is the source of invention and solutions. Welcome to the Green Revolution, and thank you for choosing to be a part of creating a healthier, happier future for all of us and our children. It's happening.

The Least You Need to Know

- ◆ Networking provides a great opportunity to raise visibility for your business.
- ◆ Working with other organizations and businesses can help you reach beyond your local market.

◆ Broadening your scope can help increase sales and profits.

◆ Creating partnerships with community and nonprofit organizations can help spread the word about your business to consumers who share your values.

Appendix A

Glossary

B corporation   A new type of corporation developed to benefit all stakeholders and that meets environmental and social standards. A company must pass a B rating test to reach these standards and amend its company documents to incorporate the interests of employees, community, and the environment.

bio-based material   An engineering material made from substances derived from living matter. It typically refers to modern materials that have undergone more extensive processing.

bio-diesel   This form of diesel fuel—manufactured from vegetable oils, animal fats, or recycled restaurant greases—is safe, biodegradable, and produces less air pollutants than petroleum-based diesel.

bioaccumulation or **bioconcentration**   The process by which an organism absorbs a toxic substance at a rate faster than it loses it. This causes even low levels of toxins to be dangerous over a long period of time in the workplace.

biodegradable material   This term describes material that can break down naturally with the help of bacteria. These are typically organic substances, but if they are nonorganic and chemically similar to organic, the microbes can also break them down. Materials such as plastics are made of stable compounds and are therefore, considered nonbiodegradable.

biodiversity   The entire diversity of all species of living organisms on Earth and the habitats in which they live.

biofuel Fuel made by living things that is renewable—in contrast to fossil fuels, made from dead organisms. Common sources of biofuel grown for the U.S. and European markets are corn, soybeans, flaxseed, and rapeseed. It can appear in solid, liquid, or gas form and is used to produce heat or electricity or to power machinery using burners, broilers, generators, internal combustion engines, turbines, or fuel cells. Although a renewable energy, there is some controversy that it is not sustainable due to the harvesting of biomass and the by-products produced during the burning of biofuels.

biomagnification Similar to bioaccumulation, with the distinction being that bioaccumulation occurs within a food chain (trophic level) and biomagnification is the same process across different trophic levels (food chains).

biomass The weight of living and dead organic matter in an ecosystem usually measured per unit area over a particular time interval. Biomass refers to organic, nonfossil material available on a renewable basis. Biomass includes all biological organisms, dead or alive, and their metabolic by-products that have not been transformed by geological processes into substances such as coal or petroleum. Examples of biomass are forest and mill residues, agricultural crops and wastes, wood and wood wastes, animal wastes, livestock operation residues, aquatic plants, and municipal and industrial wastes.

biomimicry A new science based on understanding the processes and systems in nature and using them to solve human problems.

carbon dioxide Also known as CO_2, an atmospheric gas that is a major component of the carbon cycle. Although produced through natural processes, carbon dioxide is also released through human activities, such as the combustion of fossil fuels to produce electricity. Carbon dioxide is the predominate gas contributing to the greenhouse effect and as such is known to contribute to climate change.

carbon footprint The total amount of greenhouse gases produced that directly and indirectly support human activities, usually expressed in equivalent tons of carbon dioxide.

carbon neutral The process of offsetting carbon emissions by an entity (human, business, or naturally occurring) with activities that capture or reduce carbon. Carbon-offsetting companies can measure how much carbon is needed to offset a particular activity or event.

catalyst A substance that increases the rate of a chemical reaction but which is left unchanged by the reaction.

CFC-free   Free of chlorofluorocarbons (CFC), synthetic chemicals that can damage the layer of atmospheric ozone protecting Earth. CFCs were banned from products in 1978.

clean production   A way of designing products and manufacturing processes in harmony with natural ecological cycles, which aims to eliminate toxic wastes and inputs and promotes the sustainable use of renewable energy and materials.

climate change   A study of the variation in Earth's climate or regionally over a period of time. The changes can be due to Earth itself, forces outside Earth, or human activity.

closed-loop supply chain   When a supply chain process completely reuses, recycles, or composts all material used.

cogeneration   The production of electrical and thermal energy simultaneously from the same fuel source. This could be the surplus heat energy from an electrical plant being used to heat water or used as a fuel for any other purpose.

composting   Breaking down plant and animal material using microorganisms under aerobic conditions. For successful composting, sufficient water and air is needed to enable the microorganisms to break down the material, and the compost should reach and maintain a warm temperature.

Corporate Social Responsibility (CSR)   A business's continuing commitment to behave ethically, contribute to economic development, and improve the quality of workplace life, all while benefiting the local community and society at large.

cradle to cradle   Term invented in the 1970s that sets out production techniques that are essentially waste-free; all material inputs and outputs are seen either as technical or biological nutrients. Technical nutrients can be recycled or reused with no loss of quality, and biological nutrients can be composted or consumed.

downcycle   The way in which most recycled industrial nutrients lose quality or value when they are recycled. Because of this, they can be used only in a degraded form for components other than their original use. For example, white writing paper is downcycled into cardboard and recycled writing paper rather than used to make premium writing paper.

e-waste   The waste generated from electronic devices (computers, TVs, and mobile phones). The environmental impact is considerable as technology is constantly being updated and old devices are thrown out regularly. The components used are often difficult and costly to recycle.

eco-label   It identifies a product that meets specified environmental performance criteria or standards and is awarded by a third-party organization to products or services that are determined to meet the criteria or standards. An eco-label distinguishes a product or service in terms of environmental issues.

ecological economics   A study of how the two fields (ecology and economics) interact, despite having always been considered distinct. It assumes that the economy is a subsystem of the earth's ecological system, and we can learn and benefit from understanding that relationship.

ecotourism   Responsible travel to natural areas that conserves the environment, minimizes ecological or other damage, and improves the well-being of local people.

emissions trading   The creation of economic incentives to help reduce pollution. A governing body sets a cap on the amount of a pollutants that can be emitted. Companies are given permits and credits to produce a specific amount of the pollutant. If any given company wants to exceed its pollution limit, it must buy credits from those that pollute less.

Energy Star   A U.S. government system designed in 1992 to help consumers make energy-efficient and cost-effective decisions. Energy Star endorses hundreds of products through its distinctive blue logo, from refrigerators and DVDs to vending machines and exit signs. Equally useful for the home and business, it has saved billions of dollars over recent years.

externality   The side effect on an individual or entity due to the actions of another individual or entity.

fair trade or **fairtrade**   An organized social movement and market base seeking greater equity in international trade. It helps sustainable development by giving better trading conditions to workers and producers (mainly from developing countries). The Fair Trade certification means the product was produced by workers who are paid a fair wage for their labor. The program helps ensure that developing countries and their workers are not exploited and helps generate better economies.

Floor Score   A program created by Resilient Floor Covering Institute (RFCI) and Scientific Certification Systems (SCS) that tests and certifies flooring products in compliance with California indoor air quality emission requirements. Products include vinyl, linoleum, laminate, wood, ceramic, and rubber flooring, wall base, and associated sundries.

Forest Stewardship Council (FSC)   An international nonprofit organization created in 1993 based in Bonn, Germany, whose mission is "to promote environmentally viable management of the world's forests." Forestry operations that are sustainably certified by the FSC and have their timber tracked through the supply chain can carry the FSC eco-label. Thus consumers are better informed and have the choice to buy more sustainable timber products.

global warming   The recent gradual increase in average temperature of Earth's oceans and atmosphere. Scientists believe this is caused in part by human activities, which release greenhouse gases into the atmosphere.

green   The common name given to the environmental movement, its products, associations, and anything that may be affiliated with it. The color is based on that of plants and trees.

green building   The sustainable sector of the building industry that uses methods to minimize environmental impact and reduce energy consumption of a structure. In turn, this benefits the health and productivity of its occupants.

Green Building Initiative   A nonprofit U.S. organization based in Portland, Oregon, that seeks to encourage the building industry and consumers to adopt environmentally sustainable techniques.

green design   The term given to the design of products, services, buildings, experiences, or the environment in a manner that promotes economic, social, and ecological sustainability.

Green-e   An independent certification and verification program for renewable energy and greenhouse gas emission reductions in the U.S. retail market. It has three certification programs: Green-e Climate is a voluntary certification program launched in 2007 that sets consumer-protection and environmental standards for greenhouse gas emission reductions sold in the voluntary market. Green-e Energy is an independent certification and verification program for renewable energy. Green-e Marketplace is a program that enables companies to display the Green-e logo when they have purchased a certain amount of renewable energy and their verification standards.

green manufacturing   A manufacturing method that minimizes waste and pollution achieved through product and process design. Overall, green manufacturing reduces costs, improves process efficiency, and stimulates product innovation.

green marketing   Marketing strategies developed to promote products or services that are environmentally responsible and create as little ecological impact as possible.

Green Seal   An independent, nonprofit organization based in Washington, D.C., that promotes the manufacture, purchase, and use of environmentally responsible products and services. Green Seal has its own certification process and environmental standards that companies must achieve before the seal is awarded.

green tech   New technologies developed with sustainable principles in mind.

GreenGuard Environmental Institute (GEI)   An industry-independent, nonprofit organization started in 2002 based in Atlanta, Georgia, that manages the Green-Guard certification program. This is an indoor air quality test for low-emitting products. Over 100 manufacturers across various industries offer GreenGuard-certified products. In 2006, GEI introduced the GreenGuard for building construction, which is a mold risk reduction program that certifies the design, construction, and future operations of new multifamily and commercial properties.

greenhouse effect   The term describing how greenhouse gases in the atmosphere trap heat emitted from Earth's surface, thus creating an insulating and warming effect on the planet. Scientists believe that human activities, particularly since the Industrial Revolution, have accelerated the greenhouse effect, warming the climate of Earth at a rate that will eventually cause melting of the polar ice caps and mass flooding, among other natural disasters.

greenhouse gas   A gas—such as carbon dioxide and methane—that contributes to the greenhouse effect.

greenwashing   The actions of an organization that create the image of being sustainable and environmentally responsible, even though these techniques are not actually used or not to the extent that is advertised.

indoor air quality   Measures the content of interior air quality with regard to its effect on the health of building occupants. Recent studies show that indoor air quality is often poorer than outdoor air quality, which illustrates the need for standards and thorough testing in this area.

industrial ecology   A study and practice of how industry can be developed to minimize environmental impact during the product life cycle (extraction, production, use, and disposal). This is especially important because of the historically harmful nature of this sector to the environment.

Kyoto Protocol   An agreement for industrial nations in 1997 at the United Nations Framework Convention on Climate Change (UNFCC) in Kyoto, Japan, to reduce greenhouse gas emissions by at least 5 percent below 1990 levels by 2012. The protocol was adopted in 2005 without the United States being involved, although over 200 U.S. cities have decided to adopt the Kyoto Protocols themselves.

Leadership in Energy and Environmental Design (LEED) rating   This system rates new buildings, interiors, and other components based on environmental effectiveness. LEED's checklist involves more than 60 criteria, and certification is given at four levels: certified, silver, gold, and platinum.

life-cycle assessment (LCA)   A study of the complete impact of a product or service's manufacturing, use, and disposal in terms of material and energy. The scope of the analysis is comprehensive, although few standards exist to measure and assess these impacts. LCAs are useful to companies that want to display the results of their products or services to consumers, as well as being able to identify ways to reduce energy used.

Lifestyles of Health and Sustainability (LOHAS)   This market segment of consumers is interested in health, sustainability, and the environment. In 2006, this sector was estimated at $300 billion.

materials audit   A process to analyze the costs and effects of materials used in manufacturing and to determine more efficient, less costly, less toxic, and more sustainable alternatives.

natural capital   Same as environmental capital, which is the stock of natural resources and environmental assets, and includes water, soils, air, flora, fauna, minerals, and other natural resources.

net-zero energy home   A home built with energy-efficient practices and technologies that result in an annual contribution to the energy grid that is at least the same as the amount of power used from the grid. Common sources of energy generation are solar panels, wind turbines, and geothermal heating and cooling systems. Building many of these properties would result in a significant reduction in the need for electricity plants.

nongovernmental organization (NGO)   A nonprofit organization created neither by businesses or government that often conducts humanitarian and development work around the world.

nonrenewable resources   Natural resources that cannot be regrown or regenerated at a proportion that they are being consumed. Fossil fuels such as coal and petroleum are nonrenewable resources. Examples of renewable resources are timber and some metals.

organic   Term given to the technique of developing food and agricultural products without the use of pesticides, hormones, synthetic fertilizers, and other toxic materials. Some countries have adopted a legal definition for organic.

permaculture   A design system that encompasses both permanent agriculture and permanent culture and recognizes that all living systems are organized around energy flows. It teaches people to analyze existing energy flows (sun, rain, money, and human energy) through a system (a garden, a household, or a business). When correctly designed, such a system will, like a natural ecosystem, become increasingly diverse and self-sustaining.

pollution   Any substances in water, soil, or air that degrade the natural quality of the environment or cause a health hazard. The usefulness of the natural resource is usually impaired by the presence of pollutants and contaminants.

pollution prevention   Any practice that reduces the amount of hazardous substance, pollutant, or contaminant entering the waste stream or otherwise released to the environment before recycling, treatment, or disposal. This process reduces the hazards to public health and the environment associated with the release of such substances. Often referred to as P2.

precautionary principle   When an activity raises threats of harm to the environment or human health, precautionary measures should be taken, even if some cause-and-effect relationships are not fully established scientifically.

recyclable   Material that still has useful physical or chemical properties after serving its original purpose and can therefore be reused or remanufactured into additional products. Plastic, paper, glass, tin, and aluminum cans are examples of recyclable materials.

recycle   Taking an unwanted material, processing it, and then producing a useful product again. Aluminum cans can be melted (processed) and reformed as aluminum cans or other aluminum products. Other examples include newspaper made into insulation, auto body steel made into bridge parts, or milk jugs made into park benches.

reduce   To decrease the amount of energy and materials we use in manufacturing. This also has an exponential effect, as it reduces packaging, recycling, transportation, disposal, and many other costs. Reduction is one of the most sustainable strategies that exists.

remanufacturing   The dismantling of a spent product to clean and repair it for the same use. Replacement parts must be new after-market parts that meet the same specifications as the original manufactured parts.

renewable   Any material able to be sustained or renewed indefinitely, either because of limitless supplies or new growth.

reuse   Repairing, refurbishing, washing, or recovering worn or used products, packaging appliances, furniture, or building materials for internal use. Reusing packaging and products prolongs the useful life of items and delays the final disposal or recycling.

stewardship   Taking responsibility and caring for the earth or any part of it. Includes responsibility in using resources and creating as little waste and pollution as possible.

supply chain   The system of organizations, people, activities, information, and resources involved in moving a product or service from supplier to customer.

sustainable development   Development that meets the needs of the present without compromising the ability of future generations to meet their own needs, according to the Brundtland Commission, formally The World Commission on Sustainable Development (1987).

Sustainable Forestry Initiative (SFI)   A program based on the premise that responsible environmental behavior and sound business decisions can co-exist. SFI program participants practice sustainable forestry on all lands they manage. They also influence millions of additional acres through the training of loggers and foresters in best management practices and landowner outreach programs.

take-back   An approach to encourage reuse or recycling where consumers return products back to the company that made them. Some laws mandate take-back programs and create incentives for manufacturers to make their products easily recyclable or reused.

technical nutrient   Materials made from highly stable, reusable components and designed to be captured and reused in the closed-loop cycle of sustainable manufacturing. Aluminum is an example of a technical nutrient.

telecommuting   Instead of commuting to a place of employment, the employee works from home, using the Internet and other communication devices. This reduces the use of transport, and hence, energy and pollution.

toxic   Involving something poisonous. A toxic material can cause death, disease, or birth defects in organisms that ingest or absorb them. The quantities and exposures necessary to cause these effects can vary widely.

transparency   A requirement that sits alongside accountability as a growing expectation on organizations by society. It involves an openness and willingness to accept public scrutiny that reduces the capacity for an organization to practice or harbor deception or deceit.

triple bottom line   This process, described by Theo Ferguson, includes profit, planet, and people and is designed for companies aiming for sustainability. The companies must perform not to just a single financial bottom line, but the simultaneous pursuit of economic prosperity, environmental quality, and social equity. The process is used for integrating financial, environmental, and social costs and benefits into a unified measure of business activity. Conventional objectives of profitability, competitive advantage, efficiency, and economic growth are judged successful by their compatibility with biodiversity, ecological sustainability, equity, community support, and maximized well-being for a variety of stakeholders.

triple top line   The effect that sustainable practices cause companies to increase revenues (through more desirable products and services) while reducing costs and expenses, by using more efficient processes.

upcycle   To take something that is disposable and transform it into something of similar or greater use and value. Aluminum and glass are examples of materials that can be upcycled.

volatile organic compound (VOC)   Organic chemicals containing carbon, oxygen, hydrogen, chlorine, and other atoms. Volatile chemicals produce vapors readily, and many are hazardous air pollutants and toxic.

waste reduction   Preventing or decreasing the quantity of waste being generated through waste prevention, recycling, or purchasing recycled and environmentally preferable products.

water conservation   Practices that promote the efficient use of water, such as minimizing losses, reducing wasteful use, and protecting availability for future use. This is vital as water is one of our most valuable resources.

xeriscaping   This environmentally friendly form of landscaping uses a variety of indigenous and drought-tolerant plants, shrubs, and ground cover and a limited amount of water, thus promoting water conservation.

zero waste   The theory that a society, organization, or process can reduce, reuse, or recycle all its waste, thus producing zero waste of no economic value needing final disposal. Many cities and states already have set zero-waste goals; for example, San Francisco has set a goal to create zero waste by 2020.

Resources for Going Green

In this resource guide, we've collected references to books, websites, and organizations mentioned through the book in case you want to learn more about a particular topic. For easy reference, we've organized them according to the sections in which they were discussed. You'll find more detailed descriptions of these resources in the chapters.

Books

Astyk, Sharon, and Aaron Newton. *A Nation of Farmers: Defeating the Food Crisis on American Soil*. Canada: New Society Publishers, 2009.

Benyus, Janine. *Biomimicry: Innovation Inspired by Nature*. New York: Harper Perennial, 2002.

Braungart, Michael, and William McDonnough. *Cradle to Cradle: Remaking the Way We Make Things*. New York: North Point Press, 2002.

Hawken, Paul. *Blessed Unrest: How the Largest Movement in the World came into Being and Why No One Saw It Coming*. New York: Penguin, 2008.

———. *The Ecology of Commerce*. New York: Collins Business, 1994.

Hawken, Paul, L. Hunter Lovins, and Amory Lovins. *Natural Capitalism: Creating the Next Industrial Revolution*. New York: Little Brown, 1999.

Meyerson, Mitch, and Jay Levinson. *Guerrilla Marketing on the Front Lines*. New York: Morgan James Publishing, 2008.

Part 1: Greening Your Business: Why It's the Way to Go

BBMG

www.bbmg.com

A marketing agency that specializes in working with socially responsible businesses and in identifying conscious consumers.

Kenexa Research Institute

650 East Swedesford Road

Wayne, PA 19087

1-877-971-9171

www.kenexa.com.

A company that helps organizations hire and retain employees.

MonsterTRAK.com

www.monstertrak.com

An online employment resource.

The Natural Step Framework

www.thenaturalstep.org

The Natural Step framework enables corporations to intelligently, and profitably, integrate environmental considerations into strategic decisions and daily operations.

Sustainable Business Institute

467 Saratoga Ave., #1411

San Jose, CA 95129

www.sustainablebusiness.org

Resource for sustainable business.

Part 2: Getting Started on the Green Path

B Corp

www.bcorporation.net

A B corporation is a new type of corporation that uses the power of business to solve social and environmental problems.

Bay Area Green Business Program

www.greenbiz.ca.gov

Community support for green businesses.

British Standards Institute
www.bsigroup.com
A government-chartered nonprofit corporation that provides standards and standards-related services.

The Carbon Trust
www.carbontrust.co.uk
A nonprofit corporation whose goal is to help the nation transition toward a "low-carbon" economy.

Carbonfund.org
www.carbonfund.org
Nonprofit retailer of carbon offsets.

Conservation International's Measure Your Eco Footprint
www.conservation.org/act/live_green/Pages/ecofootprint.aspx
Calculate your carbon footprint.

Devil's Thumb Ranch
www.devilsthumbranch.com
An eco-friendly resort and spa.

The Energy Star Small Business Program
www.energystar.gov/index.cfm?c=small_business.sb_index
Helps small business develop plans to reduce their energy consumption.

EPA E-Grid database
www.epa.gov/airmarkets/egrids
Find the emissions factor for your utilities.

EPA's Climate Change website
www.epa.gov/climatechange/index.html
Offers comprehensive information on the issue of climate change in a way that is accessible and meaningful to all parts of society—communities, individuals, business, states and localities, and governments.

EPA's Green Vehicle Guide
www.epa.gov/autoemissions
Guide to green vehicles.

Global Footprint Network Personal Footprint Calculator
www.footprintnetwork.org/gfn_sub.php?content=calculator
Calculate your carbon footprint.

The Global Water Tool
www.wbcsd.org/web/watertool.htm
The World Business Council for Sustainable Development (WBCSD) is a CEO-led global association of some 200 companies dealing exclusively with business and sustainable development.

Intergovernmental Panel on Climate Change
www.ipcc.ch
This United Nations–established international body of scientists publishes reports synthesizing recent research on greenhouse gases and global warming.

International Energy Agency
www.iea.org
An intergovernmental organization which acts as energy policy advisor to 28 member countries in their effort to ensure reliable, affordable, and clean energy for their citizens.

MarionEco
www.marioneco.com
Provides environmental services.

The National Institute of Standards and Technology
www.mep.nist.gov
A nationwide network of specialists that help small- and medium-size manufacturers through the Manufacturing Extension Partnerships program.

Redefining Progress's Ecological Footprint Quiz
www.myfootprint.org/en/visitor_information
Calculate your carbon footprint.

Resource Conservation and Pollution Prevention Checklist
www2.sfenvironment.org/greenbiz/files/OfficeRetail_Checklist.pdf
Check your office pollution output.

The TeleCommuter Hire Savings Calculator
www.tjobs.com/hiresavings.shtml
This online tool shows savings by employees in getting cars off the road.

Terrapass
www.terrapass.com
Carbon offset retailer and offset project owner.

United Nations Environmental Programme (UNEP)

www.wnep.org

The voice for the environment in the United Nations system.

U.S. Global Change Research Program

1717 Pennsylvania Ave. NW, Suite 250

Washington, DC 20006

202-223-6262

www.usgcrp.gov

Supports research on the interactions of natural and human-induced changes in the global environment and their implications for society.

The Water Calculator

www.h2oconserve.org/wc_disclaimer.php?pd=ca

An interactive tool to determine water usage, waste, and efficiency factors.

World Business Council for Sustainable Development

www.wbcsd.org

An international council of business leaders working toward sustainability.

World Resources Institute, an environmental think tank

www.wri.org

The World Resources Institute's "Working 9 to 5 on Climate Change Office Guide" calculates a business's greenhouse gas emissions.

Zerofootprint.net

http://goblue.zerofootprint.net/?language=en

Includes a personal carbon manager tool.

Part 3: Your Business Environment and Operations

Alaska Materials Exchange

www.greenstarinc.org/ame/ameindex.php

Free interactive web-based service for businesses and organizations to exchange items they no longer want.

The American Physical Society report

www.aps.org/energyefficiencyreport

A report on energy efficiency.

American Specialty Glass

www.americanspecialtyglass.com/landscape1.html

Sells multi-colored glass mulch for landscaping.

Association for Retail Environments

www.retailenvironments.org

Trade association for businesses that sell products and services associated with retail environments.

Barr Display

www.barrdisplay.com

A business that sells store fixtures and product display pieces.

Bicycle and Pedestrian Facilities Program in Oakland, CA

www.oaklandpw.com/bicycling

The developer of international standards pertaining to various industries and sectors.

Biomimicry Design Spiral

www.biomimicryinstitute.org

An innovation tool that helps designers incorporate sustainable design into their projects.

California Low-Carbon Fuel Standard

www.energy.ca.gov/low_carbon_fuel_standard

New law requiring low-carbon fuel efficiency.

The Clean Cargo Working Group

www.bsr.org/sustainabletransport

Network of cargo shippers working to clean up the environmental impact of ocean-going cargo.

Converted Organics

www.convertedorganics.com

Collects compostable wastes and converts to organic fertilizer products.

Denver Water

www.denverwater.org/search/searchframe.html.

Provides extensive water conservation and quality information.

Earth 911

www.earth911.org

Promotes recycling and offers a searchable list of recycling centers by region.

The Earth Policy Institute

www.earth-policy.org/Updates/2005/Update48_printable.htm

Provides information on ecological issues and the economy.

The Energy Store

www.energystore-usa.com

Independent store in South Florida that sells solar-powered products and other energy-efficient items.

The Environmental Defense Fund

www.edf.org/page.cfm?tagID=1124

Provides an updated listing of government incentives and hybrid fleet vehicle options.

EPA grants

www.epa.gov/diesel

Grants related to clean diesel engines.

EPA Indoor Air Quality Information

Environmental Protection Agency

1-800-438-4318

www.epa.gov/iaq

Information and resources for improving indoor air quality.

EPA Report

www.epa.gov/oswer/docs/iwg/cradle.pdf

Report on e-commerce packaging design challenge.

EPA Smartway Transit

www.epa.gov/smartway

Provides information, assistance, and incentives related to efficient, reduced-emissions transportation.

Flush Choice

www.flushchoice.com

Provides a retrofit kit to make toilets more water efficient.

The Green Car Journal

www.greencar.com/features/clean-fuels-deliver

Reports on fuel-efficient delivery vehicles.

Green Dwellers

www.greendwellers.com

A retail store in South Florida that sells eco-friendly home goods.

Green Globes

www.greenglobes.com

A building certification program.

Green Packaging, Inc.

650 N. Cannon Ave.

Lansdale, PA 19446

1-877-822-0552

www.greenpackaginginc.com

This Pennsylvania-based company provides sustainable packing materials to replace Styrofoam and plastics.

The GreenPostalStore.org

www.thegreenpostalstore.org

Offers eco-friendly packaging materials.

Green Restaurant Association

www.dinegreen.com

Provides support and information for sustainable restaurant practices.

Hand Motors

802-362-1754

www.handmotors.com

An auto dealership in Vermont with eco-friendly facets.

International Organization of Standards

www.iso.org

The developer of international standards pertaining to various industries and sectors.

Kendall College Sustainability for the Food Service Industry video

www.kendall.edu/SustainabilityVideo/tabid/404/Default.aspx

Video describing green restaurant practices and their importance.

Low Impact Living

www.lowimpactliving.com/providers/Solar-Power/31#

Provides a list of solar power providers.

MBDC (McDonough Braungart Design Chemistry)

http://mbdc.com/c2c/overview.php

A product and process design firm specializing in creating a sustainable future.

Miami Dade County Cooperative Extension Service
http://miami-dade.ifas.ufl.edu/environment/natural_resources.shtml
Information about native planting and xeriscaping.

Minnesota Pollution Control Agency
http://www.pca.state.mn.us/oea/
A state agency that focuses on environmental topics.

National Pesticide Telecommunications Network (NPTN)
1-800-858-PEST
http://aggie-horticulture.tamu.edu/extension/newsletters/hortupdate/mar01/art7mar.html
Information about natural pesticides.

Natural Resources Defense Council report
www.e2.org/ext/doc/NRDC-LCFSBackgrounder.pdf
A report on the Low Carbon Fuel Standard.

Packaged Facts
www.packagedfacts.com/Natural-Organic-Food-1119530/
Natural and organic food and beverage product sales statistics and trends.

PHH Arval
www.phharval.com/green
A fleet management service in North America for delivery vehicles.

Pizza Fusion
www.pizzafusion.com
An eco-friendly pizza franchise.

Rain Barrel Guide
www.rainbarrelguide.com
Instructions for building a rain barrel.

REI
www.rei.com
A retailer of outdoor sporting goods products.

Reusablebags.com
www.reusablebags.com
Online business that sells reusable bags, reusable water bottles, and other products.

Rodale Institute
www.rodaleinstitute.org/node/445
Studies and advocates organic farming.

Staples
www.staples.com
Retail store chain that sells office supplies.

The State of Massachusetts Report
www.mass.gov/?pageID=eoeeahomepage&L=1&L0=Home&sid=Eoeea
A report on advanced biofuels.

Sustainable Packaging Coalition
www.sustainablepackaging.org
Provides information on sustainable packaging.

Treecycle Recycled Paper
www.treecycle.com/recycling.html
Sells recycled paper products.

UFP Technologies
www.ufpt.com/moldedfiber/packaging.asp?gclid=CKbMs4LvhJYCFQEGQQod0y
Offers molded fiber packaging.

The United States Postal Service
www.usps.com/green
Lists efficiency innovations.

Vermont Business Materials Exchange
www.vbmx.org
Online service for selling, trading, and giving away items.

Whole Foods Market
www.wholefoods.com
National chain of environmentally friendly foods and products.

Willie Nelson's biofuel company
www.biowillieusa.com
Sells biodiesel at select fuel stations across the country.

Part 4: Your Business Practices and Cost Benefits

AccountAbility

www.accountability21.net

Established the AA1000 Framework to help organizations build their accountability and social responsibility through quality social and ethical accounting, auditing, and reporting.

All Business

www.allbusiness.com

A resource for business owners and managers.

American Public Transportation Association

1666 K. St., NW

Washington, DC 20006

www.apta.com

Provides information about public transportation.

Avego.com

www.avego.com

A new carpooling connection service that's based on emerging technologies.

BALLE (Business Alliance for Local Living Economies)

www.livingeconomies.org

An organization that performs sustainability consulting.

Carpoolconnect.com

www.carpoolconnect.com

Provides an instant, free Internet resource for finding rides going your way.

Carpoolworld.com

www.carpoolworld.com

Matches drivers and riders worldwide for free.

Ceres

www.ceres.org

This national network of investors, environmental organizations, and other public interest groups works with companies and investors who address sustainability challenges.

Commuter Choice
PO Box 15542
Washington, DC 20003
202-393-3497
Fax: 202-546-2196
www.commuterchoice.com
An organization that provides information for businesses interested in setting up a
commuter program for employees.

CorporateRegister.com
www.corporateregister.com
Offers a list on online sustainability reports.

Dividetheride.com
www.dividetheride.com
Matches carpoolers for business and kid pick-ups.

Earth 911
www.earth911.org
http://business.earth911.org/green-guides/conserve-energy-in-your-workplace/
office-energy-reduction-tips
This organization promotes recycling and other facets of sustainability.

Energy Star
www.energystar.gov/index.cfm?c=power_mgt.pr_power_mgt_faq
Tips on saving energy in the office.

EPA
http://yosemite.epa.gov/opa/admpress.nsf/dc57b08b5acd42bc852573c90044a9c4/0b24e
a327784cecf852574bf004827f4
Tips on powering down electronics.

EPA
www.epa.gov/epawaste/conserve/materials/ecycling/donate.htm
Information on recycling electronics.

eRideShare.com
www.eRideShare.com
Offers special features for employers who set up the free service for employees.

The Federal Transit Administration

www.fta.gov

Information about mass transit systems, planning, funding, and so on.

Freeconference.com

www.freeconference.com

Offers basic services for free plus a selection of premium services, such as toll-free dial-in.

FreeCycle.com

www.freecycle.com

A web-based trading organization.

The Global Reporting Initiative (GRI)

www.globalreporting.org

GRI measures an organization's performance through key performance indicators (KPI) in financial, environmental, and social areas.

GoGreenGift

www.gogreengift.com

An eco-friendly gift that can be customized for corporate events to help convey your company's sustainable philosophy.

Green America

www.coopamerica.org/cabn/resources/greenoffice.cfm

www.greenamericatoday.org

Formerly Co-Op America, a nonprofit organization supporting green businesses, this group offers tips on saving energy at the office.

Green It Group

www.greenitgroup.com

A full-service sustainability consultantcy with core competencies in sustainable business strategy, green building and building science, product assessment, green marketing, and organizational change. It specializes in the creation of strategic sustainability programs that produce measurable results.

Green Hotels

www.greenhotels.com

Find a green hotel to ease your travel footprint.

The Green Office in San Francisco
www.thegreenoffice.com
Sells supplies, including paper products with recycled content.

Hybrids.com
www.hybridcars.com
Lists companies that offer incentives to employees who purchase or lease hybrid cars, along with a host of other information about hybrid vehicles.

The Innovative Edge, Inc.
www.innov-edge.com
A consulting and training firm that helps client organizations develop innovation and creativity.

Large Software
www.largesoftware.com
Provides software for tuning up a computer's performance.

Live Office Teleconferencing
http://teleconference.liveoffice.com/features.asp
Offers several services, including recording and website access, for a per-minute fee.

The Minnesota Pollution Control Agency
www.reduce.org
Tips for reducing waste.

Native Energy Travel Calculator
www.nativeenergy.com/pages/travel_calculator/30.php
A guide to energy credits for small businesses.

Next Step Consulting
www.nextstep.co.uk
A London-based consultancy specializing in corporate environmental and social communications, policy, and strategy.

Office Depot
www.officedepot.com
Offers conference calling for a monthly or per-minute fee, including toll-free access and web-based services so conferees can review web-based material during the call.

Office tips from Waldeck's Office Supply Co.
www.waldecks.com/tipsfortheoffice.html
Office supply store in San Francisco, California, that shares some environmental tips.

OzoCar

www.ozocar.com

This business in New York City and the northeast region provides an all-hybrid fleet of Toyota Prius and Lexus cars plus free wireless and even includes a laptop in the backseat for your use.

The Paper Industry Association Council

www.paperrecycles.org/guide/work/index.html

A guide to recycling at work from the Paper Industry Association Council.

PlanetTran

1-888-756-8876

www.planettran.com

Provides similar hybrid car services in Boston and San Francisco.

RideSearch.com

www.ridesearch.com

This free service helps match up people interested in carpooling nationwide.

Sustainable Industries Green Office Guide

www.sustainableindustries.com

Resource for cutting-edge news about sustainable industries.

Tellus Institute

www.tellus.org

Assesses environment and development issues.

Virgin Airlines

www.virgin-atlantic.com

Airline working to reduce its carbon footprint through initiatives such as going paperless and serving Fair Trade teas and coffees.

The Virgin Earth Challenge

www.virginearth.com

A $25 million prize for the development of a clean airline fuel.

Zimride.com

www.zimride.com

Another carpool service that utilizes Internet technology to connect drivers with riders. They can even be found on Facebook.com.

Zipcar

www.zipcar.com

Provides temporary car rentals to members around the country and beyond.

Part 5: Marketing Your Green Message

Campaign Monitor
www.campaignmonitor.com
E-mail marketing software.

Constant Contact
www.constantcontact.com
An e-mail marketing firm.

Consumer Reports
www.consumerreports.org
Magazine that publishes reviews of consumer products based on tests and other reports.

Consumers Union
101 Truman Ave.
Yonkers, NY 10703
www.consumersunion.org
A nonprofit watchdog agency that regularly tests products for safety and value, producing reports for the public.

CSR Wire
www.csrwire.com
A news wire service that focuses on environmental and social issues.

eBlast.com
www.eblast.com
A program to help send out mass e-mails.

Ecolabels.org
www.ecolabels.org
Gives information about product labels.

Emma E-mail Marketing
www.myemma.com
An e-mail marketing firm.

Energy Star Program
www.energystar.gov
Program that certifies products that are energy efficient and sustainable.

Energy Star's rebate locator
www.energystar.gov/index.cfm?fuseaction=rebate.rebate_locator
Offers rebates for buying energy-efficient products.

Environmental Choice New Zealand (ECNZ)
www.enviro-choice.org.nz
The home of Environmental Choice—the Ecolabelling Trust of New Zealand. Gives information, licensed products, and info on joining the program.

The Environmental Choice Program (ECP)
www.epa.gov/epp/pubs/relatedintl.htm
Environment Canada's eco-label program.

EPA Green Power Partnership
www.epa.gov/greenpower
Partnership that requires a participant to buy green power in an amount based on a percentage of its annual energy consumption.

EPA Partnerships
www.epa.gov/partners/benefits/index.htm
Offers an assortment of national and regional partnering programs, including Energy Star and the Green Power Purchase program.

The European Eco-Label Catalogue
www.eco-label.com
Provides details on eco-labeled products and manufacturers.

E-Wire
www.ewire.com
News wire that reports on the environment, health, science, and technology.

Forest Stewardship Council—U.S.
1155 30th St. NW, Suite 300
Washington, DC 20007
202-342-0413
www.fscus.org/index.html
Works with landowners to bring their forests up to transparent standards.

FTC Environmental Marketing Guidelines
www.ftc.gov/bcp/grnrule/guides980427.htm
Provides a framework for the use of environmental marketing claims.

Germany's Blue Angel eco-label
www.blauer-engel.de/englisch/navigation/body_blauer_engel.htm
One of the oldest eco-labeling programs in the world.

Green America (previously Co-Op America)
1612 K St. NW, Suite 600
Washington, DC 20006
1-800-58-GREEN
www.greenamericatoday.org
A nonprofit organization that supports sustainable businesses and products.

Green Seal
1001 Connecticut Ave. NW, Suite 827
Washington, DC 20036-5525
202-872-6400
www.greenseal.org
It assesses a product using a multiple-criteria, life cycle–based method. Products that pass are awarded this seal.

The International Organization for Standards (ISO)
www.iso-14001.org.uk/iso-14024.htm
The world's largest developer and publisher of International Standards.

Mind Click
www.mindclickgroup.com
A marketing research company.

Scientific Certification Systems
www.scscertified.com
Offers a diverse range of eco-labels.

SmartWood
65 Millet St., Suite 201
Richmond, VT 05477
www.smartwood.org
Produces certified wood, including furniture, musical instruments, flooring, and picture and window frames.

Solar Energy Industries Association
805 15th St., NW, Suite 510
Washington, DC 20005
www.seia.org
Represents companies in the solar energy industry.

Staples

www.staples.com

Office supply company that won a Green Power Leadership Award in 2007 for purchasing green power equivalent to more than 20 percent of the purchased electricity in the United States.

Terra Choice consulting services

www.terrachoice.com

Administers the Environmental Choice EcoLogo.

U.S. Environmental Protection Agency (EPA)

www.epa.gov

Government agency that works on conservation and pollution prevention, among other areas.

U.S. Green Building Council

1015 18th St., NW, Suite 805

Washington, DC 20036

202-828-7422

www.usgbc.org

Administers the Leadership in Energy and Environmental Design (LEED) program.

The Vermont Business Environmental Partnership

www.vbep.org

Designates organizations Environmental Partners or Environmental Leaders based on their efforts in areas such as recycling and energy efficiency.

Index

Numbers

1605(b), 77

A

AA1000 framework, 243
accountability, 41
Accountability website, 46
active aware consumers, 263
additionality of carbon offsets, 81
agricultural run-off, 13
air fresheners, 115
air pollution, 13
alarmist consumers, 263
Alaska Materials Exchange, 146
All Business, 208
alternative health-care credits, 215
American Physical Society (APS), 171
American Public Transportation Association (APTA), 196
Anderson, Ray, 5
anti-bacterial soaps, 114
Apple MacBook, 188
appliances, 93
APS (American Physical Society), 171
APTA (American Public Transportation Association, 196
Arketype website, 33

assessment
    current operations, 33-34
    energy usage, 50
        calculating, 51
        equipment, 52-53
    fuel, 55
    life-cycle assessment, 129-130
        benefits, 130-131
        cradle to grave, 130
        impacts of materials assessment, 131-133
        ISO 14040:2006 protocol, 133
        manufacturing, 133
        phases, 133
    marketing, 270
    products, 251-252
    sustainability, 44-46
    waste, 53-55
    water, 47-49
        measuring inputs, 49
        quality, 49-50
attendee gifts, 224-225
attracting employees, 12
availability of resources, 19
Avego website, 197

B

backcasting, 28
BAN (Basel Action Network), 188
bathrooms, 113
    hand-drying options, 114
    soaps, 114
    toilets/sinks, 113

Bay Area Green Business Program, 284
Belanger, Amy, 298
benefits
    building green, 88-89
    business bottom line, 9
    employers
        attracting employees, 12
        employee retention/ productivity, 13
        healthy lives, 13
    green landscaping, 118
    life-cycle assessment, 130-131
    local sales focus, 178
    marketing, 138
    organic farming, 156
    organic foods, 154-155
    overstating, 268
    partnership programs, 284-285
    peer cooperation, 293
    planet
        eco-friendly materials, 10
        reducing dependence on oil, 10
        reducing greenhouse gases, 11
        reducing package weight, 170
bio-based solvent options, 140
biodegradability
    bottles, 167
    claims, 257

packaging materials
 molded fiber, 168
 peanuts, 168
 post-consumer recycled
  paper, 169
biodiesel fuel, 174
biofuel, 9
biological contaminants in
 indoor air, 103-104
biological nutrients, 136
biomass, 9
biomimicry
 design spiral, 134
 learning from nature,
  134-135
 website, 134
Biomimicry Institute website,
 135
bioplastic, 167
Bisphenol A (BPA), 157
Blue Angel, 280
bottom line, 4
boundaries of sustainability
 reports, 239
BPA (Bisphenol A), 157
brands
 relationships, 266
 value, 21-22
Branson, Richard, 202
Braungart, Michael, 135
buildings
 appliance efficiency, 93
 benefits of going green,
  88-89
 costs, 89
 energy efficiency, 97
 existing
  commissioning, 92
  landlord discussions, 91
  LEED EBOM
   certification, 90
  renovating, 92
  retrofitting, 92

floorings, 107
 alternatives, 107-108
 durability, 110
 reducing toxic exposure,
  109
 waste reduction, 108-109
indoor air quality
 biological contaminants,
  103-104
 chemical contaminants,
  102
 cleaning supplies, 114
 contaminants, 103
 "The Inside Story: A
  Guide to Indoor Air
  Quality," 102
 meeting venue selection,
  221
 paints/fabrics
  petrochemicals,
  104-107
 polluted, 102
 testing, 103
local materials, 94
natural lighting, 96
natural/rapidly renewable
 materials, 95
new construction, 89
reducing toxins/emissions,
 98
salvaged materials, 93
ventilation systems, 96
waste disposal, 98-99
water
 conservation, 99-100
 efficient products, 93
bulk condiments, 226
business case for sustainability
 reports, 238
Business for Social
 Responsibility organization,
 296
business programs, 56

business-related travel, 200
 promoting efficiency, 200
 reducing, 200
 sustainable vendors, 202-203
 teleconferencing, 201
 travel offsets, 202

C

calculating
 carbon footprint, 70-72
 energy usage, 51-53
 greenhouse gas emissions,
  75-76
 Green Power Equivalency
  Calculator, 287
 marketing success, 270
 unit conversion tool
  website, 77
 water inputs, 49
California
 Climate Action Registry
  (CCAR), 78
 Resource Recovery
  Association's Polystyrene
  Recycling Market
  Development Zone
  program, 139
carbon dioxide equivalent
 greenhouse gases, 82
carbon footprinting, 70
 calculating, 70-72
 carbon labels, 79
 Carbonfree certification,
  80
 cars off the road for a year,
  70
 defined, 70
 GHG Protocol, 72
  development, 71
  greenhouse gas
   emissions inventory,
   75-76

greenhouse gas
reporting standards,
77-78
Little Red Wagon, Inc.
example, 73-75
operational boundaries,
73
organizational
boundaries, 73
products, 78-80
website, 72
greenhouse gases other
than CO_2, 82
livestock, 156-157
carbon labels, 79
carbon neutral, 70
carbon offsets, 80
additionality requirement,
81
defined, 80
greenhouse gases other
than CO_2, 82
Little Red Wagon, Inc.
example, 80
overview, 80
sustainability, 81-82
Voluntary Carbon
Standard, 81
Carbon Trust, 79, 284
Carbonfree certification, 80
Carbonfund.org, 80
CARE (Carpet America
Recover Effort), 109
cargo ships, 178
Carpool Connect website, 198
Carpool World website, 198
carpooling, 197-198
cars off the road for a year, 70
cash incentives for
commuting efficiency, 199
cause marketing, 298-299
CCAR (California Climate
Action Registry), 78

CCX (Chicago Climate
Exchange), 77
certifications, 272
existing buildings, 90
genuine, 274-275
green building, 89
international, 280-282
pseudo sanctions, 275
third-party, 276
Fair Trade Certified,
278
government, 279
Green Seal, 276
LEED, 277-278
Scientific Certification
Systems (SCS), 277
types, 272-273
verification, 273-274
CFC-free eco-labels, 276
checklist for reduction, 63
emissions, 63
waste, 65
water usage, 64
chemical contamination, 14
foods, 157-158
indoor air, 102
Chicago Climate Exchange
(CCX), 77
chlorine-free paper, 192
claims of products, 256-258
Clean Cargo Working Group,
178
cleaning supplies, 114
Clif Bar
employee community
involvement support, 209
encouraging healthy food
choices, 212
nonprofit support, 300
Climate Action Plan website,
63
Climate Leaders, 77

The Climate Registry, 78
collecting rainwater, 122-124
commissioning existing
buildings, 92
communications messaging of
sustainability reports, 239
community partnerships, 298
cause marketing, 298-299
nonprofit support, 299-300
sustainable community
programs, 299
Community Supported
Agriculture (CSA), 212
Commuter Choice, 196
commuting efficiency
carpooling, 197-198
cash incentives, 199
Commuter Choice, 196
mass transit, 195-196
parking incentives, 199
remote employees, 199-200
composting
claims, 257
containers, 214
humus, 128
ingredients, 126
plates and flatware, 226
soil conservation, 125-127
worm bins, 214
computers
energy usage, 52
power management, 185
conscious consumers, 21
defining, 262-264
types, 264-265
value-driven purchasing,
265
brand relationships, 266
convenience, 266
health and safety, 265
honesty, 266
making a difference, 266

conserving. *See also* efficiency; reducing
  energy
    cost-benefit analysis, 16
    equipment, 112-113
    retail operations, 148
  soil, 125-127
  water
    buildings, 99-100
    landscaping, 121-125
    restaurants, 160
    retail operations, 148-149
    toilets/faucets, 93
    xeriscaping, 119
construction
  benefits, 88-89
  green principles
    appliance efficiency, 93
    energy efficiency, 97
    local materials, 94
    natural lighting, 96
    natural/rapidly renewable materials, 95
    reducing toxins/emissions, 98
    salvaged materials, 93
    ventilation systems, 96
    waste disposal, 98-99
    water conservation, 99-100
    water-efficient products, 93
  new, 89
consumers
  active aware, 263
  alarmists, 263
  conscious, 21
    defining, 262-264
    types, 264-265
  educating, 267
    overstating benefits, 268
    recycling products, 267-268

    enthusiasts, 263
    indifferent, 264
    nonbelievers, 264
    passive aware, 263
    targeting, 261
    value-driven purchasing, 265
      brand relationships, 266
      convenience, 266
      health and safety, 265
      honesty, 266
      making a difference, 266
consumption assessments
  energy, 50-53
  fuel, 55
  waste, 53-55
  water, 47
    assessing, 47-50
    reduction plan, 64
contaminants
  indoor air, 103
    biological, 103-104
    chemical, 102
Continental Airlines, 202
conventional consumers, 265
conventional farming compared to organic farming, 159
Converted Organics, 161
Co-Op America, 294-295
cooperating with peers, 292
  benefits, 293
  greater good, 292
copiers, 52
core stakeholders, 20
cost-benefit analysis, 15
  energy conservation, 16
  environmental, 37
  goals, 37
  meetings/events, 229
  selecting supplies, 17
  waste reduction, 16

costs
  building green, 89
  food transportation, 158
  landscaping, 118
  reducing retail supply, 145
    recycling used products, 146
    reducing waste, 145
    reusable packaging materials, 147
  sustainable supply-chain savings, 138
cotton, 106
cradle-to-cradle designs, 135-136
Cradle to Cradle: Remaking the Way We Make Things, 135
cradle to grave, 130
creating
  employee relationships, 208
    building green values into corporate culture, 209
    rewards, 211
    supporting creativity, 210
  environmental policies, 37, 59
    high-level, 60
    office practices, 61
    paper purchasing, 60
    supply chains, 62
  goals, 34
    cost-benefit analysis, 37
    one- to three-year achievement, 36
    six-month achievement, 35
  green story, 250
  greenhouse gas emissions inventory, 75-76
  marketing messages, 269
  rain barrels, 124

reduction checklists, 63
  emissions, 63
  waste, 65
  water, 64
strategic plans, 38
  accountability, 41
  prioritizing goals, 38
  roles/responsibility, 41
  strategies for achieving
    goals, 40
  timeline, 40
sustainability reports, 237
  boundaries, 239
  business case, 238
  communications
    messaging, 239
  conceptualizing, 238
  focus, 239
  information gathering,
    240-244
  integration level, 239
  medium, 239
  sharing, 245
  verification, 240-244
visions
  defining sustainability,
    30-31
  green mission
    statements, 32-33
  team gathering, 29-30
CSA (Community Supported
  Agriculture), 212
CSR Wire, 259

D

Database of State Incentives
  for Renewables and
  Efficiency (DSIRE), 286
Datschefski, Edwin, 296
daylight harvesting, 111
daylighting, 96

degradable claims, 257
delivery of products
  freight options
    cargo ships, 178
    existing commercial
      shippers, 177
    hybrid truck fleets, 176
    rail transit, 176
  local sales focus, 178
    benefits, 178
    reducing transportation
      costs, 179
    reinforcing local
      businesses, 179
    shelf time reduction, 179
  practices, 150
  vehicles, 172
    biodiesel fuel, 174
    ethanol, 173
    hybrid SUVs, 172
    low-carbon fuel
      standard, 174
Department of Energy's
  Voluntary Reporting of
  Greenhouse Gases Program,
  77
DeRocher, Cindy, 221
developing new green
  industries, 7
Devil's Thumb Ranch in
  Colorado, 220
dining at venues, 225
  bulk condiments, 226
  drinking water, 227
  local food suppliers, 226
  reusable dining ware, 226
  waste stations, 227
disposing of waste
  assessing, 53-55
  disposal of unwanted
    electronics, 187-188
  greywater, 64
  managing, 224

paper, 191-192
reducing
  building construction/
    renovation, 98-99
  cost-benefit analysis, 16
  floorings, 108-109
  restaurant, 161-162
  retail operations, 145
  venue dining, 227
reduction plan, 65
three stream waste systems,
  98
zero waste, 65
Divide the Ride website, 198
documenting marketing
  claims, 252-254
drifter consumers, 265
drinking water at venues, 227
drip irrigation systems, 121
DSIRE (Database of State
  Incentives for Renewables
  and Efficiency), 286
durability of flooring, 110

E

e-blasts, 259
e-mail campaigns, 260
e-waste, 187-188
E-Wire, 259
Earth Day Network, 296
Earth Renewable
  Technologies, 167
Earthbottles, 167
Eco-Bags, 7
eco-charrettes, 89
eco-friendly materials
  equipment, 113
  furnishings, 110
  local, 94
  natural/rapidly renewable
    building, 95

packaging
  biodegradable, 168-169
  eco-friendly options, 165
  packing materials,
    164-165
  plastic reduction, 168
  reducing package
    weights, 169-170
  shipping cartons,
    166-167
  sustainable packaging
    resources, 163-164
planet benefits, 10
salvaged building, 93
eco-labels, 272
  genuine, 274-275
  international, 280-282
  pseudo sanctions, 275
  third-party certifications,
    276
    Fair Trade Certified, 278
    government, 279
    Green Seal, 276
    LEED, 277-278
    Scientific Certification
      Systems (SCS), 277
  types, 272-273
  verification, 273-274
Eco Mark, 280
economy
  benefits of green building,
    88-89
  externalities, 6
  sustainability
    green-collar jobs, 8-9
    new green industries, 7
  system, 6
EcoPaper website, 60
ECP (Environmental Choice
  Program), 280
educating consumers, 267
  recycling products, 267-268
  sustainability, 150

efficiency
  appliances, 93
  commuting
    carpooling, 197-198
    cash incentives, 199
    Commuter Choice, 196
    mass transit, 195-196
    parking incentives, 199
    remote employees,
      199-200
  electronics, 184
    business transactions,
      184
    file storage, 184
    unplugging equipment,
      185-186
  energy
    cost-benefit analysis, 16
    equipment, 112
    retail operations, 148
  freight
    cargo ships, 178
    existing commercial
      shippers, 177
    hybrid truck fleets, 176
    rail transit, 176
  fuel, 150
  lighting
    daylight harvesting, 111
    motion-detecting
      sensors, 112
  local sales focus, 178
    benefits, 178
    reduced transportation
      costs, 179
    reinforcing local
      businesses, 179
    shelf time reduction, 179
  office paper, 192
  travel, 200
    promoting efficient, 200
    reducing travel, 200

sustainable vendors,
  202-203
  teleconferencing, 201
  travel offsets, 202
  vehicles, 172
    biodiesel fuel, 174
    ethanol, 173
    hybrid SUVs, 172
    low-carbon fuel
      standard, 174
  water
    bathrooms, 113
    retail operations, 148-149
electronics
  disposal of unwanted,
    187-188
  efficiency, 184
    business transactions, 184
    file storage, 184
    unplugging equipment,
      185-186
  publicity resources, 259-260
  purchasing/manufacturing
    processes, 186-187
  updating, 187
Ella Baker Center for Human
  Rights, 8
emissions
  greenhouse gas, 11
    inventory, 75-76
    reporting standards,
      77-78
    reducing, 11
  greenhouse gases other
    than CO$_2$, 82
  offsetting, 141
  reducing in buildings, 98
  reduction plan, 63
employees
  attracting, 12
  commuting efficiency
    carpooling, 197-198
    cash incentives, 199

Commuter Choice, 196
mass transit, 195-196
parking incentives, 199
health-care options, 214-215
healthy food choice
encouragement, 211
business meeting meals,
213
eliminating disposables,
213
incentives, 212
organizing meals with
local organic foods, 212
recycling receptacles, 214
snack rooms, 213
improving relations/
productivity, 22
relations, 208
building green values
into corporate culture,
209
rewards, 211
supporting creativity, 210
remote, 199-200
retention/productivity, 13
schedules, 203
flextime, 203
four-day workweeks, 204
increasing family time,
204
travel, 200
promoting efficiency, 200
reducing, 200
sustainable vendors,
202-203
teleconferencing, 201
travel offsets, 202
employer benefits of going
green
attracting employees, 12
employee retention/
productivity, 13
healthy lives, 13

encouraging healthy food
choices, 211
business meeting meals, 213
eliminating disposables, 213
incentives, 212
organizing meals with local
organic foods, 212
recycling receptacles, 214
snack rooms, 213
endorsements. *See* certifications
energy
assessing, 50
calculating usage, 51
equipment usage, 52-53
conservation
appliances, 279
equipment, 112-113
cost-benefit analysis, 16
retail operations, 148
emissions reduction plan,
63
Green Power Partnership
program, 286
NAM and EPA Challenge
to Save Energy, 17
reducing, 148
reducing dependence on
oil, 10
restaurant electricity, 160
solar power, 97
*Energy Future: Think
Efficiency*, 171
Energy Star, 93
appliances, 279
partnership programs,
288-289
Small Business Program,
56
website, 289
engineered wood flooring,
107
enthusiast consumers, 263

environment
benefits of green building,
88
cost-benefit analysis, 37
indicators, 44-46
preferable products, 252
policies
high-level, 60
office practices, 61
paper purchasing, 60
supply chains, 62
Environmental, Chemistry &
Hazardous Materials News,
Careers & Resources
website, 10
Environmental Choice
Program (ECP), 280
Environmental Label Award,
280
EnviroPak website, 168
EPA (Environmental
Protection Agency), 51
Climate Action Plan, 63
Climate Change Site, 56
Climate Leaders, 77
E-Grid database, 51
Energy Star, 93, 279
fuel efficiency guide, 55
Green Power Partnership
program, 286
meeting venue selection
checklist, 222
partnership programs, 284
SmartWay Transport
Program, 176
Toxic Substance Controls
Act (TSCA), 105
Waste Wise 2008 award
winners website, 287
Waste Wise program, 285
water conservation tips, 149
WaterSense program, 279
Epstein, Mark J., 20

equipment, 112
  energy conservation, 52-53,
    112-113
  sustainable materials, 113
  unplugging, 185-186
eRideShare website, 198
Essential Design, 166
ethanol, 173
European Chemicals Agency,
  105
European Commission, Green
  Public Procurement, 280
European Union Eco-Label,
  280
events
  cost-benefit analysis, 229
  dining, 225
    bulk condiments, 226
    local food suppliers, 226
    reusable dining ware, 226
    waste stations, 227
  drinking water, 227
  green options, 218
  networking, 295-296
  paper reduction, 228-229
    communication, 228
    handouts, 228
    name tags, 228
    recycling receptacles,
      229
    registration, 228
  venue selection, 218-220
    assistance, 223-224
    attendee gifts, 224-225
    building efficiency,
      220-221
    convenient location, 221
    EPA checklist, 222
    hotels, 219
    indoor air quality, 221
    nontoxic cleaning
      products, 221
    waste management, 224

existing buildings
  commissioning, 92
  green principles
    appliance efficiency, 93
    energy efficiency, 97
    local materials, 94
    natural lighting, 96
    natural/rapidly
      renewable materials, 95
    reducing toxins/
      emissions, 98
    salvaged materials, 93
    ventilation systems, 96
    waste disposal, 98-99
    water conservation,
      99-100
    water-efficient products,
      93
  landlord discussions, 91
  LEED EBOM
    certification, 90
  local materials, 94
  renovating, 92
  retrofitting, 92
existing commercial shippers,
  177
externalities, 6

F

fabrics
  nontoxic choices, 106-107
  petrochemicals, 104
    fabrics, 106
    formaldehyde, 104
Fair Trade Certified products,
  278
Fairmont Sonoma Mission
  Inn and Spa in Sonoma,
  California, 219
faucet aerators, 100
faucets, 93, 114
fax machines, 52

FedEx, 177
fertilizers, 127
festivals, 296
The Fifth Discipline, 29
file storage, 184
flextime, 203
floorings, 107
  alternatives, 107-108
  durability, 110
  reducing toxic exposure, 109
  waste reduction, 108-109
focus of sustainability reports,
  239
food suppliers
  chemicals in foods, 157-158
  livestock's carbon
    footprints, 156-157
  organic
    farming, 156
    foods, 154-155
  transportation costs, 158
forecasting, 28
Forest Stewardship Council
  certification for sustainable
  forestry initiatives, 274
formaldehyde
  EPA Toxic Substance
    Controls Act website, 105
  floorings, 107
  indoor air quality, 102
  paints/fabrics, 104
four-day workweeks, 204
FreeConference.com, 201
FreeCycle websites, 188
free-range meat, 276
freight shipping efficiency
  cargo ships, 178
  existing commercial
    shippers, 177
  hybrid truck fleets, 176
  rail transit, 176
fringe stakeholders, 20

FTC Environmental Marketing Guidelines, 255

fuel

assessing, 55

biodiesel, 174

efficiency reference guide website, 55

low-carbon fuel standard, 174

retail operation efficiency, 150

furnishings, 110-111

G

Gardens Hotel in Key West, 221

GEN (Global Ecolabelling Network), 281

general environmental benefit claims, 256

genetically modified foods, 155

genuine eco-labels, 274-275

GHG (Greenhouse Gas) Protocol, 71-72

development, 71

greenhouse gas

emissions inventory, 75-76

reporting standards, 77-78

Little Red Wagon, Inc. example, 73-75

operational boundaries, 73

organizational boundaries, 73

products, 78-80

website, 72

Global Ecolabelling Network (GEN), 281

global warming, 11

global warming potential (GWP), 83

Global Water Tool website, 49

goals

accountability, 41

creating, 34

cost-benefit analysis, 37

one- to three-year achievement, 36

six-month achievement, 35

prioritizing, 38

strategies for achieving, 40

timeline, 40

Golden Fuel Systems website, 174

Good Environmental Choice, 281

Goodwin Heartpine Company, 107

Gordon, Michael, 162

government certifications, 279

government partnership programs, 283-284

benefits, 284-285

tax credits, 285-286

GRA (Green Restaurant Association), 159

electricity, 160

marketing, 162

waste, 161-162

water, 160

website, 159

Green America

National Green Pages, 294-295

website, 294

Green Apple Festival, 296

green building principles

appliance efficiency, 93

energy efficiency, 97

local materials, 94

natural lighting, 96

natural/rapidly renewable materials, 95

reducing toxins/emissions, 98

salvaged materials, 93

ventilation systems, 96

waste disposal, 98-99

water conservation, 99-100

water-efficient products, 93

Green Chamber of Commerce organizations, 295

green-collar jobs, 8-9

Green Drinks International, 296-297

Green For All, 8

Green Globes, 89

Green Jobs Corps, 8

green manufacturing, 10

Green Mark, 281

green mission statements

creating, 32-33

examples, 33

Green Office, 190

Green Power Equivalency Calculator, 287

Green Power Partnership program, 286

Green Purchasing Network, 281

Green Restaurant Association. See GRA

Green Seal, 276

green story creation, 250

greenhouse gas emissions, 11

inventory, 75-76

greenhouse gases other than CO_2, 82

reporting standards, 77-78

reducing, 11

Greenhouse Gas Protocol. See GHG Protocol

GreenLabel, 281

greenwashing, 4, 252-255

greywater, 64, 125

group activities for employees, 215

Guayaki website, 33

Guerrilla Marketing on the Front Lines, 298

guidelines for environmental marketing, 255
  environmental claims, 256-258
  FTC Environmental Marketing Guidelines, 255
  general benefit claims, 256
  truth in advertising, 255

Guillette, Dr. Elizabeth, 154

GWP (global warming potential), 83

H

H₂O Conserve Water Calculator website, 48

hand-drying options, 114

Hand Motors, 148

Haynes, Sarah, 223

headlines, 258

health
  agricultural run-off, 13
  air pollution, 13
  employees, 214-215
  indoor air quality
    biological contaminants, 103-104
    chemical contaminants, 102
    cleaning supplies, 114
    contaminants, 103
    "The Inside Story: A Guide to Indoor Air Quality," 102
    meeting venue selection, 221

paints/fabrics petro-chemicals, 104-107
    polluted, 102
    testing, 103
  products for health issues, 137
  water pollution, 13

healthy food choices, 211
  business meeting meals, 213
  eliminating disposables, 213
  incentives, 212
  organizing meals with local organic foods, 212
  recycling receptacles, 214
  snack rooms, 213

heating, ventilating, and air conditioning (HVAC), 92

hemp, 106

HEPA (high-efficiency particulate air), 104

high-level policies, 60

HKGLS (Hong Kong Green Label Scheme), 281

hotels reducing their environmental impact, 219

humus, 128

HVAC (heating, ventilating, and air conditioning), 92

Hybridcenter.org, 286

hybrids
  cars website, 199
  SUVs, 172
  truck fleets, 176

I

implementing sustainability action plans
  continuous improvement, 65-66

environmental policies, 59
  high-level, 60
  office practices, 61
  paper purchasing, 60
  supply chains, 62
  reduction checklists, 63
  emissions, 63
  waste, 65
  water usage, 64

importance of sustainability, 18-19

improving
  brand value, 21-22
  employee relations/productivity, 22
  sustainability action plans, 65-66

indifferent consumers, 264

indoor air quality
  biological contaminants, 103-104
  chemical contaminants, 102
  cleaning supplies, 114
  contaminants, 103
  "The Inside Story: A Guide to Indoor Air Quality," 102
  meeting venue selection, 221
  paints/fabrics petrochemi-cals, 104
    fabrics, 106
    formaldehyde, 104
    nontoxic choices, 106-107
  polluted, 102
  testing, 103

Indoor Air Quality (IAQ) Information Clearinghouse, 144

indoor retail environments, 143-144

information-gathering for sustainability reports, 240-244
  key issues, 241
  mapping out the process, 241
  performance indicators, 242-243
  stakeholder engagement, 241
inks, 193
Innovation Hotel in Windsor, England, 220
inputs
  impacts assessment, 132
  water, 49
"The Inside Story: A Guide to Indoor Air Quality," 102
integrated bottom lines, 4
integration level of sustainability reports, 239
InterContinental Hotels, 219
Interface Inc., 5
interiors
  air fresheners, 115
  bathrooms, 113
    hand-drying options, 114
    soaps, 114
    toilets/sinks, 113
  cleaning supplies, 114
  equipment, 112
    appliances, 93
    energy conservation, 112-113
    sustainable materials, 113
  floorings, 107
    alternatives, 107-108
    durability, 110
    reducing toxic exposure, 109
    waste reduction, 108-109

furnishings, 110
  materials, 110
  nontoxic choices, 111
indoor air quality
  biological contaminants, 103-104
  chemical contaminants, 102
  cleaning supplies, 114
  contaminants, 103
  "The Inside Story: A Guide to Indoor Air Quality," 102
  meeting venue selection, 221
  paints/fabrics petro-chemicals, 104-107
  polluted, 102
  testing, 103
lighting, 111
  daylight harvesting, 111
  motion-detecting sensors, 112
paints/fabrics petrochemicals
  fabrics, 106
  formaldehyde, 104
  nontoxic choices, 106-107
international eco-labels, 280-282
International Energy Agency website, 51
Internet networking resources, 295
irrigation timers, 122
ISO (International Organization of Standards), 133
  14021, 1999, 253
  14040:2006 protocol, 133
  Type II Self Declared Environmental Claims guidelines, 253

J–K

Jobs in Renewable Energy Expanding, 9
Jones, Van, 8

KACO Solar, 215
Karabell, Zachary, 300
Kimpton Hotels, 220
Kirei Board, 95
Korea Eco-Label, 281
KPIs (Key Performance Indicators), 45
Kyoto gases, 82

L

landscaping
  diversity, 120
  green benefits, 118
  maintenance costs, 118
  native planting, 119-120
  pest control, 121
  plant placement, 120
  professional services, 118
  rainwater harvesting, 99
  soil conservation, 125-127
  water conservation, 121
    collecting rainwater, 122-124
    drip irrigation, 121
    irrigation timers, 122
    reusing greywater, 125
    terracing, 125
    xeriscaping, 119
Lazar, Vaughan, 162
LCA (life-cycle assessment), 129-130
  benefits, 130-131
  cradle to grave, 130
  impacts of materials assessment, 131-133

ISO 14040:2006 protocol, 133
manufacturing, 133
phases, 133
LEED (Leadership in Energy and Environmental Design), 90
2009, 91
certification, 277-278
EBOM (Existing Buildings and Operations and Maintenance), 90
ratings, 90
lens of sustainability, 5-6
Leonard, Annie, The Story of Stuff website, 6
Levinson, Jay, 298
life-cycle assessment. *See* LCA
Life Styles of Health and Sustainability (LOHAS) consumers, 264
lighting, 111
daylight harvesting, 111
motion-detecting sensors, 112
LinkedIn, 295
Little Red Wagon, Inc.
example
carbon footprinting, 73-75
carbon offsets, 80
livestock's carbon footprints, 156-157
living wages, 61
local
materials, 94
sales focus, 178-179
sourcing, 138
LOHAS (Life Styles of Health and Sustainability) consumers, 264
Lovins, L. Hunter, 4
low-carbon fuel standard, 174

low-flow
faucets, 114
toilets, 113

M

MacBook, 188
Making Sustainability Work: Best Practices in Managing and Measuring Corporate Social, Environmental, and Economic Impacts, 20
marketing
assessment, 270
cause marketing, 298-299
consumer education, 267
overstating benefits, 268
recycling products, 267-268
customizing, 269
environmentally responsible restaurants, 162
green story creation, 250
greenwashing, 252-255
guidelines/standards, 255
environmental claims, 256-258
FTC Environmental Marketing Guidelines, 255
general benefit claims, 256
truth in advertising, 255
message validity, 252-254
product assessment, 251-252
publicity, 258
electronic resources, 259-260
headlines, 258
wire services, 259
supply-chain policies' benefits, 138

targeting, 261-265
value-driven purchasing, 265
brand relationships, 266
convenience, 266
health and safety, 265
honesty, 266
making a difference, 266
mass transit, 195-196
materials
equipment, 113
flooring alternatives, 107-108
furnishings, 110
local, 94
natural/rapidly renewable building, 95
packaging
bridgeable, 168-169
eco-friendly options, 165
packing materials, 164-165
plastic reduction, 167-168
reducing package weights, 169-170
shipping cartons, 166-167
paints
nontoxic choices, 106-107
petrochemicals, 104-106
VOCs, 106
planet benefits, 10
salvaged building, 93
McDonnough, William, 135
McKenzie-Mohr, Doug, 41
measuring
carbon footprint, 70-72
energy usage, 51-53
Green Power Equivalency Calculator, 287
greenhouse gas emissions, 75-76
marketing success, 270

unit conversion tool website, 77
water inputs, 49
media outlets, 269
medium of sustainability reports, 239
Meeting Strategies Worldwide White Paper website, 227
meetings
cost-benefit analysis, 229
dining, 225
bulk condiments, 226
local food suppliers, 226
reusable dining ware, 226
waste stations, 227
drinking water, 227
green options, 218
paper reduction, 228-229
communication, 228
handouts, 228
name tags, 228
recycling receptacles, 229
registration, 228
venue selection, 218-220
assistance, 223-224
attendee gifts, 224-225
building efficiency, 220-221
convenient location, 221
EPA checklist, 222
hotels, 219
indoor air quality, 221
nontoxic cleaning products, 221
waste management, 224
Meyerson, Mitch, 298
Milliken and Company, 109
Mind Click consumer survey, 263
molded fiber packaging material, 168
monocrystal, 97

motion-detecting sensors, 112
mulches, 127
music festivals, 296

N

NAM (National Association of Manufacturers), 16-17
name tags, 228
National Institute for Occupational Safety and Health (NIOSH), 111
National Institute of Standards and Technology business program, 56
National Programme for Labelling Environmentally Friendly Products, 281
native planting, 119-120
NativeEnergy, 202
natural building materials, 95
natural fertilizers, 127
natural foods eco-labels, 275
natural lighting, 96
The Natural Step, 19, 28
naturalized consumers, 264
Nelson, Willie, 175
Net Impact, 297
networking
community partnerships
cause marketing, 298-299
nonprofit support, 299-300
sustainable community programs, 299
cooperation with peers, 292
benefits, 293
greater good, 292
events, 295-296
organizations
Business for Social Responsibility, 296

Green Drinks International, 296-297
Net Impact, 297
Social Venture Network (SVN), 297
resources, 293
Green America's National Green Pages, 294-295
Green Chamber of Commerce organizations, 295
Internet, 295
New Belgium Brewery in Fort Collins, Colorado, 251
new construction, 89
eco-charrettes, 89
green building certifications, 89
green principles
appliance efficiency, 93
energy efficiency, 97
local materials, 94
natural lighting, 96
natural/rapidly renewable materials, 95
reducing toxins/emissions, 98
salvaged materials, 93
ventilation systems, 96
waste disposal, 98-99
water conservation, 99-100
water-efficient products, 93
new green industries, 7
NF Environnement Mark, 281
Nike sweatshop incident, 234
NIOSH (National Institute for Occupational Safety and Health), 111
no sweatshop rule, 62

nonbeliever consumers, 264
nonprofit support, 299-300
nonsource point pollution, 122
nontoxic choices
  cleaners, 115
  cleaning supplies, 114
  furnishings, 111
  soaps, 114
nontoxic fabric choices, 106
nontoxic paint choices, 106

O

Odelle's Brewing in Fort
  Collins, Colorado, 251
OECD (Organization for
  Economic Co-Operation
  and Development) Environmental Directorate, 281
"An Office Building
  Occupant's Guide to Indoor
  Air Quality," 111
offices
  electronics
    business transactions,
     184
    disposal of unwanted,
     187-188
    efficiency, 184
    file storage, 184
    purchasing/
     manufacturing
     processes, 186-187
    unplugging equipment,
     185-186
    updating, 187
  paper reduction, 188-189
    chlorine-free paper, 192
    printing on both sides,
     190
    recycled paper, 189
    recycling waste, 191-192
  practice policies, 61

reducing toxins, 192
  chlorine-free paper, 192
  inks, 193
offsetting emissions, 141
oil, 10
one- to three-year
  achievement goals, 36
operations
  assessment, 33-34
  boundaries, 73
organic farming
  benefits, 156
  compared to conventional
   farming, 159
organic foods, 154-155
Organization for Economic
  Co-Operation and Development (OECD) Environmental
  Directorate, 281
organizations
  boundaries, 73
  networking
    Business for Social
     Responsibility, 296
    Green Drinks Interna-
     tional, 296-297
    Net Impact, 297
    Social Venture Network
     (SVN), 297
  partnership programs,
   283-284
    benefits, 284-285
    tax credits, 285-286
outputs, 132
overstating product benefits,
  268
ozone safe/friendly claims, 258

P

P2 (Pollution Prevention)
  website, 140
Pachauri, Dr. Rajendra, 156

packaging materials, 147
  biodegradable, 168
    molded fiber, 168
    peanuts, 168
    post-consumer recycled
     paper, 169
  eco-friendly options, 165
  packing materials, 164-165
  reducing package weights,
   169
    benefits, 170
    package size, 170
    packing materials, 169
  reducing plastic, 167-168
  shipping cartons, 166
    designing for disassembly
     and reuse, 166
    extending sustainability
     to customers, 167
  sustainable packaging
   resources, 163-164
packing materials, 164-165
paints
  nontoxic choices, 106-107
  petrochemicals, 104
    fabrics, 106
    formaldehyde, 104
    VOCs, 106
paper reduction, 188-189
  chlorine-free paper, 192
  meetings/events, 228-229
  printing on both sides, 190
  purchasing policies, 60
  recycled paper, 189
  recycling waste, 191-192
parking incentives, 199
partnership programs, 283-284
  benefits, 284-285
  community, 298
    cause marketing, 298-299
    nonprofit support,
     299-300
    sustainable community
     programs, 299

Energy Star, 288-289
EPA Green Power
Partnership, 286
recognitions, 287
strength in numbers, 288
tax credits, 285-286
PAS (Publicly Available
Standard) 2050, 79
passive aware consumers, 263
PCW (Post-Consumer Waste)
designation, 169
Pearl Pressman Liberty, 148
peer cooperation, 292
benefits, 293
greater good, 292
performance indicators, 44,
242-243
pest control, 121
petrochemicals in paints/
fabrics, 104
fabrics, 106
formaldehyde, 104
nontoxic choices, 106-107
phases of LCA, 133
photodegradable claims, 257
phthalates, 158
Pizza Fusion, 162
planet benefits of going green
eco-friendly materials, 10
reducing dependence on
oil, 10
reducing greenhouse gases,
11
plants
diversity, 120
green benefits, 118
maintenance costs, 118
native planting, 119-120
pest control, 121
plant placement, 120
professional services, 118
rainwater harvesting, 99
soil conservation, 125-127

water conservation, 121
collecting rainwater,
122-124
drip irrigation, 121
irrigation timers, 122
reusing greywater, 125
terracing, 125
xeriscaping, 119
plastic packaging materials,
167-168
Plath and Company, 213
pollution
air, 13
indoor air
biological contaminants,
103-104
chemical contaminants,
102
contaminants, 103
health issues, 102
paints/fabrics, 104-107
nonsource point, 122
preventing during
manufacturing, 140
offsetting emissions, 141
replacing solvents with
bio-based options, 140
water, 13
Pollution Prevention (P2)
website, 140
post-consumer recycled
content, 60
post-consumer recycled paper,
169
Post-Consumer Waste
(PCW) designation, 169
power management of
computers, 185
Precautionary Principle, 137
preventing pollution, 140-141
printers, 52
prioritizing goals, 38

product packaging
biodegradable, 168
molded fiber, 168
peanuts, 168
post-consumer recycled
paper, 169
eco-friendly options, 165
packing materials, 164-165
reducing package weights,
169
benefits, 170
package size, 170
packing materials, 169
reducing plastic, 167-168
shipping cartons, 166
designing for
disassembly/reuse, 166
extending sustainability
to customers, 167
sustainable packaging
resources, 163-164
products
alternative materials,
139-140
assessing, 136, 251-252
biomimicry, 134
design spiral, 134
learning from nature,
134-135
website, 134
carbon footprinting, 78-80
certifications, 272
existing buildings, 90
genuine, 274-275
green building, 89
international, 280-282
pseudo sanctions, 275
third-party, 276-279
types, 272-273
verification, 273-274
claims, 256-258
cradle to cradle, 135-136

delivery
  biodiesel fuel, 174
  cargo ships, 178
  ethanol, 173
  existing commercial
    shippers, 177
  hybrid truck fleets, 176
  local sales focus, 178-179
  low-carbon fuel
    standard, 174
  rail transit, 176
environmentally preferable,
  252
health issues, 137
life-cycle assessment,
  129-130
  benefits, 130-131
  cradle to grave, 130
  impacts of materials
    assessment, 131-133
  ISO 14040:2006
    protocol, 133
  manufacturing, 133
  phases, 133
marketing
  assessment, 270
  cause marketing,
    298-299
  consumer education,
    267-268
  customizing, 269
  environmentally
    responsible restaurants,
    162
  green story creation, 250
  greenwashing, 252-255
  guidelines/standards,
    255-258
  message validity,
    252-254
  product assessment,
    251-252
  publicity, 258-260

supply-chain policies'
  benefits, 138
  targeting, 261-265
  value-driven purchasing,
    265-266
pollution prevention
  during manufacturing,
    140-141
  Precautionary Principle,
    137
  supply-chain policies, 138
professional landscaping
  services, 118
pseudo eco-labels, 275
public transport stipends, 196
publicity, 258
  electronic resources,
    259-260
  headlines, 258
  wire services, 259
Publicly Available Standard
  (PAS) 2050, 79
publishing sustainability
  reports, 245
Putting Energy into Profits
  guide, 16

Q

quality
  indoor air
    biological contaminants,
      103-104
    chemical contaminants,
      102
    cleaning supplies, 114
    contaminants, 103
    "The Inside Story: A
      Guide to Indoor Air
      Quality," 102
    meeting venue selection,
      221
    paints/fabrics, 104-107

polluted, 102
testing, 103
water, 49-50

R

radon, 102
rail transit, 176
rain barrels, 124
rainwater harvesting, 99,
  122-124
rapidly renewable building
  materials, 95
REACH (Registration, Evaluation, and Authorization of
  Chemicals), 105
recognitions by partnership
  programs, 287
RECs (renewable energy
  credits), 97
recycling
  name tags, 228
  content claims, 257-258
  materials for products,
    139-140
  paper products, 189
  paper waste, 191-192
  poster template website,
    191
  used retail products, 146
reducing. *See also* conserving
  business travel, 200
  dependence on oil, 10
  emissions, 63, 98
  energy
    appliances, 279
    equipment, 112-113
    cost-benefit analysis, 16
    retail operations, 148
  flooring toxic exposure,
    109
  greenhouse gases, 11

package weights, 169-170
paper, 188-189
  chlorine-free paper, 192
  meetings/events, 228-229
  purchasing policies, 60
  printing on both sides,
    190
  recycled paper, 189
  recycling waste, 191-192
plastic packaging materials,
  167-168
retail supply costs, 145
  recycling used products,
    146
  reducing waste, 145
  reusable packaging
    materials, 147
toxins in offices, 98, 192
  chlorine-free paper, 192
  inks, 193
waste
  building construction/
    renovation, 98-99
  checklist, 65
  cost-benefit analysis, 16
  disposal of unwanted
    electronics, 187-188
  floorings, 108-109
  paper, 191-192
  restaurants, 161-162
  retail operations, 145
  venue dining, 227
  venue selection, 224
water usage, 47, 64
  bathrooms, 113
  buildings, 99-100
  landscaping, 121-125
  restaurant, 160
  retail operations,
    148-149
  toilets/faucets, 93
  xeriscaping, 119
refillable claims, 258

Registration, Evaluation, and
  Authorization of Chemicals
  (REACH), 105
registries for emissions
  reporting, 77-78
remote employees, 199-200
renewable energy credits
  (RECs), 97
renewable energy fields study,
  9
Renner, Michael, 9
renovations
  benefits, 88-89
  existing buildings, 92
  green principles
    appliance efficiency, 93
    energy efficiency, 97
    local materials, 94
    natural lighting, 96
    natural/rapidly
      renewable materials, 95
    reducing toxins/
      emissions, 98
    salvaged materials, 93
    ventilation systems, 96
    waste disposal, 98-99
    water conservation,
      99-100
    water-efficient products,
      93
  landlord discussions, 91
reporting
  greenhouse gas emissions
    standards, 77-78
  sustainability
    areas, 232
    boundaries, 239
    business value, 234
    communications
      messaging, 239
    conceptualizing, 238
    creating, 237-238
    defined, 232
    determining need, 236

focusing, 239
history, 233
improving stakeholder
  relationships, 235
information-gathering,
  240-244
integration level, 239
internal operations
  improvements, 235
medium, 239
reputation enhancement,
  234
sharing, 245
stakeholder interests,
  235-236
verification, 240-244
resources
  availability, 19
  Environmental, Chemistry
    & Hazardous Materials
    News, Careers &
    Resources website, 10
  networking, 293
    Green America's
      National Green Pages,
      294-295
    Green Chamber
      of Commerce
      organizations, 295
    Internet, 295
  publicity resources, 259-260
  sustainable packaging
    resources, 163-164
  WRI (World Resources
    Institute), 71
responsibility, 41
restaurants
  chemicals in foods, 157-158
  green association
    resources, 159-160
    electricity, 160
    marketing, 162
    waste, 161-162
    water, 160

livestock's carbon
footprints, 156-157
organic farming, 156
organic foods, 154-155
transportation costs of
food, 158
retail operations
educating customers, 150
energy reduction, 148
fuel efficiency, 150
indoor environment,
143-144
reducing supply costs, 145
recycling used products,
146
reducing waste, 145
reusable packaging
materials, 147
selling green products, 151
water efficiency, 148-149
retrofitting existing buildings,
92
reusing
dining ware, 226
greywater, 125
packaging materials, 147
rewarding employees, 211
RideSearch website, 197
River Recovered wood, 107
Robert, Dr. Karl-Henrik, 19
roles, 41
Rowe, Sharon, 7

S

SAIC (Science Applications
International), 130
salvaged building materials, 93
scanners, 53
schedules for employees,
203-204
SCS (Scientific Certification
Systems), 277

selecting
electronics, 186-187
meeting venues, 218-220
assistance, 223-224
attendee gifts, 224-225
building efficiency,
220-221
convenient location, 221
dining, 225-227
EPA checklist, 222
hotels, 219
indoor air quality, 221
nontoxic cleaning
products, 221
waste management, 224
waste stations, 227
nontoxic paints, 106-107
performance indicators, 46
supplies, 17
sustainability report
medium, 239
selling green products, 151
Senge, Peter, 29
sharing sustainability reports,
245
shipping cartons, 166
designing for disassembly
and reuse, 166
extending sustainability to
customers, 167
shrink wrap, 168
Silicon Valley Environmental
Partnership, 284
sinks, 113
"Six Cents an Hour" *Life*
article, 234
six Kyoto gases, 82
six-month achievement goals,
35
"Six Sins of Greenwashing,"
254-255
SmartWay Transport
Program, 176

snack room food choices, 213
soaps, 114
social indicators, 44-46
Social Venture Network
(SVN), 297
soil conservation, 125
composting, 125-127
mulch, 127
natural fertilizers, 127
Solar Energy Industries
Association, 285
solar power, 97
Solatubes, 97
solvent replacements, 140
source reduction claims, 258
soy-based inks, 193
Spitfire Agency, 223
stakeholders, 242
core, 20
fringe, 20
improving relations with
sustainability, 20-21
interests in sustainability
reports, 235-236
sustainability reports, 241
The Story of Stuff, by Annie
Leonard, website, 6
strategic plans, 40
creating, 38
accountability, 41
prioritizing goals, 38
roles/responsibility, 41
strategies for achieving
goals, 40
timeline, 40
implementing
continuous
improvement, 65-66
environmental policies,
59-62
reduction checklists,
63-65

supplies
  cost-benefit analysis, 17
  paper purchasing policies, 60
  post-consumer recycled content, 60
supply-chain policies, 62, 138
sustainability
  action plan. *See* strategic plans
  assessment, 44-46
  Brundtland definition, 4
  carbon offsets, 81-82
  community programs, 299
  defined, 17-18
  defining for your business, 30-31
  development, 4
  green-collar jobs, 8-9
  importance, 18-19
  improving
    brand value, 21-22
    employee relations/ productivity, 22
    stakeholder relations, 20-21
  lens of sustainability, 5-6
  new green industries, 7
  reports, 231-232
    areas, 232
    boundaries, 239
    business value, 234
    communications messaging, 239
    conceptualizing, 238
    creating, 237-238
    defined, 232
    determining need, 236
    focusing, 239
    history, 233
    improving stakeholder relationships, 235

information-gathering, 240-244
    integration level, 239
    internal operations improvements, 235
    medium, 239
    reputation enhancement, 234
    sharing, 245
    stakeholder interests, 235-236
    verification, 240, 244
  World Watch Institute definition, 18
Sustainable Furnishings Council website, 110
Sustainable Group, 229
SVN (Social Venture Network), 297
Swan Eco-Label, 281

T

target market, 261
  defining, 262-264
  types, 264-265
tax credits, 285-286
TCO Development, 282
TEA-21 (Transportation Equity Act for the 21st Century), 196
team gathering, 29-30
technical nutrients, 136
TeleCommuter Hire Savings Calculator, 56
telecommuting, 199-200
teleconferencing, 201
terracing, 125
testing indoor air quality, 103
Thai Green Label Scheme, 282

third-party certifications, 276
  Fair Trade Certified, 278
  government, 279
  Green Seal, 276
  LEED, 277-278
  Scientific Certification Systems (SCS), 277
three stream waste systems, 98
Timberland, 287
Timbron International, 139
timeline for goals, 40
toilet dams, 100
toilets, 93, 113
toxicity
  air fresheners, 115
  cleaning supplies, 114
  floorings, 109
  indoor air
    biological contaminants, 103-104
    contaminants, 103
    formaldehyde, 102
  paints/fabrics, 104
    fabrics, 106
    formaldehyde, 104
  reducing in buildings, 98, 192-193
transportation efficiency
  employees
    carpooling, 197-198
    cash incentives, 199
    Commuter Choice, 196
    mass transit, 195-196
    parking incentives, 199
    remote employees, 199-200
  freight options
    cargo ships, 178
    existing commercial shippers, 177
    hybrid truck fleets, 176
    rail transit, 176

local sales focus, 178
  benefits, 178
  reduced transportation costs, 179
  reinforcing local businesses, 179
  shelf time reduction, 179
travel, 200
  promoting efficiency, 200
  reducing travel, 200
  sustainable vendors, 202-203
  teleconferencing, 201
  travel offsets, 202
vehicles, 172
  biodiesel fuel, 174
  ethanol, 173
  hybrid SUVs, 172
  low-carbon fuel standard, 174
Transportation Equity Act for the 21st Century (TEA-21), 196
travel
  efficiency, 200
  promoting, 200
  reducing travel, 200
  sustainable vendors, 202-203
  teleconferencing, 201
  travel offsets, 202
offsets, 202
tree-free paper, 60
Treepac, 166
triclosan, 114
triple bottom lines, 4
truth in advertising, 255
TSCA (Toxic Substance Controls Act), 105

U

UFP Technologies website, 168
unconcerned consumers, 265
UNEP (United National Environmental Programme), 51
unit conversion tool website, 77
unplugging office equipment, 185-186
updating electronic equipment, 187
UPS, 177
U.S. Global Change Research Program website, 49
USPS (United States Postal Service), 177

V

validity of marketing messages, 252-254
value-driven purchasing, 265
  brand relationships, 266
  convenience, 266
  health and safety, 265
  honesty, 266
  making a difference, 266
VBEP (Vermont Business Environmental Partnership), 284
vegetable-based inks, 193
vehicles, 172
  biodiesel fuel, 174
  ethanol, 173
  hybrid SUVs, 172
  low-carbon fuel standard, 174
ventilation systems, 96

venues for meetings, 218-220
  assistance in finding, 223-224
  attendee gifts, 224-225
  building efficiency, 220-221
  convenient location, 221
  dining, 225
    bulk condiments, 226
    drinking water, 227
    local food suppliers, 226
    reusable dining ware, 226
    waste stations, 227
  EPA checklist, 222
  hotels, 219
  indoor air quality, 221
  nontoxic cleaning products, 221
  waste management, 224
verification
  eco-labels, 273-274
  sustainability reports, 240, 244
Vermont Business Environmental Partnership (VBEP), 284
Vermont Business Materials Exchange, 146
Vetrazzo, 94, 113
Virgin Airlines, 202
visions
  backcasting, 27
  defining sustainability, 30-31
  green mission statements, 32-33
  Natural Step's funnel diagram, 28
  team gathering, 29-30
VOCs (volatile organic compounds), 96, 106
Voluntary Carbon Standard, 81

W

Wal-Mart, 164
waste
  assessing, 53-55
  disposal of unwanted
    electronics, 187-188
  greywater, 64
  managing, 224
  paper, 191-192
  reducing, 65
    building construction/
      renovation, 98-99
    cost-benefit analysis, 16
    floorings, 108-109
    restaurant, 161-162
    retail operations, 145
    venue dining, 227
    venue selection, 224
  three stream waste systems,
    98
  zero waste, 65
Waste Wise program, 285
water
  assessing, 47-50
    measuring inputs, 49
    quality, 49-50
  conserving
    bathrooms, 113
    buildings, 99-100
    landscaping, 121-125
    restaurant, 160
    retail operations, 148-149
    toilets/faucets, 93
    xeriscaping, 119
  consumption, 47
  greywater, 64, 125
  pollution, 13
  reduction plan, 64
water-based inks, 193
waterless urinals, 113
WaterSense program, 279

WBCSD (World Business
  Council for Sustainable
  Development), 49, 71
websites
  AccountAbility, 46
  All Business, 208
  Apple MacBook, 188
  Arketype, 33
  Avego, 197
  Biomimicry Institute,
    134-135
  Carbonfund.org, 80
  Carpet America Recover
    Effort, 109
  Carpool Connect, 198
  carpool matching
    programs, 197
  Carpool World website,
    198
  Climate Action Plan, 63
  Commuter Choice, 197
  cradle-to-cradle designs,
    136
  CSR Wire, 259
  Divide the Ride, 198
  DSIRE, 286
  E-Wire, 259
  EcoPaper, 60
  Ella Baker Center for
    Human Rights, 8
  Energy Star, 289
  Energy Star Small Business
    Program, 56
  Environmental, Chemistry
    & Hazardous Materials
    News, Careers &
    Resources, 10
  EnviroPak, 168
  EPA
    Climate Action Plan, 63
    Climate Change, 56
    E-Grid database, 51

  meeting venue checklist,
    222
  Waste Wise 2008 award
    winners, 287
  water conservation tips,
    149
eRideShare, 198
European Chemicals
  Agency, 105
FreeConference.com, 201
FreeCycle, 188
fuel efficiency reference
  guide, 55
genetically modified foods,
  155
GHG Protocol, 72
Global Water Tool, 49
Golden Fuel Systems, 174
GRA, 159
Green America, 294
Green Drinks
  International, 297
Green For All, 8
Green Globes, 89
Green Office, 190
Green Power Equivalency
  Calculator, 287
Green Seal, 277
Guayaki, 33
H₂O Conserve Water
  Calculator, 48
hybrid cars, 199
Hybridcenter.org, 286
Indoor Air Quality
  (IAQ) Information
  Clearinghouse, 144
"The Inside Story:
  A Guide to Indoor Air
  Quality," 102
International Energy
  Agency, 51
ISO, 133
LEED 2009, 91

Meeting Strategies Worldwide White Paper, 227

NAM and EPA Challenge to Save Energy, 17

National Institute of Standards and Technology, 56

The Natural Step Framework, 19

Pollution Prevention, 140

Putting Energy into Profits guide, 16

rain barrels, 124

recycling poster template, 191

RideSearch, 197

Solar Energy Industries Association, 285

solar providers, 97

"The Story of Stuff" by Annie Leonard, 6

Sustainable Furnishings Council, 110

Sustainable Group, 229

TeleCommuter Hire Savings Calculator, 56

UFP Technologies, 168

unit conversion tool, 77

United National Environmental Programme, 51

U.S. Global Change Research Program, 49

WaterSense, 280

World Business Council for Sustainable Development, 49

WRI GHG Protocol 9-to-5 program, 56

Zerofootprint.net, 56

Zimride, 198

Willard InterContinental Hotel in Washington, D.C., 219

Wingspread Statement, 105

wire services, 259

workday routines, 203-204

World Business Council for Sustainable Development (WBCSD), 49, 71

worm bins, 214

WRI (World Resources Institute), 56, 71

X–Y–Z

xeriscaping, 119

Zerofootprint.net, 56

zero waste, 65

Zimride website, 198

Zipcar, 198, 203

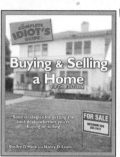

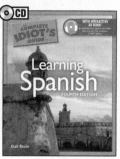

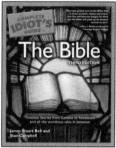

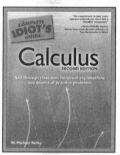

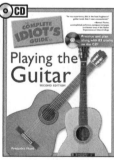

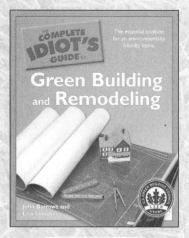
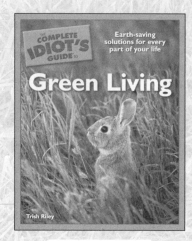
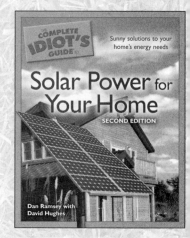
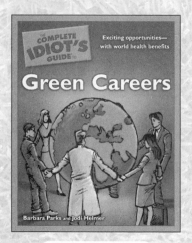

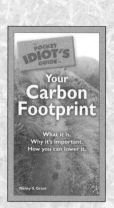